THE
LEGENDS
OF THE RABBIS

THE
LEGENDS
OF THE RABBIS

VOLUME 2

The First Generation
after the Destruction of the
Temple and Jerusalem

Judah Nadich

JASON ARONSON, INC.
Northvale, New Jersey
London

This book was set in 10-point Palacio by Lind Graphics of Upper Saddle River, New Jersey, and printed by Haddon Craftsmen in Scranton, Pennsylvania.

10 9 8 7 6 5 4 3 2 1

Library of Congress Cataloging-in-Publication Data

The Legends of the rabbis / [selected and edited by] Judah Nadich.
    p. cm.
    Includes bibliographical references and indexes.
    Contents: v. 1. Jewish legends of the second Commonwealth — v. 2. The first generation after the destruction of the Temple and Jerusalem.
    ISBN 1-56821-129-5 (coll. set). — ISBN 1-56821-130-9 (v. 1). — ISBN 1-56821-131-7 (v. 2)
    1. Legends, Jewish. 2. Aggada—Translations into English. 3. Jews—History—586 B.C.–70 A.D.—Miscellanea. 4. Tannaim—Miscellanea. I. Nadich, Judah, 1912-   .
BM530.L335 1994
296.1'2760521—dc20
                    94-1942

Manufactured in the United States of America. Jason Aronson Inc. offers books and cassettes. For information and catalog write to Jason Aronson Inc., 230 Livingston Street, Northvale, New Jersey 07647.

עוד נמשכת השלשלת

For three generations

my beloved wife, Martha Hadassah,
and our children and grandchildren
our hope for the future

Leah and Aryeh
Shira and James
Nahma and David

Natan, Adin, and Vered
Alexander, Gideon, and Benjamin
Rosina and Aliza

Contents

Introduction

This volume is a sequel to my earlier book on Jewish legends, which dealt with the period in Jewish history known as the Second Commonwealth, stretching from about 538 B.C.E. to 70 C.E. This work is concerned with a much shorter period, only one generation. But it is a richly creative generation, that of the rabbinic leaders of the Jewish people during the critical years that followed upon the destruction of the Second Temple and Jerusalem by the Romans, who ordered that they were not to be rebuilt. The very future of Judaism and of the Jewish people was threatened. The Temple service had united the Jews of the land of Israel and the Diaspora. The pilgrimages to Jerusalem had brought the people together. Now, as a mark of their humiliation, the voluntary annual contribution of half a *shekel* to the Temple was made a compulsory tax known as the *fiscus Judaicus*, to be paid each year to the Roman imperial treasury. The external symbols representing the religious and national life of the Jewish people were no more. What would take their place?

Fortunately, the answer was already in place—the teachers of the Torah and its interpreters, the rabbis who knew the traditions and who preserved them by handing them down to their disciples. Even before Jerusalem fell one of the leading scholars of his generation, Rabban Johanan ben Zakkai, had escaped from the city—according to legend he was carried out in a coffin by his students—and with the permission of the Roman general Titus had set up a school in Jabneh. The outstanding scholars joined him and with the destruction of Jerusalem the academy at Jabneh took on its prerogatives. A supreme court, to which the old name of Sanhedrin was given, became the authority for the entire scope of the religious law, including civil and criminal law, in its governance of relations among Jews. The president of the court, the *Nasi* or patriarch, as he came to be known in the outside world, was recognized by the Roman authorities as the representative of and spokesman for the Jewish people. This office continued for three and a half centuries, and after Johanan retired in favor of Gamaliel II it was passed on from father to son.

Gamaliel II, son of Simon and grandson of Gamaliel I, possessed the prestige of descent from Hillel. Recognizing the need for unity among Jews at so desperate a time, he insisted on his authority to achieve it. Academic strife between the followers of the school of Hillel and the adherents of the school of Shammai was settled in amicable fashion. A beginning was made toward indicating what the law should be when scholars disagreed, but the varying opinions were all to be studied as part of the body of the law. The strong leadership of Gamaliel II led to his humiliating colleagues who differed with him. Such conduct resulted in his being deposed and replaced by Eleazar ben Azariah in about the year 90 C.E., but he was soon reinstated.

The great majority of the population of Palestine continued to be Jewish. Salo Baron, my teacher at Columbia University, estimated the Jews in Palestine to number two million, with six million more in the Diaspora. The land, as before, was administered by a Roman governor whose seat was at Caesarea, but the Jews lived under a double system of government, that of the Romans with their officials and tax collectors and that of the rabbis, with their legal decisions emanating from the patriarch, the Sanhedrin, and the academy at Jabneh. The people voluntarily gave tithes to the priests, even though the Temple was no more, and gave contributions to charity collectors for the academy and for schools. Jewish courts were set up in every town, with the Sanhedrin as their supreme authority. The synagogue and the house of study—often the same—were the centers of Jewish life.

By and large the Jews enjoyed equal political rights with the non-Jewish subjects of the Roman Empire. Gamaliel II led a delegation of scholars to Rome, with its 50, 000 Jews, in 95 C.E. to intercede with the emperor Domitian against a proposed prohibition of Jewish proselytizing. The emperor Nerva mitigated the inequity of the annual poll tax, and after his brief reign (96–98 C.E.) his successor Trajan placed no hardships upon the Jews. For over forty years there was peace.

But in the year 114 C.E. Trajan set out to solidify the eastern regions of the Roman Empire. He subjugated Armenia and Babylonia and in the following year crossed the Euphrates, annexed Adiabene, whose rulers had converted to Judaism, and took the Parthian city of Ctesiphon. But then the news reached him that rebellion had broken out in the lands behind his armies. Jews had joined their neighbors in Babylonia in the revolt against Rome, and in Egypt Jews attacked Romans and Greeks. Jews in Cyrenaica and Cyprus took up arms against the Roman Empire. The fighting in all areas was bloody, with heavy losses on both sides until the insurrection was finally put down.

The great loss of life among Jews shocked their coreligionists in the land of Israel. Their depressed spirits led to an enactment that brides should no longer adorn themselves with wreaths. The study of Greek was prohibited except for the members of the family of the *Nasi*, since they had to deal with the Roman authorities.

Such is the historical background for the legends found in this volume. The word "legends" as used here, and as explained in the introduction to my earlier volume, may mean stories, fables, myths, fictitious narratives, or even interpretations of a biblical verse. It may include anecdotes about persons in Scriptures or about the rabbis or it may set forth ethical or moral teaching or theology or mysticism. As used in this volume, it is an all-inclusive word equivalent to *Aggadah*, the nonlegal part of rabbinic literature. The reader is referred to my earlier book's introduction for a further elaboration of *Aggadah* and for its sources in talmudic and midrashic literature plumbed by this writer.

Halakhah and *Aggadah* may be said to stand for the *Law* and the *Lore* in talmudic, midrashic, and postbiblical literature. And of *Aggadah*, Bialik, the poet laureate of the Jewish people, wrote, "Every nation has its own oral law—those popular myths and legends that draw their nourishment from the source of the nation's infancy and are carried further and added to by generation after generation and are eternally preserved in the nation's archives. The legends of a people are indeed the profoundest mirror to its soul . . ."

Hence, the study of Jewish legends has fascinated me over the years, going back to the days when I sat at the feet of Professor Louis Ginzberg, the master of Jewish law and lore.

As to the specific primary sources used by me and the dates of their composition, I refer the reader to the introduction to the earlier volume.

My thanks are extended to Professors David Weiss-Halivni and Joel Roth for their readiness to help resolve problems as they occurred.

The library of the Jewish Theological Seminary has always been helpful to me and my appreciation goes to Dr. Mayer E. Rabinowitz, its head, and Ms. Annette Muffs Botnick, reference librarian.

As always, in everything I do I am grateful to my wife, Martha Hadassah Nadich, for her encouragement and wise counsel.

Judah Nadich

New York City
2 *Tammuz*, 5753/June 21, 1993

1

Rabban Gamaliel II

Rabban Gamaliel II was the recognized leader of the Jews of the Land of Israel during the last two decades of the first century and the beginning of the second. He succeeded Rabban Johanan ben Zakkai as head of the academy at Jabneh and as *Nasi* or Patriarch he presided over the Great *Bet Din* or the Sanhedrin, the continuation of the high court that had met in the Temple before its destruction.[1]

The rabbis taught that one may understand the verse, *Justice, justice shall you pursue* (Deuteronomy 16:20) to mean also, "Seek after the sages at the academy, after Rabban Gamaliel at Jabneh." Rabbi Judah said in the name of Rabban Gamaliel: "Scripture states, *And show you mercy, and have compassion upon you, and multiply you* (Deuteronomy 13:18)—take hold of this principle: so long as you are compassionate, the All-Merciful will have compassion upon you."[2]

He said, "Provide yourself with a teacher and get a companion for study. Remove all doubt from yourself, and do not make a habit of tithing by guessing."[3]

A favorite saying of the sages of Jabneh was "I am one of God's children and the farmer is one of His children. I do my work in town while he does his work in the field. I rise early to my work and he rises early to his work. Just as he does not boast of what he does, so I do not boast of what I do. Would you say that my work is important and his is not? We have learned that whether a person achieves much or little, it matters only that he direct his heart to Heaven."[4]

Rabbi Eleazar ben Rabbi Zadok said, "When Rabban Gamaliel and his court were in Jabneh and preoccupied with the needs of the community, they did not interrupt their work for the purpose of reciting the *Shema* or 'the Prayer' in order that they not be distracted."

While a bridegroom is exempt from the recital of the *Shema* on the night following his marriage, when Rabban Gamaliel married he did recite the *Shema* on the first night. His disciples said to him, "Master, did you not teach us that a bridegroom need not recite the *Shema* on the first night?" He replied, "I will not listen to what you say, that I cast off even for a moment the yoke of the kingdom of heaven."

Once the sons of Rabban Gamaliel returned home after midnight from a wedding feast. They said to him, "We have not yet recited the *Shema*." He told them, "If the dawn has not yet risen, you must recite it."

Rabban Gamaliel gave his daughter in marriage. "Father, pray for me," she asked. "May you never return to our home," he said. When she gave birth to a son she again requested his blessing. "May the word 'woe' never leave your mouth," he replied. "Father," she exclaimed, "on both my happy occasions you have cursed me!" "Both were blessings," he told her. "Living in peace in your own home, you will have no need to return here, and as long as your son lives, 'woe' will not leave your mouth— 'Woe that he has not eaten,' 'Woe that he has not drunk,' 'Woe that he has not gone to school.' "[5]

The benediction referring to the heretics that was added to "the Prayer" was instituted at Jabneh.[6]

It was taught that Rabbi Judah said in the name of Rabban Gamaliel, "Look, the verse reads, *Let nothing that has been doomed stick to your hand, in order that the Lord may turn from His blazing anger and show you compassion, and in His compassion increase you as He promised your fathers on oath* (Deuteronomy 13:18). Let this sign be in your hand. So long as you are merciful, He will have mercy on you. When you are not merciful, the Omnipresent will not have mercy on you."[7]

Abba Urion of Sidon reported five sayings in the name of Rabban Gamaliel: When corrupt judges multiply, false witnesses multiply. When informers multiply, plundering of property increases. When effrontery becomes usual, people are robbed of their dignity, respect, and honor. When the lesser person says to the greater, "I am superior to you," men's years are cut short. When the favorite sons provoke their Father in heaven by their actions, He sets over them a godless king and punishes them. To whom does this apply? To Ahasuerus.[8]

Imma Shalom, wife of Rabbi Eliezer and sister of Rabban Gamaliel, had a certain Christian wise man and judge living in her vicinity whose reputation was that he would never take a bribe. She and her brother decided to test him. Imma Shalom appeared before him with a golden lamp as a gift and declared, "I want a share in my father's estate." He promptly declared that the estate be divided between her and her brother. Rabban Gamaliel said to him, "But in our law it is stated that where there is a son, the daughter does not inherit." The judge answered, "From the day you were exiled from your land, the law of Moses has been removed, and another law set in its place, in which it is written that a son and a daughter inherit equally." The next day Rabban Gamaliel brought him a Lybian ass and said, "Look further on in your book and you will find that it is written, 'I came not to destroy the law of Moses, nor to add to it.' And the law of Moses says clearly that when there is a son, the daughter does not inherit." His sister, in a broad hint to the judge, said, "Let your light shine forth now as a lamp." Rabban Gamaliel quickly retorted, "The ass came and kicked over the lamp."[9]

Rabban Gamaliel said that in four ways do heathen states devour their inhabitants: by taxes, bathhouses, theaters, and annual levies. He used to say that the words of Torah are as difficult to acquire as fine woolen clothes but are as easily lost as linen garments. Foolish and frivolous words are easily acquired, but are as hard to lose as a sack. Often a man buys a sack in the market for a *sela* and continues to use it for four or five years.[10]

Abba Judin of Sidon said in the name of Rabban Gamaliel, "How do we know that a person ought not say, 'I am unworthy to pray for the Temple or for the land of Israel?' Because the Torah says, *I will heed their outcry as soon as they cry out to Me* (Exodus 22:22)."[11]

The Roman government sent two officers to study the Torah under Rabban Gamaliel. They studied with him Scripture, Mishnah, Midrash, *Halakhah*, and *Aggadah*. As the officers were taking their leave they said to him, "All of the Torah is beautiful and praiseworthy except for one thing, and that is your saying 'That which is stolen from a non-Jew is permitted, while that which is stolen from a Jew is forbidden.' However, we shall not report this to the government."

At that moment Rabban Gamaliel issued a decree against stealing from a non-Jew, declaring it is forbidden because it is an act that profanes the name of God.[12]

Proklos ben Philosophos asked Rabban Gamaliel in Acre while he was washing in the bathhouse dedicated to Aphrodite, "It is written in your Torah, *Let nothing that has been devoted* [to idolatrous purposes] *stick to your hand* (Deuteronomy 13:18). Why then do you bathe in Aphrodite's bathhouse?" He answered, "One may not give an answer while bathing." When he came out, he said, "I did not come into her domain, she came into mine! For people do not say, 'Let us make a bathhouse for Aphrodite.' They say, 'Let us make an Aphrodite as an ornament for the bathhouse.' Moreover, even if you were given much money you would not enter the temple of your goddess naked or suffering a flux, nor would you urinate in her presence. Yet this idol stands here at the head of the gutter and everyone urinates right in front of her. It is written only . . . *their gods* (Deuteronomy 7:16, 12:2–3); meaning, that which is treated as a god is forbidden, but that which is not venerated as a god is not forbidden."[13]

Once it happened that a certain pagan asked Rabban Gamaliel where the Holy One, blessed be He, sits and Rabban Gamaliel replied, "I do not know." The man said, "How do you pray and what is your wisdom, you who pray to God every day and yet do not know where His place is?" To that Rabban Gamaliel replied, "Look, you ask me about something that is a journey of thirty-five hundred years away from me. Let me ask you about something that sits with you day and night and you tell me where its place is." The man asked, "And what is that?" Rabban Gamaliel replied, "It is the soul that sits within you. Tell me exactly in what place it is set." When the man answered, "I do not know," Rabban Gamaliel exclaimed, "May the breath of life blow out of this man! Although you do not know the place of something that sits inside you, you ask me about something that is a thirty-five hundred years' journey distant from me!"

The pagan continued and said to Rabban Gamaliel, "We do rightly in bowing down to the work of our hands for it is something we can always see." Rabban Gamaliel retorted, "You can see the work of your hands, but it cannot see you. The Holy One, blessed be He, sees the work of His hands, but the work of His hands cannot see Him, as it is written, *You cannot see My face, for man may not see Me and live* (Exodus 33:20). You can see for yourself that this is so. It is clearly stated by Ezekiel that when he saw the likeness of God, he fainted away. About this it is written, *When I beheld it, I flung myself down on my face* (Ezekiel 1:28)."[14]

Once the emperor said to Rabban Gamaliel, "Your God is a thief, for it is written, *So the Lord God cast a deep sleep upon the man; and, while he slept, He took one of his ribs . . .* (Genesis 2:21)." His daughter said, "Let me answer him." To the emperor she said, "May I have a military commander?" "For what reason?" he asked. She replied, "Thieves broke in on us last night and stole a silver pitcher, leaving a gold pitcher in its place." "Would that such a thief come to us every day," he exclaimed. "So," she retorted, "was it not better for Adam to lose one rib and to receive in its place a wife to serve him?" "But that is what I said," answered the emperor. "He should have done it while Adam was awake." She said to him, "Let me have a piece of raw meat." It was brought to her. She placed it under her armpit, then took it out and offered it to him, saying, "Eat some of this." He snorted, "I find it repulsive!" "Ah," she rejoined, "such would have been Adam's reaction had Eve been taken out of his body while he was awake."[15]

The emperor told Rabban Gamaliel, "I know what your God is doing and where He is seated." Rabban Gamaliel became faint and sighed, "I have a son in one of the coastal cities, and I am concerned about him. Please tell me about him." The emperor replied, "Do I then know where he is?" The rabbi retorted, "You do not know what is on earth. How can you claim to know what is in heaven?"[16]

The emperor said to Rabban Gamaliel, "It is written, *He reckoned the number of the stars* (Psalms 147:4). What is so wonderful about that? I, too, can count the stars." Rabban Gamaliel brought some quinces, put them in a sieve, whirled them around while saying, "Count them." To which the emperor replied, "Stop their motion." Rabban Gamaliel answered, "But the heavens also move!"

Some say that the story went this way. The emperor told Rabban Gamaliel, "I can count the stars." The rabbi said to him, "How many molars and other teeth have you?" He put his hand in his mouth and was counting them, when Rabban Gamaliel said to him, "You do not know what you have in your own mouth, yet you claim to know what is in the heavens!"[17]

The emperor said to Rabban Gamaliel, "He who created the mountains did not create the wind, and he who created the wind did not create the mountains, for it is written, *He who formed the mountains, and He who created the wind* (Amos 4:13)." The rabbi responded, "Would you then say that because the following two verses have two different verbs that two gods are involved—*And God created man in His image* (Genesis 1:27) and . . . *the Lord God formed man* . . . (Genesis 2:7)? Moreover, there is a part of the human face that is but one handbreadth square and contains two kinds of openings, eyes and ears. Would you say that the creator of the one kind did not create the other because the verbs are different in the verse, *Shall He who implants the ear not hear, He who forms the eye not see* (Psalms 94:9)?" The emperor replied, "Yes, I would." "Yet," the rabbi retorted, "Your supposed two different creators must come to an agreement at the time the person dies, to have the eyes and ears die together!"[18]

The emperor once said to Rabban Gamaliel, "You maintain that whenever ten Jews come together for prayer, God's presence is with them. How many gods are there then?" Rabban Gamaliel called the emperor's servant and lightly struck him on the neck. The emperor asked, "Why did you strike him?" "Because," the rabbi answered, "he let the sun shine into the emperor's house." "But the sun is everywhere," the emperor declared. To which Rabban Gamaliel exclaimed, "The sun is but one among the countless tens of thousands of the servants of the Holy One, blessed be He, and yet its presence is everywhere. How much more so the presence of the Holy One Himself!"[19]

A certain philosopher said to Rabbi Gamaliel, "It is written in your Torah, *For the Lord your God is a consuming fire, a jealous God* (Deuteronomy 4:24). But is there any power in the idol that it should provoke jealousy? A hero may be rightly jealous of another hero, a wealthy man of another wealthy man, but has an idol any power that one should be aroused to jealousy of it?"

Rabban Gamaliel said to him, "Suppose a man were to call his dog by his father's name, so that when taking a vow, he would swear, 'By the life of this dog.' Against whom would the father be provoked, against the dog or against the son?"

The philosopher responded, "Some idols have worth." Rabban Gamaliel asked, "What makes you think so?" The man explained, "There was a fire in a certain province, and the temple of the idol was saved. Was it not because the idol extended its protection over it?"

Rabban Gamaliel answered, "Let me tell you a parable to which the matter may be compared. A king of flesh and blood goes forth to war. Against whom does he wage war? Against the dead or against the living?" The philosopher replied, "Against the living." But he continued with another question to Rabban Gamaliel, "If idolatrous objects of worship have no worth, why then does not your God destroy them?" Whereupon Rabban Gamaliel retorted, "Do you then worship only one object? Look, you worship the sun and the moon, the stars and the planets, the mountains and the hills, the springs and the glens—even human beings. Shall He destroy His world because of fools? *Shall I sweep everything away from the face of the earth? declares the Lord, Shall I sweep away man and beast; shall I sweep away the birds of the sky and the fish of the sea, the stumbling-blocks of the wicked* (Zephaniah 1:2-3)? Because the wicked stumble over these things should He destroy them? Do they not worship the human being, so *am I to sweep away man from the face of the earth* (Zephaniah 1:2-3)?"[20]

An idolater asked a question of Rabban Gamaliel, "Why did the Holy One, blessed be He, reveal himself to Moses in a thorn bush?" The rabbi replied, "Had He appeared in a carob tree or a fig tree you would have asked me a similar question. However, I must not let you go without an answer. It teaches us that there is no place without God's presence and He spoke to Moses even from a lowly bush."[21]

Agnitus, the Roman general, asked Rabban Gamaliel, "How many Torahs were given to the Jewish people?" The rabbi responded, "Two, one oral and one written."[22]

A certain philosopher asked Rabban Gamaliel, "Your God is certainly a great artist, but surely He found good materials to work with." "What are they?" the rabbi inquired. "*Tohu, vohu*, darkness, water, wind, and the deep (see Genesis 1:2)," the man replied. "Woe to that man!" the rabbi exclaimed. "The expression 'created' is used by Scripture in connection with them all: *tohu and vohu—I make weal and create woe* (Isaiah 45:7); darkness—*I form light and create darkness* (Isaiah 45:7); water—*Praise him, highest heavens, and your waters that are above the heavens* (Psalms 148:4), and why? *For it was He who commanded that they be created* (Psalms 148:5); the wind, *Behold, He who formed the mountains, And created the wind* (Amos 4:13); the deep, *There was still no deep when I was brought forth* (Proverbs 8:24)."[23]

Again, a philosopher asked Rabban Gamaliel, "Is it possible that you still say, 'We wait for the Lord who will remember us?' " The rabbi answered, "Yes." The philosopher asserted, "You are uttering a lie! God will never return to you, for does not Scripture say *He has cast them off* (Hosea 5:16)? Can a childless widow who, performing the ceremony of *halitzah*, draws the shoe off her brother-in-law's foot, expect to have her dead husband return to her? And therefore does it not follow that God will not return to you?" Whereupon Rabban Gamaliel asked him, "In the ceremony of *halitzah*, who draws off the shoe, the woman or the man?" The other replied, "The woman draws off the shoe." The rabbi then said to him, "God has drawn off from us, but we have not drawn off from Him. If the surviving brother drew the shoe off the woman's foot, what validity would such an act have? Does Scripture state, 'He has allowed them to draw off from Him?' Not at all. It says only, *He has cast them off.* Similarly Scripture says, *I opened the door for my beloved, But my beloved had turned and gone* (Song of Songs 5:6). Therefore the Children of Israel have continued to cry out, *Why, O Lord, do you stand aloof* (Psalms 10:1)."[24]

It is related of Rabbi Halafta that when he visited Rabban Gamaliel, he found him sitting at his table on the Sabbath with the Targum of Job in his hand, reading it. He said to him, "Master, will you permit me to tell you what my own eyes saw." "Tell me," he replied. "I was watching your father's father, Rabban Gamaliel the Elder, while he was sitting at the side of the building in the course of construction on the Temple Mount, when a Targum on the book of Job was brought to him. 'Remove a layer of stones,' he ordered the builder, and bury this under it.' "[25]

The story is told that Rabban Gamaliel, Rabbi Joshua, Rabbi Eleazar ben Azariah, and Rabbi Akiba were traveling on a ship and only Rabban Gamaliel had a *lulav* with him. He had paid one thousand *zuzim* for it. It was the time of the festival of Sukkot, and Rabban Gamaliel took it and performed the necessary rites with it. He then gave it to Rabbi Joshua, who gave it to Rabbi Eleazar, who then gave it to Rabbi Akiba, and he returned it to Rabban Gamaliel. Thus they all fulfilled the obligation.

What do the four species of growth used on Sukkot symbolize? They symbolize the four righteous men whom the Holy One, blessed be He, placed in every kingdom to redeem His people and to spread the knowledge of the Torah. These are they: in Babylon—Daniel, Hananiah, Mishael, and Azariah; in Persia—Haggai, Zechariah, Malachi, and Nehemiah; in the Hellenist world—the four Hasmonean brothers, Judah the eldest having already lost his life; in the Roman world—Rabban Gamaliel, Rabbi Joshua, Rabbi Eleazar ben Azariah, and Rabbi Akiba.[26]

Rabban Gamaliel and Rabbi Joshua were traveling aboard ship. Rabban Gamaliel brought bread with him for the journey, while Rabbi Joshua brought both bread and flour. The ship went off course, and the journey was unduly delayed. When Rabban Gamaliel had consumed his bread, Rabbi Joshua shared his flour with him. "Did you know," the former asked him, "that we should be so much delayed that you brought flour with you?" The latter answered him, "A certain star rises once in seventy years and leads the sailors astray, and I suspected it might rise during our journey and send us off course." "You possess so much knowledge!" Rabban Gamaliel exclaimed. But Rabbi Joshua interjected, "Rather than be surprised at me, why do you not wonder at the knowledge of your two disciples, Rabbi Eleazar Hisma and Rabbi Johanan ben Gudguda, who are able to calculate how many drops of water there are in the sea! And yet they have neither bread to eat nor clothing to wear!" Rabban Gamaliel decided to appoint the two as supervisors in the academy. When the ship returned to port he sent for them, but they did not come, not wishing to have the honor. He sent for them a second time and said to them, "Do you imagine that I offer you power? It is servitude that I offer you, as it is said, *If you will be a servant to these people today and serve them* (1 Kings 12:7)."[27]

Rabban Gamaliel and the elders were approaching the end of their sea journey on a Friday, but they did not enter the harbor until the Sabbath. They asked Rabban Gamaliel, "Is it all right for us to disembark?" He replied, "I was watching carefully and we were within the Sabbath limit before dark." At that moment a Gentile laid a gangplank. They inquired of Rabban Gamaliel, "May we disembark upon it?" He said to them, "Since he did not make it in our presence—and, therefore, specifically for our need—we are permitted to disembark upon it," and they did. Rabban Gamaliel had a tube for measuring distances, through which he could take a visual citing of the distance for two thousand cubits on sea or dry land. With it one could measure the depth of a valley or the height of a date palm.[28]

It is told of Rabban Gamaliel, Rabbi Joshua, Rabbi Eleazar ben Azariah, and Rabbi Akiba that they went to Rome. There they taught that the ways of God are not the ways of man. Man makes a decree ordering others to do a certain thing while he himself does nothing, but God is not so. There happened to be a sectarian who heard them. As they were leaving, he accosted them with the taunt, "Your words are only lies. Did you not say that God commands a thing and also fulfills it Himself? Why does He not observe the Sabbath? He makes the winds blow and breaks out the storms on a Sabbath!" They replied, "Wretch! Is a man not permitted on the Sabbath to carry in his own courtyard?" He answered, "Yes." Whereupon they said to him, "Both the higher and the lower regions are the courtyard of God, as it says, *His presence fills all the earth* (Isaiah 6:3). And even if a man carry a distance equivalent to his own height, does he transgress?" The sectarian agreed that he does not. "Then," they said, "it is written, *For I fill both heaven and earth* (Jeremiah 23:24)."[29]

Once when Rabbi Eliezer, Rabbi Joshua, and Rabban Gamaliel were in Rome, the Royal Senate adopted a decree that ordered that after thirty days there were to be no more Jews in the world. One of the emperor's senators was a God-fearing man. He came to Rabban Gamaliel and revealed the matter to him. Our rabbis were greatly distressed. That God-fearing man said to them, "Do not be troubled; within the next thirty days the God of the Jews will stand up for them." When twenty-five days had elapsed he told his wife about the decree. She said, "But twenty-five days have already gone by." To which he responded, "There are still five days left." She was even more righteous than he and she asked, "Do you not have a ring with poison in it? Suck it and you will die, the Senate will then have to suspend sessions for thirty days because of your death, and the decree will lapse." He did as she suggested, and died. The rabbis heard of it, and they visited her to express their sympathy. They said to her, "Alas for the ship that entered the harbor without having paid the fee"—that is, this righteous man had not been circumcised before entering the harbor of eternity. She said, "I know of what you speak. By your lives, the ship did not go by without paying the fee." She at once went into a bedroom and brought out a box containing her husband's foreskin with bloody rags upon it. The rabbis applied this verse to her: *The great of the peoples are gathered together, the retinue of Abraham's God; for the guardians of the earth belong to God; He is greatly exalted* (Psalms 47:10).[30]

The story is told about the four sages, Rabban Gamaliel, Rabbi Joshua, Rabbi Eleazar ben Azariah, and Rabbi Akiba, that they once journeyed to a kingdom in the interior where they had a friend who was a philosopher. Rabbi Joshua asked Rabban Gamaliel, "Master, would you like us to call on our friend, the philosopher?" He answered, "No." In the morning Rabbi Joshua asked him again and this time, Rabban Gamaliel said, "Yes." Rabbi Joshua went and knocked on the door. The philosopher thought, "This can be the manners only of a sage." When a second knock came, he got up and washed his hands, face, and feet. On the third knock he rose and opened the door and saw the sages of Israel standing there together, with Rabban Gamaliel in the middle, Rabbi Joshua and Rabbi Eleazar ben Azariah on his right and Rabbi Akiba on his left. The philosopher thought to himself, "How shall I greet these wise men of Israel? If I say, 'Peace be upon you, Rabban Gamaliel,' I shall offend the other sages. If I say, 'Peace upon you, sages of Israel,' I shall offend Rabban Gamaliel." As soon as he came close to them, he greeted them with the words, "Peace be upon you, sages of Israel, headed by Rabban Gamaliel."[31]

Sectarians asked Rabban Gamaliel, "How is it known that the Holy One, blessed be He, will resurrect the dead?" He answered that it may be known from the Torah, the prophets, and the Writings, but they rejected his proofs. He said, "From the Torah: as it is written, *The Lord said to Moses: You are soon to lie with your fathers and rise up* (Deuteronomy 31:16)." "But," they said to him, "perhaps the *rise up* refers to *this people who will rise up and go after alien gods* (Deuteronomy 31:16)?" "From the prophets: as it is written, *Oh, let Your dead revive! Let corpses arise! Awake and shout for joy, You who dwell in the dust! For your dew is like the dew on fresh growth; and the earth shall cast out its dead* (Isaiah 26:19)." "But," they replied, "perhaps this refers to the dead brought to life by Ezekiel." "From the Writings: as it is written, *And your mouth like choicest wine that goes down sweetly, causing the lips of those that are asleep to speak* (Song of Songs 7:10)." "But," they again argued, "perhaps the word does not mean *to speak* but *to move*." They remained unconvinced until he told them this verse, "*In the land that the Lord swore to your fathers to give to them* (Deuteronomy 11:21)—to you, it is not written, but *to them*, hence the fact of resurrection may be deduced from the Torah." Others maintain that he proved it from this verse, *While you, who held fast to the Lord your God, are all alive today* (Deuteronomy 4:4), just as you are all alive today, so will you all be alive in the world to come.[32]

The emperor said to Rabban Gamaliel, "You say that the

dead will live again, but they become dust, and can dust come to life?" His daughter intervened, "Let it be and I shall answer him. There are two potters in our town; one creates from water and the other from clay. Who deserves more praise?" He replied, "The one who creates from water." To which she retorted, "If He can create the human being from water—the sperm—how much more likely is it that He can create out of dust?"

The rabbis set forth from Brindisi. Their large ship sailed on the sea and on the Sabbath Rabban Gamaliel and Rabbi Eleazar ben Azariah walked about the entire ship. But Rabbi Joshua and Rabbi Akiba did not go beyond four cubits for they wanted to impose a strict ruling upon themselves with regard to the distance a person may walk on the Sabbath.[33]

Rabbi Akiba said, "I was watching Rabban Gamaliel and Rabbi Joshua during the Sukkot services. All the people waved their palm branches at the recital of *Praise the Lord, for He is good* (Psalms 118:1) and during the next three verses, but the rabbis waved their branches only at *O Lord, deliver us! O Lord let us prosper!* (Psalms 118:25)."[34]

During the festival of Sukkot, if they had to leave the *sukkah* at night where they had been sleeping, because of rain, great heat, or mosquitos, Rabban Gamaliel and Rabbi Eliezer would go in and out all night long.[35]

A woman in the neighborhood of Rabban Gamaliel lost a son, and she used to weep for him at night. When Rabban Gamaliel would hear her, he would also weep until his eyelashes fell out. When his disciples noticed this, they removed her from the neighborhood.[36]

On the verse concerning the suspected wife, *as the Lord causes your thigh to sag and your belly to distend* (Numbers 5:22), Rabban Gamaliel commented, Whence can we infer that as the water tests the woman so too does it test the adulterous man? From the verse just stated, for the verse cannot refer to the woman, since she is the subject of a later verse . . . *so that her belly shall distend and her thigh shall sag* (Numbers 5:27).[37]

In the same connection the verse reads, *And he shall bring as an offering for her one-tenth of an* ephah *of barley flour* (Numbers 5:15); *barley flour*, but not fine flour, *barley*, but not wheat. Rabban Gamaliel said, "The scribes have left me an opportunity, so I shall enlarge upon this in a symbolic way, but in a way that seems appropriate: Just as her actions were the actions of an animal, so is her offering the food of an animal."[38]

Rabban Gamaliel stated, "It is said, *To the end that you and your children may endure* (Deuteronomy 11:21) and it is said again, *Parents shall not be put to death for their children* (Deuteronomy 24:16). From these verses we learn that when the parent prolongs his days, the child also prolongs his days, and when the parent does not prolong his days, the child does not prolong his days."[39]

It once happened that Rabban Gamaliel was going along the road from Acco to Kheziv, with his servant Tabi walking in front of him and Rabbi Ilai behind him. He noticed a loaf of bread lying on the road and he said to Rabbi Ilai, "Ilai, pick up that loaf of bread from the road." Soon they saw a pagan and Rabban Gamaliel called out, "Mabgai, take that loaf from Ilai!" Rabbi Ilai began conversing with the pagan and he asked him, "Where do you come from?" He answered, "From one of those station-keepers' villages." "And what is your name?" "Mabgai," he replied. "Has Rabban Gamaliel ever seen you before?" "No," was his response. From this it can be seen that Rabban Gamaliel hit upon his name by means of the Holy Spirit. And three things do we learn from this happening: that it is forbidden to pass by food lying in the road, that we follow the status of the majority of those who travel along a road, and that the leaven of a non-Jew is permitted immediately after Passover.

They entered Kheziv and after they had taken food and drink a man came to Rabban Gamaliel and asked him to annul a vow he had sworn. Rabban Gamaliel asked Rabbi Ilai, "Do you think that each of us has drunk a fourth of a *log* of wine according to the Italian measure?" "Yes," he replied. Rabban Gamaliel said, "Let the man walk after us until the effect of the wine wears off." He went on foot after them about three miles until they reached the Ladder of Tyre. When they arrived there Rabban Gamaliel got down off his donkey and, wrapping himself in his cloak, he sat down and annulled the man's vow. From this we learn several things: that a fourth of a *log* of wine according to the Italian measure befuddles the mind; that he whose mind is befuddled is not to render a judicial decision; that traveling awhile will cause the effect of drinking to wear off; that the annulment of vows should not be done while riding or walking or standing but only when sitting.[40]

There was a certain member of the household of Rabban Gamaliel who was so strong that he could carry as much as a bag of forty *se'ah* of corn to the baker. Someone said to him, "You have such great strength and yet you do not devote it to the study of Torah?" The man commenced the study of Torah, and then he could only carry a bag of thirty *se'ah*. As he studied, he could carry less and less—twenty, then twelve, then eight. By the time he finished the study of his first book, he could not even carry a bag containing just one *se'ah*. Even his garment, some say, had to be removed from him for he could not do it himself, thus bearing out the words, *Adorned with sapphires* (Song of Songs 5:14).[41]

The members of the household of Rabban Gamaliel would not say "Healing!" when someone sneezed because to do so would be to imitate the ways of the heathen.[42]

It was taught in a tannaitic statement that slaves are not to be called "Mister So-and-so" or "Madam So-and-so." But the members of the household of Rabban Gamaliel did refer to the family's slaves as "Mister Tabi" and "Madam Tabita."[43]

Tabita, the maidservant of Rabban Gamaliel, was examining herself in between her carrying each jug of wine. When she felt the commencement of menstruation, she ceased carrying the wine and said to Rabban Gamaliel, "My lord, I have noticed a bloodstain on my undergarment." He exclaimed, "Alas, all the wine has become ritually impure!" She explained, "I examined myself before touching each jug but I felt nothing until now." He responded, "May your life be preserved even as you have preserved mine!"[44]

It once happened that Rabban Gamaliel knocked out the tooth of Tabi, his slave. He came before Rabbi Joshua and said to him, "Now I have an excuse to free my slave Tabi." But Rabbi Joshua said, "You do not have the power to do so, for such a penalty may be applied only in a case in which there are witnesses who may testify in court. But here there are none, so there are no grounds for freeing Tabi."[45]

Rabbi Simon related that it actually happened that Tabi, Rabban Gamaliel's slave, slept under the bed in a *sukkah*, and Rabban Gamaliel said to the elders, "Do you see Tabi my slave— he is learned in the law so he knows that slaves are exempt from keeping the commandment of dwelling in a *sukkah* during the feast of Tabernacles. That is why he is sleeping under the bed!"[46]

Tabi, the slave of Rabban Gamaliel, used to put on *tefillin* when he recited his morning prayers on weekdays, and the sages did not object to his doing so because of his known piety. Rabban Gamaliel was once asked, "Master, have you not taught us that slaves are exempt from the requirement of *tefillin*?" He replied, "My slave Tabi is unlike all other slaves; he is a worthy man."[47]

When Tabi died, Rabban Gamaliel accepted condolences on his death. His students asked him, "Did you not teach us that one does not receive condolences upon the death of slaves?" He said to them, "My slave Tabi was unlike all other slaves; he was a worthy man."[48]

It happened that Rabban Gamaliel appointed Rabbi Johanan ben Nuri and Rabbi Eleazar Hisma to serve as supervisors of students in the academy, but they were so unobtrusive that the students were unaware of them, for they sat among the students. It was the practice of Rabban Gamaliel that when he entered the academy and said, "Ask your questions," that meant that no supervisor was present. If a supervisor was present, he would not say it. On this particular day, when he came in and found that Rabbi Johanan ben Nuri and Rabbi Eleazar Hisma were seated among the students, he said to them, "Johanan ben Nuri and Eleazar Hisma, you are doing a disservice to the group in that you do not seek to exercise control over it. In the past you were your own masters, but henceforward you are servants of the public."[49]

Rabbi Eleazar ben Zadok said, "Once we were in session before Rabban Gamaliel in the study-house in Lod, and Zonen, who was in charge, came along and announced that it was time to burn the leaven. So father and I went along to the house of Rabban Gamaliel where we burned the leaven."[50]

It once happened on the first night of Passover that Rabban Gamaliel and the sages were reclining in the house of Boethus ben Zeno in Lod, and they were discussing the laws of Passover that entire night until the cock crowed. Then each pushed aside his table, stretched, and went along to the study-house.[51]

On another occasion Rabban Gamaliel and the elders were seated at a table in Jericho. They were served dates after they had finished the meal and recited grace. After eating the dates, Rabbi Akiba on his own recited one blessing. Rabban Gamaliel reproached him, "Akiba, why do you poke your head into disputes?" Rabbi Akiba answered him, "Was it not you who taught us that one should follow the majority in adopting a decision in law?"[52]

Once Rabban Gamaliel gave a banquet for the sages. All of them were reclining while Rabban Gamaliel served them. They said, "We are not doing the right thing, letting Rabban Gamaliel serve us." But Rabbi Joshua said to them, "Let him do it. We know that someone greater than he served others." They asked, "Who was that?" He replied, "Our father Abraham, who served the ministering angels, thinking that they were mortal creatures, Arabs who worshiped idols. How much more appropriate is it for Rabban Gamaliel to serve sages, scholars in the Torah!" Rabbi Zadok also said, "Let him continue to serve, for we can find someone greater than he and even greater than our father Abraham who serves human beings." They inquired, "Who?" He answered, "The Holy One, blessed be He, for He provides every person with his needs and everyone with what he lacks. And not only to the righteous but even to the wicked and even to idol-worshipers as well. How much more so should Rabban Gamaliel wait upon sages, scholars in the Torah!"[53]

It is written, *The man who does these things shall never be shaken* (Psalms 15:5). When Rabban Gamaliel came to this verse he would weep. He would say that it means, "Whoever does *all* the preceding things mentioned in the psalm, he is the one who will never be shaken: *He who lives without blame, who does what is right, and in his heart acknowledges the truth; whose tongue is not given to evil, and who has never done harm to his fellow* and all the rest (Psalms 15:5). But if a person embodies only one of these qualities he will fall." But Rabbi Akiba said to him, "How about the verse, *Do not defile yourself in any of these ways* . . . (Leviticus 18:24), does that mean also that a person must violate *all* the previous commandments against immorality before he be judged immoral? It surely means the violation of any *one* of the commandments makes a person immoral. So too here, if a person embodies any of the virtues mentioned, *he shall never be shaken.*"[54]

Rabban Gamaliel said, "Whoever has a trade, to what is he compared? To a vineyard surrounded by a fence, to a cultivated furrow protected by a border. And if he does not have a trade, to what is he compared? To a vineyard not surrounded by a fence, to a furrow not protected by a border."

Rabbi Jose said in the name of Rabban Gamaliel, "Whoever has a trade, to what is he compared? To a woman who has a husband. Whether she pretties herself or not, people do not stare at her. And if a person does not have a trade, to what is he compared? To a woman who does not have a husband. Whether she pretties herself or not, everyone stares at her."

Rabbi Jose ben Rabbi Eleazar said in the name of Rabban Gamaliel, "Whoever has a trade, to what is he compared? To a fenced-in vineyard in which cattle and beasts cannot enter. And people going past it do not trample on it and they do not see what is in it. But whoever does not have a trade, to what is he compared? To a vineyard with a broken-down fence into which cattle and beasts can enter. People going past it trample upon it and everyone sees what is in it."[55]

Once Rabbi Yeshevav went ahead and divided all his possessions as charity for the poor. Rabban Gamaliel sent him this message: "How could you do this? Did not the sages say that one may set aside no more than one fifth of his possessions for the performance of a religious duty?"[56]

Rabbi Meir quoted Rabban Gamaliel to explain why the Torah levies a heavier punishment upon the thief than upon the robber. To what may the matter be compared? To two persons, each of whom made a banquet in the same town. The first invited the people of the town but not the king. The second invited neither the king nor the people. For which of the two should the king's punishment be more severe? Surely it should be for the one who did invite the townspeople but not the king.[57]

Rabbi Abbahu told the story that once Rabban Gamaliel and Rabbi Joshua were walking along the road and because of the mud they moved over to the side of the road, which was private property. Soon they saw Rabbi Judah ben Pappos walking in the center of the road and sinking into the mud as he walked. Rabban Gamaliel asked Rabbi Joshua, "Who is this man who singles himself out as so righteous a person that he does not step on private property even though he is sinking into the mud?" Rabbi Joshua replied, "It is Judah ben Pappos whose every action is for the sake of heaven."[58]

The sages came together in the vineyard at Jabneh and said, "The time is coming when a person will go looking for a teaching of the Torah and will not find it or for a teaching of the scribes and will not find it, for it is said, *A time is coming—declares my Lord God—when I will send a famine upon the land: not a hunger for bread or a thirst for water, but for hearing the words of the Lord. Men shall wander from sea to sea and from north to east to seek the word of the Lord, but they shall not find it* (Amos 8:11–12)."[59]

Rabban Gamaliel once said that in the generation when the Messiah, the descendant of David, comes, the synagogue will be a brothel, Galilee will be in ruins, and the inhabitants of Gablan will wander about begging from city to city without anyone showing pity. The wisdom of the scribes will be dishonored and God-fearing men despised, while the people's leaders will be without shame. Truth will be lacking, and the person who shuns evil will be thought demented.[60]

The story is told that once Rabban Gamaliel took a seat by the bench of the Gentiles on the Sabbath in Acco. He was told by some Jewish onlookers that it is not the practice to do so. He did not want to tell them that it is permitted according to Jewish law, so he got up and went on his way.[61]

On one occasion it happened that Rabban Gamaliel and Aquila the proselyte came to Ashkelon and Rabban Gamaliel went to the bathhouse to bathe while Aquila bathed in the sea. But Rabbi Joshua ben Kevusai said, "I was with them and Rabban Gamaliel bathed only in the sea."[62]

Rabban Gamaliel said, "Anyone against whom the sages pronounce excommunication, even if later they annul the ban and receive him back, does not leave the world in peace."[63]

It was said by Rabban Gamaliel that just as the New Moons are sanctified and renewed in this world, so will Israel be sanctified and renewed in the future world, as it is said, *Speak to the whole Israelite community and say to them: You shall be holy, for I, the Lord your God, am holy* (Leviticus 19:2).

Once the heavens were covered with clouds but the likeness of the moon was seen on the twenty-ninth of the month. The people felt that the New Moon should be declared and the *Bet Din* wanted to sanctify it, but Rabban Gamaliel said to them, "I have it on the authority of the house of my father's father that the renewal of the moon occurs after at least twenty-nine days and a half plus two thirds of an hour and seventy-three parts." On that same day the mother of Ben Zaza died and Rabban Gamaliel delivered a lengthy eulogy, not because she deserved it, but so that people would know that the *Bet Din* had not sanctified the month.[64]

Once it happened that more than forty pairs of witnesses on their way to the court to testify to the appearance of the New Moon were detained in Lod by Rabbi Akiba. Rabban Gamaliel sent him a rebuke, "If you detain the many, the result will be that you will place a stumbling block in their way in the future. Will not your action result in preventing many from performing a religious precept? And anyone who detains the multitude from carrying out a religious commandment deserves to be excommunicated!" Rabbi Judah the baker said, "Heavens forfend! Rabbi Akiba was not put under the ban. It was Zekher the head of Gir whom Gamaliel removed from his office."[65]

Rabban Gamaliel had a diagram with pictures of different phases of the moon on it. The diagram was on a tablet on the wall in his upper chamber. This he would show to people not expert in the subject and he would ask them, "Did you see the moon like this or like that?" Once two witnesses came and said, "We saw it in the morning in the east and in the evening in the west." Rabbi Johanan ben Nuri exclaimed, "They are false witnesses!" But when they came to Jabneh, Rabban Gamaliel accepted their testimony. Later two other witnesses came and said, "We saw the moon at its expected time yet on the added intercalated night it did not appear." Rabban Gamaliel accepted their testimony. Rabbi Dosa ben Harkinas said, "They are false witnesses! How can people testify one day that a woman has given birth if on the next day her belly extends to her teeth?" Rabbi Joshua said to him, "I agree with you."

When Rabban Gamaliel heard of it, he sent for Rabbi Joshua and said, "I order you to come to me with your staff and your money on the day that according to your calculation is Yom Kippur. Rabbi Akiba visited Rabbi Joshua and found him distressed, and he said to him, "I can show that all that Rabban Gamaliel has done is legitimate because the verse reads, *These are the set times of the Lord, the sacred occasions, which you shall celebrate each at its appointed time* (Leviticus 23:4). Whether they be in their proper time or not, there are no 'appointed times' except those that the court enjoins." Rabbi Joshua then went to Rabbi Dosa ben Harkinas, who said to him, "If we come to judge the decisions of the court of Rabban Gamaliel, then we must weigh the decisions of every court from the days of Moses until now, for it is written, *Then Moses and Aaron, Nadab and Abihu, and seventy elders of Israel* (Exodus 24:9). Why were not the names of the elders specified? In order to teach you that every court of three judges appointed since the days of Moses must be considered equal to the court of Moses."

Rabbi Joshua then took his staff and his money in hand and

went to Jabneh to Rabban Gamaliel on the very day that was Yom Kippur according to the calculation of Rabbi Joshua. When Rabban Gamaliel saw him, he arose and kissed him on his head and said to him, "Come in peace, my master and disciple—my master in wisdom and my disciple, because you accepted my words."[66]

Rabbi Zadok had a firstborn animal. He set down barley for it in wicker baskets made of peeled willow twigs. As it was eating, it slit its lip. He came before Rabbi Joshua for his decision. He asked him, "Have we made any difference between a priest who is a *haver* and one who is not learned?" Rabbi Joshua answered, "Yes." Then he went and asked Rabban Gamaliel and he replied, "No." Rabbi Zadok said to him, "But Rabbi Joshua told me yes." He told him, "Wait until the scholars come into the academy." When they did, Rabbi Zadok arose and asked, "Have we made any difference between a priest who is a *haver* and one who is not learned?" Rabbi Joshua answered, "No." Rabban Gamaliel then said, "Was not your reply in the affirmative reported to me? Joshua, stand on your feet and let them testify against you!" Rabbi Joshua stood and said, "How should I act? If I were alive and the witness against me dead, the living can contradict the dead. But since both he and I are alive, how can the living contradict the living?" Rabban Gamaliel continued to sit and expound the subjects of study while Rabbi Joshua remained standing, not having been given permission to sit, until all the people voiced their protest and called out to Huzpit the Meturgaman, "Stop! Bring the study session to an end!" And he did.[67]

Our rabbis taught that once a student came to Rabbi Joshua and asked him, "Rabbi, is the evening service optional or obligatory?" Rabbi Joshua answered, "Optional." The student then went to Rabban Gamaliel and asked the same question and Rabban Gamaliel replied, "Obligatory." The student interposed, "But Rabbi Joshua told me it was optional!" Rabban Gamaliel then said to him, "Just wait until the scholars enter the academy." As soon as they arrived, the questioner arose and asked, "Is the evening service optional or obligatory?" "Obligatory," was Rabban Gamaliel's response. Then he inquired, "Is there anyone among you who differs?" "No," Rabbi Joshua spoke up. "But," said Rabban Gamaliel, "you have been quoted as saying it is optional. Get up on your feet and let them testify against you!" Rabbi Joshua stood up and said, "Were I alive and he, the witness, dead, I would be able to deny it, but the fact is that I am alive and he is alive, how can I deny what he says?" Rabban Gamaliel continued to sit and expound the subjects of study, and Rabbi Joshua remained standing—not having been given permission to be seated—until all those present shouted out to Huzpit the Meturgaman, "Stop! Bring the study session to an end!" And he did. The persons present said, "How long shall we allow Rabbi Joshua to be humiliated? Last Rosh Hashanah Rabban Gamaliel humiliated him, again on the subject of firstborn animals he humiliated him—with reference to Rabbi Zadok—and now too he has humiliated him. How long shall we permit this to continue? Come, let us depose Rabban Gamaliel from his post as head of the academy. And whom shall we put in his place? Shall it be Rabbi Joshua? But he is the one who is involved here. Shall it be Rabbi Akiba? Perhaps Rabban Gamaliel will pray that he be punished and Rabbi Akiba has no ancestral merit to protect him. Let us then make Rabbi Eleazar ben Azariah head of the academy for he is wise, rich, and possesses ancestral merit, being the tenth descendant in direct line from Ezra, so no prayer by Rabban Gamaliel can do him harm." They then went to Rabbi Eleazar and asked him, "Is the master willing to become head of the academy"?" He replied, "Let me go to consult with the members of my family." He went home and asked his wife her advice. She told him, "Perhaps they will depose you too." He responded, "There is a saying, 'Make use of a precious vessel if only for a day even though it be broken tomorrow.'" "But," she interjected, "you have no gray hair and how will they respect you?" That day he was only eighteen years of age, but a miracle occurred and eighteen of his locks of hair turned gray. This explains what Rabbi Eleazar said, "Behold I am like a seventy-year-old man," and not "Behold I am seventy years old."

We learned that on that day of Rabbi Eleazar's elevation to the seat of head of the academy, the doorman of the academy was dismissed and all students who wanted to learn were admitted. Before then Rabban Gamaliel had announced that only the integrated personality—whose innermost self matched his outward being—could enter the academy. But on that day many benches for students were added. Abba Joseph bar Dostai and the rabbis differed about the number; one said four hundred additional benches, the other, seven hundred. When Rabban Gamaliel witnessed the tremendous increase, he felt faint and said to himself, "Heavens forfend, perhaps I have kept many Jews from studying the Torah." In a dream he was shown white earthen jugs filled with ashes, as if to tell him that the new students would amount to nothing. But in reality this was not so—the dream came only to put his mind at ease. On that day the treatise of *Eduyyot* was studied, and wherever the phrase "On that day" occurs in rabbinic literature it refers to that day when Rabbi Eleazar became head of the academy. And there was no legal question hitherto undecided that was not resolved on that day. Even Rabban Gamaliel did not absent himself from the academy for even one hour. That is evident from our having learned that on that day Judah the Ammonite, a would-be convert, appeared before the academy and asked, "May I become a convert to Judaism?" Rabban Gamaliel told him, "You are forbidden as an Ammonite from becoming a Jew." But Rabbi Joshua said to him, "You are permitted to join the Jewish people." Rabban Gamaliel retorted, "But the verse declares, *No Ammonite or Moabite shall be admitted into the congregation of the Lord* (Deuteronomy 23:4)." To which Rabbi Joshua replied, "Do the Ammonites and Moabites still remain in their original place? Did not Sennacherib king of Assyria mix up all the peoples he conquered? It is so stated, *I have erased the borders of peoples; I have plundered their treasures, Even exiled their vast populations* (Isaiah 10:13). Therefore, since we are not certain, we must assume that this candidate for conversion is of the majority of the present population of Ammon who are not true Ammonites." However, Rabban Gamaliel responded, "But is it not also said, *But afterward I will restore the fortunes of the Ammonites—declares the Lord* (Jeremiah 49:6)?" To which Rabbi Joshua rejoined, "Is it not said too, *I will restore My people Israel* (Amos 9:14)? We have not been restored and the Ammonites have likewise not been returned to their land." Thereupon the would-be proselyte was at once admitted to the Jewish people.

Whereupon Rabban Gamaliel concluded, "Since the opinion of Rabbi Joshua has been accepted, I shall go to him to effect a reconciliation." When he arrived at the home of Rabbi Joshua, he noticed that the framework of his house was blackened and he said to Rabbi Joshua, "From the walls of your house it is evident that you are a blacksmith." Rabbi Joshua replied, "Woe to the generation whose leader you are, for you are completely unaware of the anxieties of scholars or what their occupations are or how they earn a livelihood!" Rabban Gamaliel pleaded, "I have rebuked you, forgive me." But Rabbi Joshua did not even look at him. Rabban Gamaliel continued, "Please do it for the sake of my father's honor." Rabbi Joshua then forgave him and they were reconciled. They said, "Who will go and tell the rabbis?" A laundryman who was there said, "I will go." Through him Rabbi Joshua proposed to send this message: "He who once wore the priest's cloak, let him again wear it and he who does not wear the cloak say to him who wears it, take off the cloak and I shall wear it." Somehow Rabbi Akiba learned of it early and said to the other rabbis, "Let the gates to the academy be closed so that the servants of Rabban Gamaliel not come in to inflict pain upon us."

Rabbi Joshua thought better of his original plan to send the laundryman and said, "It will be better if I go to the rabbis and tell them." So he went and, reaching the academy, he knocked on the door and called out to Rabbi Eleazar, "He who is a priest authorized to sprinkle the water of purification, or the son of one so authorized to sprinkle, let him sprinkle. But the one who is not a sprinkler nor the son of a sprinkler shall he say to the sprinkler son of a sprinkler, 'Your water is only the water of a cave and your ashes are but from the stove'?" Rabbi Akiba then spoke to Rabbi Joshua, "Have you been appeased? You know that what we did to depose Rabban Gamaliel was only for the sake of your honor. If so, then tomorrow early you and I shall be at Rabban Gamaliel's door to return him to his previous post." Yet Rabbi Eleazar ben Azariah was not altogether removed. Rabban Gamaliel would lecture for two successive Sabbaths, and then Rabbi Eleazar would lecture the following Sabbath. Thus the question and answer that someone asked may be understood, "Whose Sabbath was it?" and the answer, "It was the Sabbath of Rabbi Eleazar."

The student who originally asked whether evening services are obligatory or optional and so initiated the entire affair was Rabbi Simon ben Johai.[68]

It is related of Rabban Gamaliel that when his wife died he bathed on the first night after the burial. His disciples said to him, "Master, have you not taught us that a mourner is forbidden to bathe?" He replied, "I am not like other men. I am delicate."[69]

At first the expenses of a funeral were harder on the family than the actual bereavement so that it would happen that a body would be left in the street and the members of the family would run away. But Rabban Gamaliel ordered a simple funeral for himself when his time would come. When he died they carried him out for burial in a linen shroud. Afterward all the people followed his example and buried the dead in shrouds of linen.[70]

When Rabban Gamaliel died, as soon as his body was removed past the door of his house, Rabbi Eliezer said to the family of Rabban Gamaliel, "Overturn your beds." After the rolling stone had been placed, closing the tomb, Rabbi Joshua said to them, "Overturn your beds." They told him, "We have already done so by order of Rabbi Eliezer."[71]

When Rabban Gamaliel died, Aquila the proselyte burned more than seventy *maneh* worth in his honor.[72]

"There were a thousand young men in my father's house; five hundred of them studied the Law, while the other five hundred studied Greek wisdom," said Rabban Simon the son of Rabban Gamaliel the Patriarch.[73]

Our rabbis taught that from the days of Moses up to Rabban Gamaliel the Torah was taught only while standing. When Rabban Gamaliel died, feebleness descended on the world and students studied the Torah while sitting. We also learn that from the time that Rabban Gamaliel died, full honor was no longer paid to the Torah, and levitical purity and abstinence came to an end.[74]

2

Rabbi Eliezer ben Hyrcanus

Rabbi Johanan ben Zakkai had five disciples, whom he described in the following way. Eliezer ben Hyrcanus was "a cemented cistern that loses not a drop" and "a glazed pitcher that preserves its wine." Joshua ben Hananiah was "a threefold cord not readily broken" (Ecclesiastes 4:12). Jose the priest was "a saint of the generation." Ishmael ben Hananiah was "an oasis in the desert that retains its waters"—happy the disciple whose teacher acknowledges and describes him in such a manner! Eleazar ben Arakh was "a swift-running stream and a vigorous fountain whose waters increase and overflow," thus fulfilling the verse, *Your springs will gush forth/In streams in the public squares* (Proverbs 5:16).[1]

Rabbi Johanan ben Zakkai used to say that if all the sages of Israel were placed on one side of the scales and Eliezer ben Hyrcanus on the other, he would outweigh them all. But Abba Saul said in the name of Rabbi Johanan ben Zakkai that if all the sages of Israel together with Eliezer ben Hyrcanus were placed on one side of the scales and Eleazar ben Arakh on the other, he would outweigh them all.[2]

How did Rabbi Eliezer begin his life of Torah? He was twenty-eight years old and had not as yet studied Torah. It happened that once his brothers were plowing arable land belonging to his father, while he was given stony land to plow. He sat down and wept. His father asked him, "Why are you crying? Are you unhappy because you have been given stony soil to plow? Until now you have been plowing a stony plot but now you will have arable land to plow." But when Eliezer started to work the fertile ground, again he sat down to cry. His father asked him, "Why are you weeping? Is it because you do not like working on the arable plot?" Eliezer answered, "No, that is not the reason." His father persisted, "But then why are you crying?" Eliezer replied, "I weep only because I desire to learn Torah." Hyrcanus said to him, "Look, you are twenty-eight years old, and you want to study Torah? Get married, have children and take *them* to school!"

A short while later Eliezer told his father, "I shall go to Jerusalem to study Torah with Rabban Johanan ben Zakkai." His father said, "You will not go until you have plowed a full furrow." The next morning Eliezer woke up early and plowed the furrow, but as he finished, his cow fell and was maimed. He thought, "It is fortunate for me that this accident occurred, for now I shall flee to Rabban Johanan ben Zakkai." Because he lacked food, on the way he ate clods of earth. He reached the academy of Rabban Johanan, sat down before him, and wept. When Rabban Johanan asked him why he was weeping, Eliezer told him, "It is my desire to study Torah." The rabbi questioned him. "Have you never studied at all?" The answer was no. Rabban Johanan began by teaching him the *Shema*, the Prayer, the grace after meals, and two laws each day. On the Sabbath Eliezer would review what he had learned and would absorb it. Because of his poverty he went eight days without eating and emitted a foul odor from his mouth. Rabban Johanan noticed it and asked him, "Eliezer, my son, have you eaten anything today?" Eliezer remained silent. Again the question was put to him and again he did not reply. Rabban Johanan declared, "By our life! Today you will eat with me." Eliezer spoke up, "I have already eaten at my lodgings." Rabban Johanan ordered his students, "By your lives, investigate this matter!"

They went through all the streets of Jerusalem, asking the innkeepers, "Do you have a student in your rooms?" The answer was always in the negative until they came to a certain woman and to their question she replied, "Yes." They inquired, "Does he have anything here?" She told them, "He has a single sack into which he places his head and sucks as on a wine sack." They asked her to show it to them, which she did at once. They looked into it and saw only some earth. They asked her, "Has not Eliezer eaten with you at all today?" She answered, "No, I thought he was eating with his teacher."

They went and told Rabban Johanan, who cried out, "Woe to you, Eliezer, that your lot was cast among us, but I tell you now that as a foul odor came from your mouth, so in the future will the fragrance of Torah be spread from your mouth to the ends of the earth." Rabban Johanan provided him with food on a regular basis and soon he was completely healed. He studied with Rabban Johanan for three years.

His brothers told their father Hyrcanus, "See what your son Eliezer has done to you. He left you in your old age and went off to Jerusalem. Go up there and pronounce a vow that he will never inherit any of your property." Hyrcanus listened to them and went. It happened that the day he arrived was a day of celebration for Rabban Johanan ben Zakkai and all the greatest men of the land were his guests, among them Ben Zizit Ha-Kaset, Nakdimon ben Guryon, and Ben Kalba Savua. When Rabban Johanan heard that Hyrcanus had come, he had him seated among these important people. Hyrcanus felt uneasy. Rabban Johanan fixed his eyes upon Eliezer and said to him, "Begin and expound." But Eliezer begged off. "I cannot; I am like a cistern that cannot give off more water than has been poured into it. So too I am unable to speak words of Torah other than what you have taught me." But Rabban Johanan spoke up, "No, my son, you are more like an ever-flowing fountain that brings forth its own waters." He urged him to begin and his fellow students also pressed him. Whereupon he stood up and began. He expounded upon subjects of learning that had never been heard before. His face shone as with the brilliance of the sun, and beams of light emanated from his head as they had from the head of Moses, and so absorbed were they all that no one noticed if it was day or night. Then Rabban Johanan stood up, kissed Eliezer on his head and said, "Blessed are you, Abraham, Isaac, and Jacob, that such a descendant has come from your loins!" Hyrcanus inquired, "Of whom is he speaking this way?" They told him, "Of Eliezer, your son." He declared, "Then he should not have spoken so. Instead it should have been, 'Blessed am I that such a person came from my loins!' "

Hyrcanus then stood up on a bench and called out to the people of Jerusalem who were there, "My masters, I have come here only to disinherit my son Eliezer by an oath. But now all my possessions will go to him and his brothers will inherit nothing." But Rabbi Eliezer said to him, "Had I sought landed property from the Holy One, blessed be He, He would have granted it to me, as it is said, *The earth is the Lord's and all that it holds* (Psalms

24:1). Had I asked Him for silver and gold, He would have given it to me, as it is said, *Silver is Mine and gold is Mine—says the Lord of Hosts* (Haggai 2:8). All that I seek from the Holy One, blessed be He, is to study Torah."[3]

The elders assembled in the upper room in Jabneh and they heard a mysterious voice that said to them, "There are among you two men who are worthy of receiving the Holy Spirit and Samuel the Small is one of them," and they all gazed at Rabbi Eliezer ben Hyrcanus. They were overjoyed that their own prior opinion was at one with the opinion of the Holy Spirit.[4]

Rabbi Judah said in the name of Rav, "A Sanhedrin must not be established in a city that does not contain at least two persons who can speak the seventy languages and one additional person who understands them." In the city of Betar there were three who could speak them and in Jabneh, four: Rabbi Eliezer, Rabbi Joshua, Rabbi Akiba, and Simon the Temanite, who would take part in their discussions while he sat on the ground.[5]

Rabbi Eliezer said, "Let the honor of your fellowman be as precious to you as your own. Do not be quick to anger, and repent one day before your death. Warm yourself at the fire of the wise but beware of their hot coals that you not burn yourself. Their bite is like the bite of a fox, their sting is like a scorpion's sting, their hiss like the hiss of a serpent, and all their words are like coals of fire."

When Rabbi Eliezer taught this to his disciples they asked, "But does a person know the day of his death?" He answered, "Let him then repent today for perhaps he will die tomorrow. Thus his entire life will be spent in repentance."[6]

The verse reads, *Happy are those who act justly, who do right at all times* (Psalms 106:3). Is it then possible to do right at all times? Our masters in Jabneh explained it—some say it was Rabbi Eliezer—as referring to the person who feeds his sons and daughters when they are young.[7]

The rabbis taught: *Justice, justice shall you pursue* (Deuteronomy 16:20). This means, seek out a court whose judgments are proper, like the court of Rabban Johanan ben Zakkai or the court of Rabbi Eliezer.[8]

The study hall in Rabbi Eliezer's academy was shaped like an oval with seats on both sides and there was a rock on which he would sit while teaching.[9]

Rabbi Eliezer said: "Whoever greets his teacher without

calling him 'My master and teacher' forfeits his life." Ben Azzai said: "Whoever greets his teacher without calling him 'My master and teacher' or whoever does not respond in similar fashion to his teacher's greeting or whoever opposes the opinion of his master's school forfeits his life." Who for this purpose is considered a man's teacher? Whoever has taught him Mishnah and *Shas*, not only Scripture—such is the opinion of Rabbi Meir. Rabbi Judah said: "One from whom he has learned the greater part of his knowledge." Rabbi Jose said: "Whoever has enlightened his eyes in the study of the Mishnah. If his teacher is blind, he should not say to him, 'The sun has set' but 'Remove your *tefillin*.' "[10]

Again, Rabbi Eliezer said: "Whoever prays behind his teacher or greets his teacher in the ordinary way or responds similarly to his teacher's greeting or differs with the decision of his master's academy or utters a point of view that he did not hear from his master causes the Heavenly Presence to depart from the Jewish people."[11]

Rabbi Eliezer taught that it is forbidden for a disciple to give a legal decision in the presence of his master. He may not give such a decision until he is at least twelve *mils* distant, this being the length of the encampment of the Children of Israel from one end to the other in their journey to the Promised Land. This may be inferred from the text, *They encamped by the Jordan from Beth-jeshimoth as far as Abel-shittim* (Numbers 33:49). How far apart were these places? Twelve *mils*.[12]

A disciple rendered a legal decision in the presence of his master, Rabbi Eliezer. The latter said to his wife, Imma Shalom, "This young man will not live out the week." His students asked him, "Rabbi, are you then a prophet?" He answered, "I am neither a prophet nor the son of a prophet, but this is the tradition I have received: 'Any disciple who teaches a law in the presence of his master brings the death penalty upon himself.' " And the disciple who had rendered a legal decision in the presence of his master, Rabbi Eliezer, did not live out the week.[13]

We have learned that Rabbi Eliezer said the Ark was brought into exile in Babylonia, as it is said, *At the turn of the year, King Nebuchadnezzar sent to have him brought to Babylon with the precious vessels of the House of the Lord* . . . (2 Chronicles 36:10).[14]

Rabbi Eliezer was asked, "Are the later generations worthier than the early generations?" He replied, "What happened to the Temple shrine because of your conduct gives you the answer.

Your forefathers caused the Temple roof to collapse, as it is said, *And the covering of Judah was laid bare* (Isaiah 22:8). But we, we were responsible for the destruction of the very walls, as it is said, *Raze it, raze it, Even to the foundation thereof* (Psalms 137:7)."[15]

Rabbi Eliezer and Rabbi Joshua discussed the verse, *And moreover I saw under the sun, in the place of justice, that wickedness was there; and in the place of righteousness that wickedness was there* (Ecclesiastes 3:16). Rabbi Eliezer said that the meaning is that the place where the Great Sanhedrin had once sat and decided the lawsuits of Israel, there *All the officers of the king of Babylon entered, and took up quarters at the middle gate* (Jeremiah 39:3), that is, in the very place where the law used to be decided. The proverb has it, "Where the master hangs up his armor, there the shepherd hangs up his pitcher." And the Holy Spirit exclaims, "In the place of righteousness, there was wickedness perpetrated," that is, in the place of which it is written, *The faithful city that was filled with justice* (Isaiah 1:21); *But now murderers* (Isaiah 1:21), that is, they commit murders—there they killed Zechariah and Uriah.

Rabbi Joshua explained the verse in this way: "In the place of justice, there was condemnation," that is, in the place where the Divine Attribute of Justice displayed itself in the story of the Golden Calf . . . there punishment was carried out, there the Lord smote the people because they had made the Calf. The Holy Spirit exclaimed, *In the place of righteousness, there was the wickedness,* the place where I attributed righteousness to them and called them godlike, as I said, *I had taken you for divine beings, sons of the Most High* (Psalms 82:6), *there was wickedness,* there they acted wickedly by making the Golden Calf and prostrating themselves before it.[16]

Rabbi Eliezer the Great said, "From the day the Temple was destroyed, sages began to be like schoolteachers, the schoolteachers like synagogue officials, the synagogue officials like the ordinary run of people, the ordinary run of people became feeble, and there is no one to seek compassion for them. On whom can we rely? On our Father in heaven."[17]

It is told that once Rabbi Eliezer unknowingly sat on a bed on which a Torah scroll lay. When he became aware of it, he jumped up as if a snake had bitten him.[18]

Our rabbis taught: What was the historic method of learning? Moses learned from the mouth of the Almighty. Then Aaron entered and Moses taught him. When Aaron had finished, he took his seat at Moses' left and his sons then entered. Moses taught them and they left except for Eleazar, who took a seat at Moses' right, and Ittamar, who sat at Aaron's left. Rabbi Judah interposed, "Aaron was always at Moses' right." The elders then came in and Moses taught them. The elders took their place and Moses then taught the people generally. So it can be seen that Aaron learned the same lesson four times, his sons three times, the elders twice, and the people once. Moses then departed and Aaron studied the same lesson with them all. He left and his sons became the teachers. After Aaron's sons the elders taught. The result was that each of them studied the text four times. Therefore, Rabbi Eliezer said a teacher must teach the text to his students four times. For if Aaron, who learned the passage from Moses and Moses from the Almighty, reviewed the text four times, the ordinary student who learns from the ordinary teacher, how much more so![19]

Rabbi Eliezer said that a husband should speak pleasantly to his wife at the time of their having relations. Rabbi Judah said that he should aim at making her happy at the time when he is engaged in fulfilling the commandment toward her, as it is stated, *Whoever keeps the commandment shall know no evil thing* (Ecclesiastes 8:5).[20]

Imma Shalom, the wife of Rabbi Eliezer and sister of Rabban Gamaliel, was asked, "Why are your children beautiful? And during intercourse how does your husband conduct himself toward you?" She replied, "He does not converse with me during the first or last watch but only during the middle watch and [when he has relations with me] he uncovers a handbreadth and covers a handbreadth, and it is as though he was urged on by a demon. When I questioned him as to the reason for the middle watch, he replied, 'So that another woman should not come to my mind and my children consequently come within the category of bastards.' "[21]

Rabbi Eliezer and Rabbi Eleazar expounded the verse, *And Moses said to Aaron, "Take a jar, put one omer of manna in it, and place it before the Lord"* (Exodus 16:33). For how long? Rabbi Eleazar said, "For generations to come." Rabbi Eliezer said, "Until the days of the Messiah." For when Jeremiah reproached the Jewish people, "Why are you not engaged in the study of the Torah?" they answered, "If we do, how shall we earn food to eat?" At that time Jeremiah took out the jar of manna, showed it to them and said, "O generation, behold the word of the Lord! Have I been like a desert to Israel, Or like a land of deep gloom? Then why do My people say, 'We have broken loose, We will not come to You any more'? (Jeremiah 2:31). See how your ancestors who engaged in study of Torah got their food! And you involve yourselves in the study of Torah and I shall feed you in similar manner." Rabbi Eliezer also taught, "He who has a piece of bread in his basket and says, 'What shall I eat tomorrow?' belongs to those of little faith."

Yet Rabbi Eliezer said, "Great is work, for Adam tasted no food until he had done some work. . . ." Further said he, "Great is work, for just as Israel was commanded concerning the Sabbath, so too were they commanded concerning the duty to labor, as it is written, *Six days you shall labor and do all your work* (Exodus 20:9)."[22]

Rabbi Eliezer the Great said that from the fifteenth day of the month of Av the sun's strength becomes weaker and therefore they no longer would cut wood for the altar.[23]

Rabbi Jose ben Joezer of Tzeredah taught: Let your house be a meeting place for the wise; sit in the very dust at their feet and drink in their words with thirst. Some interpreted "sit in the very dust at their feet" as referring to Rabbi Eliezer and "drink in their words with thirst" as referring to Rabbi Akiba.[24]

Rabbi Aha taught in the name of Rabbi Jose bar Hanina that when Moses went up to heaven, he heard the voice of the Holy One, blessed be He, as He sat studying the section dealing with the Red Heifer, quoting the law in the name of its author: "Rabbi Eliezer says that the heifer whose neck is to be broken must be not more than one year old and the Red Heifer not more than two years old." Moses then said to the Holy One, blessed be He, "Master of all worlds, the worlds above and the worlds below are in Your domain, yet You sit and quote a law taught by a mere mortal human being!"

The Holy One, blessed be He, replied, "Moses, there will arise in My world a righteous man who [in his concern for the purification of Israel], will begin his instruction in the Oral Law and so I [also concerned for the purification of Israel] say, 'Rabbi Eliezer taught that the heifer whose neck is to be broken must be not more than one year old and the Red Heifer not more than two years old.' "

Moses said, "Master of universes, may it please You to decree that Eliezer be my descendant."

The Holy One replied, "By your life, I decree that Eliezer be your descendant"; therefore, the words, *And the other was named Eliezer* (Exodus 18:4), as if to say—the name of that gifted one.[25]

We have learned that Rabbi Eliezer said that the souls of the righteous are placed beneath the Throne of Glory, but the souls of the wicked get more and more filthy, as it is said, *The life of my lord will be bound up in the bundle of life; but He will fling away the lives of your enemies as from the hollow of a sling* (1 Samuel 25:29).[26]

Rabbi Eliezer said that all the dead will arise at the resurrection, dressed in their shrouds. Know that this is so for see what happens when one plants seeds in the earth. One plants naked seeds and they arise out of the earth with many coverings. How much more so that people who are placed in the earth dressed with their garments! Will they not rise up dressed in their garments? Not only this, but come and learn from Hananiah, Mishael, and Azariah, who went into the fiery furnace dressed in their garments, as it is said, *The satraps, the prefects, the governors, and the royal companions gathered around to look at those men, on whose bodies the fire had had no effect, . . . whose shirts looked no different . . .* (Daniel 3:27).[27]

Rabbi Eliezer said that all the host of heaven will in the future pass away and then will be renewed. What is written about them? *All the host of heaven will molder away* (Isaiah 34:4). Just as the leaves fade from off the vine and the fig tree and the tree remains standing dry but again blossoms afresh and bears buds and produces new fresh leaves, so too in the future all the host of heaven will fade away like a vine and a fig tree and will again be renewed before Him. To make it known that there is a passing away that does not really pass away. No more shall there be evil and no more shall there be plague, and there shall not be the former misfortunes, as it is said, *For behold! I am creating a new heaven and a new earth* (Isaiah 65:17).[28]

Rabbi Eliezer declared, "I heard with my ear the Lord of Hosts speaking. And what did He say? He said, *See, I have set before you this day life and good, and death and evil* (Deuteronomy 30:15)." The Holy One, blessed be He, said, "Behold, these two ways have I given to Israel, one is good, the other is evil. The one that is good is that of life; and the one that is evil is that of death. The good way has two byways, one of righteousness and the other of love." Elijah, may he be remembered for good, is placed exactly between these two ways. When a man comes to enter one of these ways, Elijah, may he be remembered for good, cries aloud on his behalf, *Open the gates, and let a righteous nation enter* (Isaiah 26:2). And Samuel the prophet comes and he places himself between these two byways. He says, "On which of these two shall I go? If I go on the way of righteousness, the way of love is better. If I go on the way of love, the way of righteousness will seem to be better. But I call heaven and earth to be my witnesses that I will not give up either of them."[29]

Rabbi Eliezer taught that all heathen are excluded from a share in the world to come. Rabbi Joshua said to him, "But there are righteous people among all the nations who do have a share in the world to come!"[30]

In the name of Rabbi Eliezer it was taught: *O hope (mikveh) of Israel! O Lord!* (Jeremiah 17:13) means that as the ritual pool of purification (*mikveh*) is near so that the impure may cleanse themselves, so the Holy One is near to cleanse Israel. Therefore Hosea, admonishing Israel, says to them, *Return, O Israel to the Lord your God* (Hosea 14:2).

In the name of Rabbi Eliezer it was taught: *O hope (mikveh) of Israel! O Lord!* (Jeremiah 17:13). Hence the Holy One declared to Israel! I say to you that you are to pray in the synagogue of your city. When you cannot, pray in an open field. If that is not possible, pray in your house. If that is not feasible, pray upon your bed. If you cannot speak the words, commune with your heart. *Commune with your own heart upon your bed and be still* (Psalms 4:5). At the conclusion of the *Amidah* Rabbi Eliezer would recite this prayer of his: "May it be Your will, O Lord my God and God of my fathers, that hatred for us shall not enter the heart of any man nor hatred for any man enter our heart; that no one shall envy us, nor we envy anyone else; that Your Torah be our preoccupation all the days of our life; and that our words be an effective petition before You."[31]

Rabbi Eliezer and Rabbi Joshua differed as to the explanation of the verse, *Righteousness exalts a nation; but lovingkindness (hesed) is a sin for other peoples* (Proverbs 14:34). Rabbi Eliezer said that *righteousness exalts a nation*—that is, Israel; but *lovingkindness is a sin for other peoples*—even deeds of lovingkindness become a sin for heathen peoples because they boast of such deeds. Rabbi Joshua read the verse differently: *Righteousness exalts a nation*—that is, Israel; but *sin is a boon (hesed) for other peoples*—that is, when Israel sins, it is a boon for the peoples of the world because they can again impose bondage upon Israel.

Rabbi Eliezer said, "Because God loves the righteous, He chastises them in this world, as it is said, *But He who loves him disciplines him early* (Proverbs 13:24)." He said further, "Because God loves Israel, He disciplines them by handing them over to enslavement by the kingdoms in this world, so that they will thereby achieve atonement for their sins in the coming future, as it is said, *But He who loves him disciplines him early* (Proverbs 13:24)."[32]

Rabbi Eliezer interpreted another verse, *Honor the Lord with your wealth* (Proverbs 3:9) to mean honor your Physician even before you have need of Him.[33]

It was taught that when the maidservant of Rabbi Eliezer died and his students came to offer their sympathy, he did not wish to accept their expressions of condolence. He went out into the courtyard to avoid them but they followed him. He went back into the house but they came after him. He said to them, "It seems to me that you did not take my mild hint, when I went out to the courtyard to avoid you. Nor did you take my second hint, when I went back into the house again to avoid you. Has it not been taught that condolences are not to be accepted when slaves die because slaves are property like one's animals? If for freemen, who are not related, condolences are not to be accepted, then surely for slaves that should be so."[34]

If a person is going through a place of danger frequented by robbers and the time for prayer comes, he need offer only a brief prayer. What is termed "a brief prayer"? Rabbi Eliezer says that it may be, "Do Your will in the heavens above and grant gratification to those who revere You on earth. Do that which is good in Your eyes. Blessed be the One who hears prayer."[35]

The story is told that a certain man was reading from the Scriptures before Rabbi Eliezer and he read the verse, *O mortal, proclaim Jerusalem's abominations to her* (Ezekiel 16:2). Rabbi Eliezer said to him, "Go and proclaim your mother's abominations!"[36]

With reference to the verse, *He led Israel out with silver and gold* (Psalms 105:37), Rabbi Eliezer the Great taught: Out of Egypt the lowliest among the Children of Israel brought forth with him ninety asses laden with silver and gold.[37]

Commenting on *awesome as bannered hosts* (Song of Songs

6:10), Rabbi Eliezer and Rabbi Joshua differed. Rabbi Eliezer said that to the other nations Israel resembled the ministering angels who stand arrayed like troops with banners. Rabbi Joshua said that when Israel went out of Egypt they looked like troops under banners drawn up in their places.[38]

With regard to the verse, *Hand upon the throne of the Lord! The Lord will be at war with Amalek throughout the ages* (Exodus 17:16), it is taught in a *baraita* in the name of Rabbi Eliezer that the Holy One swore a solemn oath: "By My right hand and again by My right hand, by My throne and again by My throne, I swear that if would-be proselytes come from any of the peoples of the earth I will receive them, but if they be descendants of Amalek I will never receive them."[39]

When Rabbi Eliezer came to the verse, *For anyone who does such things is abhorrent to the Lord* (Deuteronomy 18:12), he would say, "How unfortunate we are! Since he who clings to anything unclean, the spirit of uncleanness rests upon him, he who clings to the *Shekhinah*, the holy spirit should surely rest upon him. What causes this not to happen? *But your iniquities have been a barrier between you and your God* (Isaiah 59:2)."[40]

Rabbi Eliezer said, "Why are they called *other gods* (Deuteronomy 11:16)? Because every day men create new deities. If the original idol was made of gold and one needs a duplicate, he will make a copy in silver, or if of silver, he will make another in copper, or if of copper, he will make the second in iron, or if of iron, he will make a copy in tin, or if of tin, he will make another of lead, or if of lead, he will make a different one in wood."[41]

The men of Sodom will neither come to life in the world to come nor be brought to judgment, for it is said, *Now the inhabitants of Sodom were very wicked sinners against the Lord* (Genesis 13:13): *wicked* toward one another; *sinners* with incest; *against the Lord* refers to their profaning God's name; *very* implies that they deliberately set out to sin. This is the view of Rabbi Eliezer. Rabbi Joshua said that they will be brought to judgment, as it is stated, *Therefore the wicked shall not stand in the judgment nor will sinners, in the assembly of the righteous* (Psalms 1:5). They will not stand in the assembly of the righteous but they will stand in the assembly of the wicked. Rabbi Nehemiah said that they will not even enter into the assembly of the wicked for judgment, as it is said, *May sinners disappear from the earth, and the wicked be no more* (Psalms 104:35).[42]

Korah and his group will neither come to life in the hereafter nor be brought to judgment, as it is stated, *The earth closed over them and they vanished from the midst of the congregation* (Numbers 16:33). This is the view of Rabbi Eliezer. But Rabbi Joshua said: They shall enter into the world to come and will be brought to judgment and of them Scripture declares, *The Lord deals death, and gives life, casts down into the grave and raises up* (1 Samuel 2:6). In connection with Korah the word *grave* is mentioned: *They went down alive into the grave, with all that belonged to them* (Numbers 16:33), and in the Samuel passage the word *grave* is also mentioned. As in the latter verse Scriptures speak of bringing down into the grave and also bringing up, so here with Korah they went down but will come up again in the hereafter. Rabbi Eliezer asked him, "How then do you explain the words, *The earth closed over them and they vanished from the midst of the congregation?*" He replied, "They vanished from the midst of the congregation, but they did not vanish from the world to come."

The generation of the wilderness will neither come to life in the hereafter nor be brought to judgment, as it is said, *In this very wilderness they shall die to the last man* (Numbers 14:35). And there is also the statement, *Concerning them I swore in anger, they shall never come to My resting place* (Psalms 95:11). This is the view of Rabbi Eliezer. But Rabbi Joshua said: They will enter the world to come and they will be brought to judgment. Concerning them, Scriptures state, *Bring in My devotees, who made a covenant with Me over sacrifice* (Psalms 50:5). Rabbi Eliezer said to him, "How then do you explain the words, *I swore in anger?*" He replied, "That refers to the spies and the wicked of that generation." Rabbi Joshua then asked Rabbi Eliezer, "How do you explain *Bring in my devotees?*" "That," Rabbi Eliezer answered, "refers to Moses and Aaron and all the pious generation of the tribe of Levi."[43]

Young children of the wicked—children who died as minors—will neither live in the world to come nor be brought to judgment, as it is said, *For lo! That day is at hand, burning like an oven. All the arrogant and all the doers of evil shall be straw, and the day that is coming—said the Lord of Hosts—shall burn them to ashes and leave of them neither root nor branch* (Malachi 3:19). This is the view of Rabbi Eliezer. But Rabbi Joshua said that they will enter the world to come and of them Scriptures say, *He called loudly and said: 'Hew down the tree, lop off its branches, Strip off its foliage, scatter its fruit'* (Daniel 4:11). But the text continues, *'But leave the stump with its roots in the ground, in fetters of iron and bronze'* (Daniel 4:12). Now the word *root* is mentioned here and it is also found in the former verse. As here the word *root* refers to the tree being hewn down—meaning the wicked man—so in the earlier verse Scriptures speak of the wicked man.[44]

Rabbi Eliezer taught that where is no judgment, there will be judgment and where there is judgment, there will be no judgment. How so? Because when courts on earth render judgment, there will be no judgment in heaven; but when no judgment is rendered on earth, there will be judgment in heaven. For the Holy One, blessed be He, will sit in judgment upon the guilty and make them pay. But when judgment is rendered on earth, the Holy One, blessed be He, will say, "What is there for Me to do? This was My calling," as it is said, *For the Lord is a God of justice* (Isaiah 30:18).[45]

Rabbi Eliezer said that all the prophets begin their books with words of reproof and end with words of comfort except Jeremiah, who ends his book with words of reproof, saying, *A regular allotment of food was given him* [Jehoiachin] *by order of the king of Babylon for each day, to the day of his death—all the days of his life* (Jeremiah 52:34).[46]

What should a man do in order to have children? Rabbi Eliezer said, "Let him distribute charity generously to the poor, as it is said, *He gives freely to the poor; his beneficence lasts forever; his horn is exalted in honor* (Psalms 112:9). Or else let him fulfill the wishes of his wife." Rabbi Eliezer continued, "He should speak seductively to her at the time of intercourse." Rabbi Judah said, "He should try to make her happy when he is engaged in fulfilling the commandment toward her, as it is said, *Whoever keeps the commandment shall know no evil* (Ecclesiastes 8:5)."[47]

For what sin do a man's children die young? Rabbi Eliezer said, "For the sin of unfulfilled vows, as it is said, *Don't let your mouth bring you into disfavor . . . and destroy your possessions* (Ecclesiastes 5:5)." Rabbi Natan said, "For the sin of neglecting the *mezuzah*, as it is written, *And inscribe them on the doorposts of your house and on your gates* (Deuteronomy 11:20), which is followed by *To the end that you and your children may endure* (Deuteronomy 11:21)." Rabbi Nehorai said, "For the sin of neglecting the study of the Torah one's children die young, as it is stated, *Because you have spurned the teaching of your God, I, in turn, will spurn your children* (Hosea 4:6)."[48]

We have learned in a *baraita* that Rabbi Eliezer said that he who does not participate in producing children is as though he were a murderer. For it is said, *Whoever sheds the blood of man, by man shall his blood be shed* (Genesis 9:6) and immediately afterward it is written, *Be fertile, then, and increase* (Genesis 9:7). Indeed, Abba Hanan quoted Rabbi Eliezer as saying that he who does not participate in producing children deserves death, as it is said concerning Nadab and Abihu, *and they left no sons* (Numbers 3:4); whence it may be inferred that if they had sons, they would not have died.[49]

Bar Kappara taught that anyone who calls Abraham Abram violates a positive commandment, as it said, *But your name shall be Abraham* (Genesis 17:5). Rabbi Eliezer said that such a person violates a negative commandment, as it is said, *And you shall no longer be called Abram* (Genesis 17:5).[50]

The verse states, *On one of the heights which I will point out to you* (Genesis 22:2). Rabbi Huna quoted Rabbi Eliezer's comment: The Holy One, blessed be He, first places the righteous in doubt and suspense and then He reveals to them the real meaning of the matter.[51]

It was taught that Rabbi Eliezer explained the verse, *On the vine there were three branches* (Genesis 40:10): *the vine* is the world, the *three branches* are Abraham, Isaac, and Jacob. *It had barely budded when out came its blossoms*, these are the matriarchs; *and its clusters brought forth grapes*, these are the tribes. But Rabbi Joshua said to him, "Is a man shown in a dream what has already happened? Surely he is shown only what is yet to happen. Therefore, I say, *The vine* is the Torah, the *three branches* are Moses, Aaron, and Miriam, and *it had barely budded when out came its blossoms*, these are the members of the Sanhedrin, *and its clusters brought forth grapes* are the righteous people of every generation." Rabban Gamaliel said, however, "We still stand in need of the Modaite, for he explains the verse as referring to one place." For Rabbi Eleazar the Modaite explained, "*The vine* is Jerusalem, the *three branches* are the Temple, the King, and the High Priest and . . . *when out came its blossoms* are the young priests, and *its clusters ripened into grapes* are the drink-offerings."[52]

Rabbi Eliezer said, "Just as the thornbush is the lowliest of all the trees in the world, so the people of Israel were lowly and humble in Egypt. Therefore, did God reveal Himself to them and redeem them, as it is said, *I have come down to rescue them from the Egyptians* (Exodus 3:8)."[53]

Rabbi Eliezer applied the verse, *Like a lily among thorns* (Song of Songs 2:2) to the redemption of Israel from Egypt. Just as it is difficult to pluck a lily from among thorns, so the deliverance of Israel was a difficult matter for the Holy One, blessed be He. And so the verse reads, *Or has any god ventured to go and take for himself one nation from the midst of another by prodigious acts* (Deuteronomy 4:34).[54]

Whence did God bring darkness upon the Egyptians? Rabbi Eliezer answered, "From the darkness that is in Gehenna, *A land whose light is darkness* (Job 10:22)." Rabbi Eliezer said further that the earth drinks only from the waters of the Great Sea. But Rabbi Joshua asked, "Are not the waters of the Great Sea salty?" Rabbi Eliezer replied, "The waters of the sea are made sweet in the clouds, as it is said, *The clouds . . . distill* (Job 36:28). Where are the waters of the sea distilled? In the clouds." But Rabbi Joshua maintained that the earth drinks from the upper waters, as it is said, *The land . . . soaks up its water from the rains of heaven* (Deuteronomy 11:11). The clouds rising up from earth to heaven take water as from a gourd's mouth. They distill drops as through a sieve, so that not one drop touches another, as it is said, *Distilling waters from the thick clouds* (2 Samuel 22:12).[55]

Rabbi Eliezer ben Hyrcanus said that the Egyptians were smitten with forty plagues in Egypt—not just ten—but at the Red Sea they were smitten with two hundred. For every plague that visited them in Egypt was accompanied by three more, as the verse says, *He killed their vines with hail* (Psalms 78:47) and *He inflicted His burning anger upon them, wrath, indignation, trouble, a band of deadly messengers* (Psalms 78:49). *Wrath* is one, *indignation* is two, *trouble* is three, and *a band of deadly messengers* is four. And if these forty plagues were the work of one finger [*And the magicians said to Pharaoh, "This is the finger of God!"* (Exodus 8:15)], then with a whole hand they were smitten with two hundred plagues. [*And when Israel saw the great hand* (Exodus 14:31)].[56]

The verse reads, *Go follow the tracks (ikvei) of the sheep* (Song of Songs 1:8). Rabbi Eliezer, Rabbi Akiba, and the rabbis gave different explanations of it. Rabbi Eliezer said, "From the unleavened cakes that the Israelites took with them from Egypt you may know what I shall do for them subsequently (*ekev*). And so it is written, *Let abundant grain be in the land* (Psalms 72:16)." Rabbi

Akiba said, "From the way I surrounded them with clouds of glory, as it is said, *The Lord went before them in a pillar of cloud by day . . . that did not depart from before the people* (Exodus 13:21-2), you may know what I shall do for them subsequently (*be-ekev*). And so it is written, *A pavilion for shade . . . by day* (Isaiah 4:6)." The rabbis say, "From the way I give them food in the wilderness, food sweeter than milk and honey, you may know what I shall do for them subsequently, as it says, *And in that day the mountains shall drip with wine* (Joel 4:18)."[57]

Now consider the text, *You led (nahita) Your people like a flock in the care of Moses and Aaron* (Psalms 77:21). The word *nahita* is an acronym. Rabbi Eliezer said that it represents the first letters of the following words: *nissim*, "miracles," did You do for them; *hayyim*, "life," that You gave them; *yam*, "the sea," that You divided for them; *Torah* that You gave them. And through whom? Through the care of Moses and Aaron. Rabbi Joshua said that *nahita* stands for *niflaot*, "wonders," that You have performed for them; *herut*, "freedom," that You have given them; *yeminekha*, "Your right hand," that has saved them; *telui rosh*, "the raising of their pride," that You have given them—all through the care of Moses and Aaron. The rabbis, however, said that *nahita* stands for *neviim*, "prophets," whom You have raised up from among them; *hasidim*, "pious men," whom You have raised up from among them; *yesharim*, "upright men," whom You have raised up from among them; *temimim*, "men of integrity," whom You have raised up from among them—all through the care of Moses and Aaron. Still another explanation of the word, *nahita*. Rabbi Akiba said that it stands for *noraot*, "tremendous things," have You done against their enemies; *haron af*, "hot anger," have You directed against their foes; *yadekha*, "Your hand," fought against them; *tehomot*, "the depths," into which You have plunged them—all through the care of Moses and Aaron.[58]

Rabbi Simon, in the name of Rabbi Eliezer, suggested four lines of thought on the verse, *If your brother is in straits and has to sell part of his holding, his nearest redeemer shall come and redeem what his brother has sold* (Leviticus 25:25). Who was it, he asked, who showed kindness to those who did not need it? It was Abraham to the angels. It is written, *And he waited on them under the tree as they ate* (Genesis 18:8). Now did they really eat? Rabbi Judan explained that they seemed to be eating and drinking, the courses disappearing in the order of their arrival. What recompense did the Holy One, blessed be He, give to Abraham's children? The manna fell for them, the well came up for them, the quails were provided for them, the clouds of glory encircled them, and the pillars of fire journeyed before them. Now from this can one not learn *a minori ad majus*? If in the case of one who showed kindness to those who did not need kindness, the Holy One, blessed be He, rewarded his children, how much more so in the case of one who shows kindness to one who really needs it!

The second line of thought suggested by Rabbi Simon, quoting Rabbi Eliezer, is this: Who were they who did not show kindness to those who were not in need of it? The Ammonites and the Moabites to Israel. It is written, *Because they did not meet you with bread and water* (Deuteronomy 23:5). Now did Israel need bread and water? Is it not a fact that during all those forty years that Israel spent in the wilderness the manna fell for them, the well came up for them, the quails were provided for them, the clouds of glory encircled them, and the pillars of fire journeyed before them? This is all true, but courtesy requires that when people come from a journey they should be welcomed with food and drink. How did the Holy One, blessed be He, punish them? As a consequence of their misbehavior it was decreed that *No Ammonite or Moabite shall be admitted into the congregation of the Lord* (Deuteronomy 23:4). Now can one not learn *a minori ad majus*? If in the case of those who did not show kindness to those not in need of it, we see that they were punished, how much more so in the case of one who did not show kindness to someone who really needed it!

A third line of thought in this connection quoted by Rabbi Simon in the name of Rabbi Eliezer: Who was it who showed kindness to one to whom he was indebted? Jethro to Moses. Scripture says that Jethro spoke to his daughters about Moses, *Ask him in to break bread* (Exodus 2:20) . . . When did the Holy One, blessed be He, give Jethro his reward? . . . In the days of Saul, as is proven by the text, *Saul said to the Kenites, Come, withdraw at once . . . That I may not destroy you . . . for you showed kindness to all the Israelites* . . . (1 Samuel 15:6). Did Jethro show kindness to all the Israelites? Did he not show kindness only to Moses? True, but it teaches us that when a person shows kindness to one of the great men in Israel, it is considered as if he did it to all Israel. Now can one not learn *a minori ad majus*? If in the case of one who shows kindness to one to whom he is indebted, we see how the Holy One, blessed be He, repays him, how much more so in the case of a person who shows kindness to one to whom he is not indebted!

A final line of thought in this connection suggested by Rabbi Simon in the name of Rabbi Eliezer. Who was it who showed kindness to one who needed kindness? It was Boaz to Ruth. For the verse says, *At mealtime, Boaz said to her, "Come over here and partake of the meal, and dip your morsel in the vinegar"* (Ruth 2:14), for it was the custom of the reapers to dip their bread in the vinegar during the dry heat. *So she sat down beside the reapers* (Ruth 2:14). Of course! *He handed her kali,* that is, a little *(kalil),* a small quantity at the tips of his fingers. Yet it is written, *she ate her fill and had some left over* (Ruth 2:14). Rabbi Isaac observed that we might infer one of two things from this: either a blessing rested in the hand of the righteous man, Boaz, or a blessing rested in the bowels of that righteous woman. From the fact that it is written, *she ate her fill and had some left over,* we may learn that the blessing rested in the bowels of that righteous woman.[59]

The verse reads, *And the Lord put a word in Balaam's mouth* (Numbers 23:5). This implies that He twisted his mouth—as with a bit—and pierced it, like a man who drives a nail into a board. Rabbi Eliezer says that an angel was speaking, while Rabbi Joshua says that it was the Holy One, blessed be He.[60]

There are the verses: *If any man's wife has gone astray and broken faith with him, in that a man has had carnal relations with her unbeknown to her husband, and she keeps secret the fact that she has defiled herself . . .* (Numbers 5:12-13). How much is the minimum period for her secluding herself with another man to compel her to be subjected to the water ordeal (Numbers 5:16-28)? Sufficient to cause defilement. How much for defilement? Sufficient for intercourse. How much for intercourse? Sufficient for reaching the first stage of sexual contact. How much for this? Rabbi Eliezer says, "The time it takes for a palm tree to swing back into position against the wind." Rabbi Joshua says, "The time it takes to mix a cup of wine." Ben Azzai says, "The time it takes to drink it." Rabbi Akiba says, "The time it takes to roast an egg by rolling it in ashes." Rabbi Judah ben Batyra says, "The time it takes to swallow three such roasted eggs one after the other." Rabbi Eleazar ben Phineas says, "The time it takes a weaver to knot a thread." Penimon says, "The time she would need to stretch out her hand and take a loaf of bread out of the basket." Although it is no real proof of this last statement, there is at least a hint of it in the verse, *The last loaf of bread will go for a harlot; a married woman will snare a person of honor* (Proverbs 6:26). Rabbi Jose observed that all these minima begin only after her unfastening her *sinnar*. Rabbi Johanan commented that each one of these rabbis based his estimate upon personal experience. But did Ben Azzai ever take a wife? Some guess that he warmed up, others hold that he had married but had separated, while still others assert, *The counsel of the Lord is for those who fear Him; to them He makes known His covenant* (Psalms 26:14).[61]

Another verse on the same subject *But if the woman has not defiled herself and is pure, she shall be unharmed and able to retain seed* (Numbers 5:28). Rabbi Eliezer interpreted the verse to mean the suffering was sufficiently great to entitle her to be given children as a reward, and so if she was barren she is remembered with a child. Rabbi Joshua objected, "If that be the case all the barren women will go and act in a suspicious manner in order that they be subjected to the water ordeal, found innocent, and be remembered with a child, while the woman who remains at home will be the loser! In fact, what is meant by *she shall be unharmed and able to retain seed* is that if hitherto she has suffered in childbirth, she will henceforth be delivered with ease; if, until now, she has given birth to daughters only, she will now give birth to sons; if hitherto, she gave birth to dark-complexioned children, now she will have fair children; if undersized ones, she will have children of normal weight; if before this she gave birth once in two years, she will now have a child every year; if she had single births, she will in the future have twins." Rabbi Simon held that no reward is given for a transgression, but since, from the fact she had been previously been forbidden to her husband as long as she is under suspicion, it might be supposed that she should continue to be so in the future, Scripture explicitly states, *she shall be unharmed and able to retain seed*, making it clear that from now onward she is permitted to her husband and will give birth.[62]

Abba Hanan said in the name of Rabbi Eliezer that as a reward for their merit in counseling the princes of Israel to present the wagons on which the Tabernacle was to be carried, the tribe of Issachar was privileged to have understanding given to their tribe. And so it says, *of the Issacharites, men who had understanding of the times* (1 Chronicles 12:33). It says, in addition, *And Issachar's chiefs were with Deborah* (Judges 5:15).[63]

It was taught that Rabbi Eliezer asked, "If it has already been said that *You shall love the Lord your God . . . with all your soul* (Deuteronomy 6:5), why did the verse also say *with all your might*? And if it said *with all your might*, why did it have to say also *with all your soul*? But the answer is that if there be an individual who values his person more than his wealth, to him are the words directed, *with all your soul*. And if the individual values his wealth more than his person, to him are directed the words, with *all your might*."[64]

On the verse, *And if, for (ad) all that, you do not obey Me* (Leviticus 26:18), Rabbi Eliezer and Rabbi Joshua commented. Rabbi Eliezer explained that the Holy One, blessed be He, does not bring punishment upon Israel without first warning them. That is what is written, *And if, for (ad) all that*—reading *ad* as *ed*, "witness." Rabbi Joshua said the meaning of the verse is so that Israel shall not declare, "The afflictions are exhausted—He has no others to bring upon us." Therefore, Scripture states, *And if, for (ad) all that*—reading *ad* as *od*, "more." He does have other afflictions to bring upon us if we deserve them.[65]

We have learned that Rabbi Eliezer the Great said that when Moses died a heavenly voice was heard over a space of twelve miles square, equal to the area of Israel's encampment, announcing, "Moses, the great teacher of Israel, has died."[66]

On the verse, *While the king was at his table* (Song of Songs 1:12), Rabbi Eliezer commented: While the supreme King of kings, the Holy One, blessed be He, was at His table in the firmament, Mount Sinai was already sending up pillars of smoke, as it says, *The mountain was ablaze with flames* (Deuteronomy 4:11). Rabbi Akiba explained: While the supreme King of kings, the Holy One, blessed be He, was yet at His table in the firmament, *already the glory of the Lord abode on Mount Sinai* (Exodus 24:16). Rabbi Eliezer ben Jacob said: While the supreme King of kings was still at His table in the firmament, Michael, the great prince, had already descended and delivered our father Abraham from the fiery furnace.[67]

On the verse, *I have likened you* (dimitikh), *my darling* (Song of Songs 1:9), Rabbi Eliezer said, "Israel is like a king's daughter who has been carried away captive, and when her father was getting ready to ransom her she, out of fear, made signs to her captors and said to them, 'I am yours and I belong to you and will follow you.' Her father said to her, 'What! Do you think that I am unable to rescue you? Hold your peace *(dumah dimitikh)*, yes, be silent.' So too when the people of Israel was encamped at the Red Sea and *the Egyptians gave chase to them . . . and overtook them encamped by the sea* (Exodus 14:9), the Israelites made signs to the Egyptians out of fear and said to them, 'We are yours and we belong to you and will follow you.' Then the Holy One, blessed be He, said to them, 'What? Do you think that I am unable to rescue you? Be quiet!' The word *dimitikh* here means *shitaktikh* ('I made you silent'). Therefore, it is written, *The Lord will battle for you; you hold your peace*! (Exodus 14:14)."[68]

Rabbi Eliezer and Rabbi Joshua jointly commented on the verse, *His head is finest gold, his locks are curled and black as a raven* (Song of Songs 5:11). They said, "Curled *(taltalim)*—as if it were written *tillei tillim*—that is, 'piles upon piles' of legal teachings of the Torah. With whom are these preserved? With those who occupy themselves with them at dawn and late in the evening." Rabbi Eliezer said, "Woe to him who puts aside words of Torah but rises early for wine!"[69]

Rabbi Eliezer and Rabbi Joshua commented upon the verse, *Distribute portions to seven or even eight* (Ecclesiastes 11:2). Rabbi Eliezer's comments were as follows: Distribute *portions of seven* refers to the seven days of the week, as the word is used in *And it came to pass on the seventh [day]* (1 Kings 18:44), that is, the Sabbath day. *Or even eight* refers to the eight days of circumcision, for it is written, *and put his face between his knees* (1 Kings 18:42). Why between his knees? He, Elijah, spoke before the Holy One, blessed be He, "Lord of the universe, even if Your children possess only these two commandments, the Sabbath and circumcision, it is fitting that You should have mercy upon them."

Rabbi Joshua's comments were these: *Distribute portions to seven* refers to the seven days of Passover; or *even eight* to the eight days of the festival of Sukkot. How do we know that Shavuot, Rosh Hashanah, and Yom Kippur are to be included? The text states *even* and the word denotes inclusion.[70]

Rabbi Eliezer and Rabbi Joshua discussed the text, *Sow your seed in the morning, and don't hold back your hand in the evening* (Ecclesiastes 11:6). Rabbi Eliezer understood it to mean that if you have sown in the early season, sow also in the later season because you do not know which will succeed for you. Rabbi Joshua understood it differently. If you marry in your youth and your wife dies, marry again in your older years. For if you have children in your youth, have them again in your older years, as the verse states, *Sow your seed in the morning, and don't hold back your hand in the evening, since you don't know which is going to succeed, the one or the other.*

A different source gives another understanding of the verse by Rabbi Joshua. If a poor man comes to you in the morning, help him; if a second poor man comes in the evening, help him too because you do not know which of them the Holy One, blessed be He, has allotted to you, *the one or the other or if both are equally good.*[71]

The verse reads, *Meanwhile, Boaz had gone to the gate and sat down there. And now the redeemer* [or *kinsman*] *whom Boaz had mentioned passed by* (Ruth 4:1). Was the kinsman waiting behind the gate that he should so quickly come along? Rabbi Berekhiah said that the great men, Rabbi Eliezer and Rabbi Joshua, explained it. Rabbi Eliezer said that Boaz played his part, Ruth played hers, and Naomi hers. Whereupon the Holy One, blessed be He, said, "I too must play My role," and He called out, "Hello there, *Peloni Almoni* (So-and-so) come along now!" But Rabbi Joshua maintained that *Peloni Almoni* was the name of the kinsman.[72]

Rabbi Eliezer, Rabbi Joshua, and Rabbi Akiba commented upon the verse, *Who closed the sea behind doors/When it gushed forth out of the womb* (Job 38:8). Rabbi Eliezer said that just as a house has doors, so a woman too has doors, as it is written, *Because it shut not up the doors of my mother's womb* (Job 3:10). Rabbi Joshua said that just as for a house there are keys, so too for a woman, as it is written . . . *God heeded her and opened her womb* (Genesis 30:22). Rabbi Akiba said that just as a house has hinges (*tzirim*), even so does a woman have labor pains (*tzirim*), as it is written, . . . *she was seized with labor pains, and she crouched down and gave birth* (1 Samuel 4:19).[73]

Rabbi Simon the Pious told Rabbi Eliezer, "I once entered the area between the hall leading to the interior of the Temple and the altar without having washed my hands and feet." Rabbi Eliezer said to him, "Who is more dear, you or the high priest?" Rabbi Simon did not answer. Rabbi Eliezer said, "You are embarrassed to say that even the dog of the high priest is more precious than you!" Rabbi Simon answered, "My master, you have said it." To which Rabbi Eliezer responded, "By the holy service! If even the high priest were to have entered that area in the Temple without having washed his hands and feet, they would have broken his head with clubs. How fortunate you were that a Temple superintendent did not find you!"[74]

Rabbi Eliezer was leaning on Rabbi Simon bar Kahana when they passed by a fence. He said to him, "Bring me a sliver of wood from the fence that I may use it as a toothpick." But he thought better of it and said, "Do not bring me a thing, for if you do, everyone will do the same and ruin the man's fence."[75]

Rabbi Abbahu in the name of Rabbi Eliezer said that we ought to be grateful to the imposters who beg, pretending to be poor, because were it not for the fact that they are imposters, the person who refused their begging would at once incur the penalty of death. For it says, *He will cry out to the Lord against you and you will sin* (Deuteronomy 15:9), and it says further, *The person who sins he shall die* (Ezekiel 18:4).[76]

It was taught in the name of Rabbi Eliezer that vengeance against Israel comes through the hands of the poor, as is proved by the text, *He will cry out to the Lord against you and you will sin* (Deuteronomy 15:9). And vengeance against Edom is by the hands of Israel, for it says, *I will wreak My vengeance on Edom through My people Israel* (Ezekiel 25:14).[77]

Rabbi Eliezer the Great applied the verse, *O God, heathen have entered Your domain* (Psalms 79:1) to the Emperor Trajan, who came and seized Alexandria of Egypt, in which there were one hundred and twenty myriads of people [Jews], and persuaded them to assemble in the Valley of Yedayim, where that people (the Greek inhabitants?) would not have the upper hand over them. They went out and stood in the Valley of Yedayim and he posted fifty thousand swordsmen at their rear and butchered them until not one was left alive; as Scripture says, *Their blood was shed like water . . .* (Psalms 79:3).[78]

Rabbi Eliezer the Great also said, "There are two streams in the Valley of Yedayim, one running this way and the other that way. It was estimated by the sages that at one time they ran red, two parts water to one part blood. A *baraita* tells us that for seven years the Gentiles fertilized their fields with the blood of Jews, it being unnecessary for them to use ordinary fertilizer.[79]

Our rabbis taught that once it happened that Rabbi Eliezer was sitting and lecturing the entire day of the festival on the laws of the festival. When the first group left the study hall he said, "These are people of large barrels." When the second group left he said, "These are people of casks." Upon the departure of the third group, he said, "These are people of pitchers, and after the next group left, he said, "These are people of flasks." When the fifth group walked out, his comment was, "These are people of beakers." When the sixth group began to go he said, "These are the people of the curse." He then looked at his disciples who still remained, and their faces grew pale; whereupon he said to them, "My sons, I did not speak this way about you, but of those who walked out. They put aside eternal life and instead occupy themselves with ephemeral life." When his students took leave of him after the studies had come to an end, he said to them, "*Go, eat choice foods and drink sweet drinks and send portions to whoever has nothing prepared, for the day is holy to our Lord. Do not be sad, for your rejoicing in the Lord is the source of your strength* (Nehemiah 8:10)."[80]

It was taught that Rabbi Eliezer said, "The dead whom Ezekiel resurrected stood up on their feet, gave voice to song, and then died immediately. Which song did they sing? 'The Lord slays in righteousness and revives in mercy.' " Rabbi Joshua said, "This was the song they sang, *The Lord deals death and gives life,/Casts down into Sheol and raises up* (1 Samuel 2:6)." Rabbi Judah ben Batyra rose and said, "I am one of the descendants of those resurrected dead and these are the *tefillin* that my grandfather left me from them." Rabbi Eliezer ben Rabbi Jose the Galilean said, "The dead whom Ezekiel revived went up to the land of Israel, married wives, and fathered sons and daughters."[81]

With regard to the hundred and eighty-five thousand slain soldiers in the army of Assyria besieging Jerusalem, with what were they struck down? Rabbi Eliezer said, "He smote them with His hand, as it is written, *And when Israel saw the great hand which the Lord had wielded against the Egyptians* (Exodus 14:31). That was the hand that would some day wreak vengeance upon Sennacherib." Rabbi Joshua said, "He struck them down with His finger, as it is said, *And the magicians said to Pharaoh, 'This is the finger of God!'* (Exodus 8:14). That was the finger that would some day take vengeance against Sennacherib." Rabbi Eliezer ben Rabbi Jose said, "The Holy One, blessed be He, said to the angel Gabriel, 'Is your scythe sharpened?' He answered, 'Master of the universe! It has been sharpened since the six days of Creation,' as it is written, *For they have fled before swords: before the sharpened sword* (Isaiah 21:15)." Rabbi Simon ben Johai said, "It was the time for the ripening of fruits, so the Holy One, blessed be He, said to

Gabriel, 'When you go forth to ripen the fruits, attack them,' as it is written, *He shall catch you/Every time he passes through;/He shall pass through every morning,/Every day and every night,/And it shall be sheer horror/To grasp the message* (Isaiah 28:19).

Rabbi Judah of Sikhnin said in the name of Rabbi Eliezer, "There is no place in the world in which a *bet rova* measure of seed can be planted that does not contain nine *kav* measures of evil spirits."[82]

Once Rabbi Eliezer and Rabbi Joshua went on a mission to collect funds for the support of scholars. They came to the valley of Antiokhia, where lived a man by the name of Abba Judan. He would always fulfill the commandment of supporting the sages in a generous manner. But he had become impoverished, and when he caught sight of Rabbi Eliezer and Rabbi Joshua he hid himself from them. He went into his house and remained indoors for two days, not venturing out into the street. His wife asked him, "Why have you not gone out for two days?" He answered, "The rabbis have come to gather funds for those who labor in the Torah and I am not in a position to give them anything. I am therefore ashamed to go out into the street." His wife, who was even more righteous than he, said, "We still have one field left. Sell one half of it and give the proceeds to them." He went and did so, selling half his field for five gold pieces, which he gave to the rabbis, saying to them, "Pray for me." They prayed for him and blessed him, "May God fulfill your need." They left to collect funds elsewhere. After some time Abba Judan went to plow the half of the field he had retained. As he was plowing, his cow fell and broke its leg. As he went down to lift her up, the Holy One, blessed be He, opened his eyes and he found a treasure there. He exclaimed, "My cow's leg was broken but it turned out for my benefit!" He became richer than ever before. On their return journey the rabbis again passed through that place and they inquired about him, "How is Abba Judan doing?" People replied, "You mean Abba Judan with all the servants, with all the oxen, with all the camels, with all the goats? Who can even catch a glimpse of him!" When Abba Judan learned of their arrival he went to meet them. They asked, "How are you doing?" He gave them one thousand gold pieces and said, "Your prayers have borne fruit and fruit from fruit." They told him, "As you live, even though others gave more than you, we wrote down your name at the very top of the list." They applied to him the verse,

A man's gift eases his way and gives him access to the great (Proverbs 18:16).[83]

A certain woman came to Rabbi Eliezer and said to him, "In a dream I saw the loft of the upper story of my house split open." He told her, "You will give birth to a son." She went away, and it happened as she had been told. Again she dreamed the same dream and came and told it to Rabbi Eliezer, who gave her the same interpretation. She subsequently had a second son. A third time the identical dream came to her and she went to Rabbi Eliezer but she could not find him, so she told her dream to his disciples. "You will bury your husband," they told her. Soon afterward her husband died. When Rabbi Eliezer heard a cry of wailing he asked what had happened and he was told the story. He rebuked his disciples, "You have killed a man—is it not written, *And as he interpreted for us, so it came to pass* (Genesis 41:13)?"[84]

It has been taught that Rabbi Eliezer said that the days of the Messiah will last forty years, as it is written, *Forty years shall I take hold of that generation* (Psalms 95:10). Rabbi Eleazar ben Azariah said the period would last for seventy years, as it is written, *In that day, Tyre shall remain forgotten for seventy years, equaling the lifetime of one king* (Isaiah 23:15). Now who is *the one king*? The Messiah, of course. Rabbi Judah ha-Nasi said that the days of the Messiah would extend over three generations, for it is written, *Let them fear You as long as the sun shines, while the moon lasts, a generation and generations* (Psalms 72:5).

Another *baraita* taught that Rabbi Eliezer said that the days of the Messiah will last forty years. In one place, it is written, *He subjected you to the hardships of hunger and then gave you manna to eat* (Deuteronomy 8:3). In another place it is written, *Give us joy for as long as you have afflicted us* (Psalms 90:15)—just as we suffered in the wilderness for forty years, so shall we rejoice with the Messiah for forty years. Rabbi Dosa said that the time of the Messiah will last for four hundred years. In one place it is written, *And they shall be enslaved and oppressed four hundred years* (Genesis 15:13), while elsewhere it is written, *Give us joy for as long as You have afflicted us* (Psalms 90:15). Rabbi Judah ha-Nasi said that the years of the Messiah will cover three hundred and sixty-five years, according to the number of days in a solar year, as it is written, *For I had planned a day of vengeance/And My year of redemption arrived* (Isaiah 63:4).[85]

It has been taught that there never was "a condemned city" and there never will be. With whom does that agree? With Rabbi Eliezer who said that no city containing even a single *mezuzah* can be condemned. Why not? Because it is written, *Gather all its spoil into the open square, and burn the town and all its spoil* (Deuteronomy 13:17). But if it contains a single *mezuzah*, this is impossible because it is written, *Cut down the images of their gods, obliterating their name. . . . You shall not do so to the Lord your God* (Deuteronomy 12:3–4). Rabbi Jonathan said, "I saw a condemned city and sat upon its ruins."[86]

Rabbi Eliezer was asked by his disciples, "How far should one go in the practice of honoring one's parents?" He answered, "Go and see the behavior of a certain non-Jew in Ashkelon, Dama ben Natina by name. His mother was not altogether well mentally and she used to slap him with her slipper in the presence of his colleagues. All he would say was 'Mother, it is enough.' Once she dropped the slipper. He stooped and picked it up so that she would not have to trouble herself. It happened that the sages came to him to buy a precious stone to replace one that had been lost from the vestments of the high priest. They agreed with him upon a price of one thousand gold pieces. He went in to get the jewel and saw that his father had fallen asleep with his leg stretched across the box that contained it. He did not want to disturb him and came out empty-handed. The sages saw that he did not bring out the stone and they thought he wanted a higher price, so they raised their offer to ten thousand gold pieces. When his father awoke Dama entered his room and brought out the stone. The sages offered the ten thousand gold pieces, but he exclaimed, "Heavens forfend! I will not make a profit of honoring my father. I shall take from you the price of one thousand gold pieces that I had originally set with you." And what reward did the Holy One, blessed be He, give him? The following year a red heifer was born in his flock and when the sages came to purchase it for the Temple sacrifice, he told them, "I know that you will give me any price I ask, but I want only the money I lost at your earlier visit because I would not profit from honoring my father."

He had so much respect for his father that during his father's entire life Dama would never sit upon the stone seat upon which his father customarily sat. In addition, when his father died, he venerated the stone.[87]

Rabbi Eliezer was once asked, "How far does one have to go

in honoring one's father and mother?" He replied, "Even to the point of one's parent throwing a money bag of *dinars* into the sea while the son or daughter remains silent in order not to embarrass the parent."[88]

The son of a certain widow once asked Rabbi Eliezer, "Suppose one's father asked for a drink of water and at the same time one's mother asked for a drink of water, whom does one serve first?" He answered, "Delay honoring the mother and honor the father first, since both the son or daughter and the mother are to give honor to the father." The man then went to Rabbi Joshua who gave him the same answer. "But, Rabbi," the man asked him, "suppose the mother and father were divorced, what then?" Rabbi Joshua said, "From looking at your eyelids it may be seen that you are the son of a widow. But to answer your question—pour some water for them into a basin and screech for them like roosters."[89]

There was a case of a fast decreed on Hanukkah in Lod and it was reported that Rabbi Eliezer got a haircut and Rabbi Joshua took a bath on the same day. The latter told those who had decreed the fast on a day during Hanukkah, "Go and carry out a second fast because you fasted on Hanukkah."[90]

It once happened that because of a drought Rabbi Eliezer ordered the people to fast for thirteen different days. On the last fast day, with no rain as yet, the people began to leave the place of prayer. Whereupon Rabbi Eliezer said to them, "Have you prepared your burial places that you are giving up?" They burst out weeping and the rains came.

On another occasion of sustained dry weather, Rabbi Eliezer led the people in the recital of twenty-four prayers, but he was not answered. Rabbi Akiba followed him and prayed, "Our Father, our King, You are our Father; Our Father, our King, we have no King but You; Our Father, our King, we have sinned before You; Our Father, our King, have compassion upon us; Our Father, our King, do it for the sake of Your name." Immediately he was answered and the rains came. The people thought that it was because he was greater than Rabbi Eliezer. But a heavenly voice at once spoke up and said, "It was not because Rabbi Akiba is greater than Rabbi Eliezer that his prayer was answered but that he forgoes retaliating against those who do him harm while Rabbi Eliezer does not."[91]

The story is told that once Rabbi Ilai went to Lod to pay his respects to his teacher, Rabbi Eliezer, on a festival. Rabbi Eliezer said to him, "Ilai, are you not among those who rest on a festival?" For Rabbi Eliezer used to say, "I speak the praise of the so-called lazy people who do not even leave their homes on a festival, for it is said, *You shall rejoice on your festival with your son and daughter* (Deuteronomy 16:14)."[92]

We have learned that Rabbi Eliezer said that on a festival a person should either eat and drink, or sit and study. Rabbi Joshua said that a person should divide the day, half for eating and drinking and half for the study hall.[93]

It is told that Rabbi Eliezer once spent the festival in Upper Galilee and was resting in the *sukkah* of Rabbi Johanan ben Ilai in Caesarea. When the sun shone into the *sukkah* his host asked Rabbi Eliezer, "My master, shall I spread a sheet over the thatch on the *sukkah*?" He answered, "There was no tribe in Israel that did not produce a judge." The sun soon covered half of the *sukkah*. Again, Rabbi Johanan asked, "Shall I spread a sheet over the *sukkah* roofing?" Rabbi Eliezer replied, "There was not a single tribe in Israel that did not produce prophets, and the tribes of Judah and Benjamin produced kings crowned by word of the prophets." The sun now covered Rabbi Eliezer completely. Rabbi Johanan took a sheet and covered the top of the *sukkah*. Rabbi Eliezer fastened his cloak, threw it over his shoulder, and walked out—not because he had a different opinion as to the law but because he never uttered a decision that he had not heard from his teacher.[94]

There is another story about Rabbi Eliezer when he was staying in Upper Galilee. He was asked thirty questions pertaining to the laws of the *sukkah*. About twelve he said, "I have heard a precedent," about eighteen he stated that he had not heard any prior decision. Rabbi Jose ben Rabbi Judah said, "It was the other way around—concerning eighteen, he had a precedent, concerning twelve he had not." The questioners asked Rabbi Eliezer, "Rabbi, are all your legal decisions based only on what you have already heard?" He said to them, "You wish to compel me to say that which I have not heard from my masters, but I tell you that first, no one came into the study hall earlier than I; second, I never fell asleep there, not for a deep sleep nor for even a nap; third, no man did I leave behind when I left the study hall; fourth, I never engaged in idle talk; and last, I never uttered a legal decision that I had not heard from my teacher."[95]

Who is to be considered an *am ha-aretz*? He who does not

recite the *Shema* morning and evening—this was the opinion of Rabbi Eliezer. Rabbi Joshua said that it is the man who does not put on *tefillin*. Ben Azzai said that it is he who does not wear *tzitzit* on his garment. Rabbi Nathan said that it is the person who has no *mezuzah* on his doorpost. Rabbi Jonathan ben Joseph said that it is he who has sons and does not raise them in the study of the Torah, while others said that even the man who has studied Scripture and the laws derived from it but who has not served scholars as a disciple is to be considered an *am ha-aretz*.[96]

Rabbi Eliezer said, "If it were not that they need us for purposes of trade, the *amei ha-aretz* would kill us."[97]

The verse reads, *And all the peoples of the earth shall see that the Lord's name is proclaimed upon you, and they shall stand in fear of you* (Deuteronomy 28:10). We have learned that Rabbi Eliezer the Great said, "This refers to the *tefillin* on the head."[98]

Neither in winter nor summer would Rabbi Eliezer remove his *tefillin*—in imitation of the practice of his teacher, Rabban Johanan ben Zakkai. In the winter, when Rabban Johanan could tolerate it, he wore both the *tefillin* on the head and arm. But in the summer when, because of the heat, he could not tolerate it, he wore the *tefillin* only on the arm.[99]

It once happened that Rabbi Eliezer went to Ubelin where he stayed with a certain homeowner. It was the practice there to bathe in a cave. When Rabbi Eliezer took his clothes off and removed his *tefillin*, his host said to him, "Rabbi, is not the water of the next cave better than the water of this one?" Although there was only a distance of four cubits between the two caves, Rabbi Eliezer dressed and put on his *tefillin* to go to the next cave because he never walked four cubits without wearing *tefillin*. In this manner did Rabbi Eliezer make the commandment of *tefillin* a permanent practice. Thus Rabbi Eliezer used to say, "Great is the commandment of *tefillin*, for the Holy One, blessed be He, said to Israel, . . . *but you shall meditate therein day and night* (Joshua 1:8). 'Sovereign of the universe,' said Israel to the Holy One, blessed be He, 'Is it possible for us to meditate in the Torah day and night?' The Holy One, blessed be He, answered them, 'My children, put *tefillin* on your heads and on your arms and I shall account it to you as if you meditated in the Torah day and night'; as it is written, *And this shall serve you as a sign on your hand and as a reminder on your forehead—in order that the teachings of the Lord may be in your mouth* (Exodus 13:9)."

Rabbi Joshua argued, "What Rabbi Eliezer teaches makes the

point impossible. The verse reads, *In His law does he meditate day and night* (Psalms 1:2), but the ordinance of *tefillin* can be observed only during the day, as it is said, *You shall keep this institution at its set time from day to day* (Exodus 13:10)."

Rabbi Eliezer asked Rabbi Joshua, "Then, according to you, how can the words, *In His law does he meditate day and night* be observed?" Rabbi Joshua answered, "By the recital of the *Shema*, for when a person recites the *Shema* morning and evening, the Holy One, blessed be He, reckons it for him as if he had labored day and night in the study of the Torah."[100]

Rabbi Eliezer began a discourse with the verse, *Who can tell the mighty acts of the Lord, proclaim all His praises?* (Psalms 106:2). "Is there any man who can utter the mighty acts of the Holy One, blessed be He, or can proclaim all His praise? Not even the ministering angels are able to narrate God's praise. But to investigate a part of His mighty deeds pertaining to what He has done and what He will do in the future is permissible, so that His name should be exalted among His creatures whom He has created, from one end of the world to the other, as it is said, *One generation shall laud Your works to another* (Psalms 145:4)."[101]

We have learned that Rabbi Eliezer stated that the world was created in the month of *Tishri*. In *Tishri* the patriarchs were born and in the same month they died. Isaac was an exception, for he was born during Passover. On Rosh Hashanah Sarah, Rachel, and Hannah conceived. On Rosh Hashanah Joseph was freed from prison and slavery ended for our ancestors in Egypt. During *Nisan* they were redeemed and during *Tishri* they will be redeemed by the Messiah. Rabbi Joshua said that the world was created during the month of *Nisan*. During the same month the patriarchs were born, and they died in *Nisan*. Isaac was born during Passover itself. On Rosh Hashanah, Sarah, Rachel, and Hannah conceived. On the same holiday, Joseph was freed from prison and slavery ended for our ancestors in Egypt. They were redeemed during *Nisan*, and during the same month in the future they will experience the final redemption.[102]

The verse reads, *Both* [man and beast] *go to the same place; both came from dust and both return to dust* (Ecclesiastes 3:20). Rabbi Eliezer and Rabbi Joshua differed. The former said that all that the Holy One, blessed be He, created in heaven has its origin in heaven, and all that He created on earth has its origin on earth. On what is this statement based? On the following verses: *Praise the Lord from the heavens;/praise Him on high./Praise Him all His angels . . . Praise the Lord, O you who are on earth,/all sea monsters and ocean depths,/fire and hail, snow and smoke*, etc., to the end of the psalm (Psalms 148:1–7). But Rabbi Joshua said that all that the Holy One, blessed be He, created in heaven and on earth had its origin in heaven. Although it is written about snow: *He commands the snow, "Fall to the ground!"* (Job 37:6), yet its origin is surely from heaven, as it is stated, *For as the rain or snow drops from heaven* (Isaiah 55:10). Just as the snow is created out of heaven, though its existence is on the earth, so everything that is in heaven and on earth was created only in heaven.[103]

Rabbi Eliezer said that the world was created beginning with its center, as it is written, *Whereupon the earth melts into a mass,/ And its clods stick together* (Job 38:38)—that is, first the center piece was created, then the other parts adhered to it. Rabbi Joshua said that the world was created beginning with its outermost parts, as it is written, *He commands the snow, "Fall to the ground!"/And the downpour of rain, His mighty downpour of rain* (Job 37:6). Rabbi Isaac said that the Holy One, blessed be He, threw a stone into the sea and from that place the world was founded, as it is written, *Onto what were its bases sunk?/Who set its cornerstone?* (Job 38:6). And the sages said that the world was created beginning with Zion, as it is written—*A psalm of Asaph: God, the Lord God spoke/and summoned the world from east to west./From Zion, perfect in beauty, God appeared* . . . (Psalms 50:1–2); that is, from Zion appeared the beauty of the world.[104]

Rabbi Eliezer said that the world is like an exedra whose north side is not enclosed, and so when the sun reaches the northwest corner in the evening, it turns around and goes back to the eastern side of the sky. Rabbi Joshua, however, said that the world is like a tent whose north side is enclosed. When the sun reaches the northwest corner it goes around to the back part of the tent until it reaches the east, as it is written, *It goes toward the south and turns again toward the north* . . . (Ecclesiastes 1:6); that is, *it goes toward the south* by day and *turns again toward the north* by night. *It turns about continually in its course, and the wind returns again to its circuits* (Ecclesiastes 1–6)—this refers to the eastern and western sides of the heaven, which the sun sometimes traverses and sometimes goes around.[105]

The verse reads, *All streams flow into the sea* (Ecclesiastes 1:7). Whence does the earth drink? Rabbi Eliezer and Rabbi Joshua offered different answers. Rabbi Eliezer said that it drinks from the waters of the ocean, for it is written, *But a flow would well up from the ground and water the whole surface of the earth* (Genesis 2:6). Rabbi Joshua said to him, "But are not the waters of the ocean salty?" He answered, "They are sweetened by the clouds, as it is written, *The skies rain;/They pour down on all mankind* (Job 36:28). When are the waters sweetened? In the skies." Rabbi Joshua, on the other hand, said that the earth drinks from the waters above, as it is written, the land . . . *soaks up its water from the rains of heaven* (Deuteronomy 11:11). The clouds raise themselves from the earth to heaven and receive the waters as from the mouth of a bottle, as it is written, *Which cluster into rain, from His mist* (Job 36:27). And the clouds distill the water as through a sieve, one drop not touching another, as it is written, *Darkness of waters, thick clouds of the skies* (Psalms 18:12). Why are the skies called *shehakim* in Hebrew? Because they grind (*Shohekim*) the water into separate drops.[106]

Our rabbis taught that Rabbi Eliezer said that all the songs and words of praise voiced by David in the Book of Psalms were uttered with reference to himself. But Rabbi Joshua said that David spoke them with reference to the community, while the sages said that some refer to the community and others to himself. Those uttered in the singular refer to himself and those spoken in the plural refer to the community.[107]

It happened once that a student led the prayer service in the presence of Rabbi Eliezer and made it longer than usual. His students said to Rabbi Eliezer, "Our master, how this fellow stretches out the service!" Rabbi Eliezer replied to them, "Was he any longer than Moses our master of whom it is written, *When I lay prostrate before the Lord those forty days and forty nights* (Deuteronomy 9:25)?" Again it happened that another disciple led the prayer service in the presence of Rabbi Eliezer and he made the service very short. His disciples said to Rabbi Eliezer, "What an abbreviator is this fellow!" He said to them, "Was he any shorter than Moses, our master, whose prayer was *O God, pray heal her!* (Numbers 12:13)?"

Rabbi Eliezer stated that the Holy One, blessed be He, said to Moses, "There is a time to pray briefly and a time to pray at length. When My children are in great danger, with the sea shutting them in and the enemy in hot chase, and all the while you stand here, piling prayer upon prayer! *Tell the Israelites to go forward* (Exodus 14:15). For Rabbi Eliezer used to say, "There is a time to be brief in prayer and a time to be lengthy."[108]

Aquila the Proselyte asked Rabbi Eliezer, "Since the performance of circumcision is so beloved by the Holy One, blessed be He, why did He not include it in the Ten Commandments?" Rabbi Eliezer answered, "Because it is a commandment given before the Ten Commandments. It is written *and keep My covenant* (Exodus 19:5), which refers not only to the covenant of the Sabbath but also to the covenant of circumcision."[109]

Rabbi Eliezer said, "If you will succeed in keeping the Sabbath you will escape three bad periods of time: the day of Gog, the suffering preceding the coming of the Messiah, and the Great Judgment Day."[110]

We have learned that Rabbi Eliezer said that the night has three watches and at the start of each watch the Holy One, blessed be He, roars like a lion over the loss of His abode, the Temple, as it is said, *The Lord roars from on high,/He makes His voice heard from His holy dwelling* (Jeremiah 25:30). And the division of the night may be recognized by these signs. At the first watch the donkey brays, at the second dogs bark, and at the third the infant suckles from its mother's breast and the wife speaks with her husband.[111]

Do not be astonished at the virtue of Rabbi Akiba. Look at Rabbi Eliezer, who was more distinguished than he. Rabbi Eliezer raised his sister's daughter for thirteen years and she slept with him in the same bed until the signs of her puberty appeared. Then he said to her, "Go now and get married." She replied, "Am I not your maid, content to be a servant to wash the feet of your disciples?" He said to her, "My daughter, I am now an old man. Go and marry a young man of your age." She answered, "Have I not already told you that I am your maid, content to be a servant to wash the feet of your disciples?" When he heard what she had said, he asked her consent to be betrothed and married her.[112]

Rabbi Eliezer said that if a man teaches Torah to his daughter it is as though he has taught her lechery. But Ben Azzai said that a man ought to give his daughter a knowledge of the Torah.[113]

A Roman lady asked Rabbi Eliezer, "How is it that though the Israelites committed only one sin in worshiping the Golden Calf, they died through three kinds of death?" He said to her, "A woman has no wisdom except at the distaff, for it is written, *And all the skilled women spun with their own hands* (Exodus 35:25)."

Hyrcanus, his son, said to him, "Because you did not answer her with one teaching of the Torah, she will deprive you of three hundred *kor* of tithe every year." To which Rabbi Eliezer replied, "Let the words of the Torah be burned rather than be entrusted to women!" When Hyrcanus left, Rabbi Eliezer's students said to him, "Master! You warded off this woman with a reed, but what answer will you give us?"[114]

Once a woman who wished to become a convert came to Rabbi Eliezer and said, "Rabbi, receive me." He said to her, "Tell me about your past life." She told him, "My youngest son was conceived through my eldest son." He stormed at her, so she went to Rabbi Joshua, who received her as a convert. His disciples asked him, "Rabbi Eliezer drove her away and you accept her?" He answered, "When she set her mind on becoming a convert, she no longer lived in her past world, as it is written, *All who go to her cannot return* (Proverbs 2:19), and if they do return to their evil ways, *neither do they find again the paths of life* (Proverbs 2:19). Rabbi Eliezer taught, "Why did the Torah warn in thirty-six places—and some say forty-six—against the mistreatment of converts? Because they have a tendency to do wrong."[115]

The verse reads, *All streams flow into the sea,/Yet the sea is never full* (Ecclesiastes 1:7). Once Rabbi Eliezer and Rabbi Joshua were traveling on the Great Sea when their ship entered an area where the water did not flow. Rabbi Eliezer said to Rabbi Joshua, "We must have been brought here for the purpose of carrying out an experiment. They filled a barrel with water from that place. When they arrived in Rome the emperor Hadrian asked them, "What is the nature of the ocean water?" They replied, "It is water that absorbs other water." He further asked them, "Is it possible that the rivers should run into the sea without it becoming full?" They answered, "It absorbs whatever water in the world that flows into it." He said to them, "I shall not believe it until you prove it to me." They took a flask, filled it with the ocean water from their barrel, then poured other water into the flask. The ocean water in the flask absorbed the new water.[116]

A large ship was once sailing on the ocean when a gale caught it and drove it to a place where the water stood still and the ship could not move. When the passengers saw that they were in great danger—for they were stranded and their food might give out—they said, "Come, let us share our provisions, so that if we die, we all die and if we live, we all live." As a reward for their concern for each other, the Omnipresent enlightened their eyes and they thought of a plan. They took a kid, slaughtered and roasted it, and hung it up on the west side of the ship. A large sea animal, attracted by the smell, came and began to drag the ship until it sailed into an area where the water was flowing and was able to continue the voyage. When the people reached their destination and entered Rome, they narrated the story to Rabbi Eliezer and Rabbi Joshua, who applied to them the text, *Cast your bread upon the waters* (Ecclesiastes 11:1).[117]

Once Rabbi Eliezer and Rabbi Joshua were sailing aboard a ship and Rabbi Eliezer fell asleep while Rabbi Joshua was awake. Suddenly Rabbi Joshua shook with fright and so woke Rabbi Eliezer, who asked, "What happened, Joshua?" Rabbi Joshua answered, "I saw a brilliant light in the sea." Rabbi Eliezer said, "Perhaps you saw the eyes of the leviathan about whom it is written, *And his eyes are like the glimmerings of dawn* (Job 41:10)."[118]

There was a dispute between Rabbi Eliezer and the other sages on the question of a baking oven that had been cut up into rings with sand placed between each ring. This was the kind of oven made by Akhnai. Rabbi Eliezer declared such an oven insusceptible to ritual uncleanness, but the other sages stated that it is susceptible. On that day Rabbi Eliezer raised every possible argument to support his opinion but the sages did not accept them. Then he said to them, "If the law is as I say, let this carob tree prove it," and the carob tree uprooted itself and moved one hundred cubits. Some say it was four hundred cubits. The sages told him, "One does not bring a proof from a carob tree." Again he said to them, "If the law is as I say, let the walls of the study hall prove it." The walls leaned over, about to fall, when Rabbi Joshua rebuked them, saying, "When scholars are engaged in a legal dispute, what right have you to interfere?" The walls did not fall, out of respect for Rabbi Joshua, nor did they revert to a vertical position because of their respect for Rabbi Eliezer. They stood like that afterward, leaning over. Again, Rabbi Eliezer said to the sages, "If the law is as I say, let heaven prove it!" A heavenly voice then cried out, "Why do you dispute with Rabbi Eliezer since in all matters the law is as he says!" But Rabbi Joshua stood up and exclaimed, "*It is not in the heavens* (Deuteronomy 30:12)." What did he mean by that? Rabbi Jeremiah explained, "Since the Torah has already been given at Mount Sinai, it is no longer in heaven and we need pay no attention to a heavenly voice because it is written in the Torah, *Follow after the majority* (Exodus 23:2)."

The prophet Elijah appeared to Rabbi Natan, who asked him, "How did God react at that hour?" Elijah replied, "God laughed and said, 'My sons have gotten the better of me! My sons have gotten the better of me!'"

It was said that on that day all the items declared ritually clean by Rabbi Eliezer were brought into the academy and burned. Then they voted to place him under the ban. The question arose as to who would go and give him the news, until Rabbi Akiba said, "I shall go and tell him lest someone unfit break the news to him suddenly and that would cause the world's destruction." What did Rabbi Akiba do? He dressed himself all in black, wrapped himself around in black, and when he came to Rabbi Eliezer he sat at a distance of four cubits away from him. Seeing all this, Rabbi Eliezer asked, "Akiba, why is today different from previous days?" He answered, "My master, it appears that your colleagues have separated themselves from you." Rabbi Eliezer at once rent his garments, took off his shoes, and sat on the ground, tears flowing from his eyes. At that time the crops failed everywhere by a third—the olives, the wheat, and the barley. Others say that even the dough ready for baking in the hands of women spoiled. They say that Rabbi Eliezer's grief was so great on that day that wherever his eye fell, a fire broke out. Rabbi Gamaliel was on his way home by ship when a gale suddenly roared, almost sinking the vessel. He said, "It seems to me that this storm is because of Rabbi Eliezer ben Hyrcanus," and he arose and prayed, "Master of the Universe, it is revealed and known to You that the decree of excommunication that I acted upon I did not for my honor and not for the honor of my father's house, but for Your honor so that controversies in law shall not multiply among the Jewish people." The sea ceased storming and was calm.

Imma Shalom was the wife of Rabbi Eliezer and the sister of Rabban Gamaliel. From the day of his excommunication onward she would not permit her husband to recite the personal *tahnun* prayers. A certain day she mistook for Rosh Hodesh when those prayers are not recited. She had thought that the month just ending was a defective month and therefore the next day was the beginning of the new month, when in fact it was a full month and therefore the next day was the last day of the month just ending.

Others say that the reason she was not with her husband to prevent his reciting the *tahnun* prayers was that a poor man was standing at the door and she brought out some bread to him. On her return she found that her husband was already reciting the *tahnun* prayers. She called out to him, "Get up, you have killed my brother." It did not take long before the news came from Rabban Gamaliel's home that he had died. Rabbi Eliezer asked his wife, "How did you know that this would happen?" She answered, "I have a tradition from my father's house that all the heavenly gates may at times be closed but never the gates of wounded feelings."[119]

Once Rabbi Eliezer was walking through the market and he saw a woman cleaning her house. She threw out the dirt and it fell on his head. He said, "It would appear from what has just happened that my colleagues will bring me near, as it is written, *He raises the poor from the dust* (Psalms 113:7)."[120]

Rabbi Eliezer was once arrested by the Romans for heresy on the charge that he was a Christian. He was made to go up and stand on a raised platform to be tried before the governor. The Roman governor asked him, "Is it possible that a scholar like you should be involved with such worthless matters?" He answered him, "I believe the Judge can be relied upon." The governor thought that the rabbi was referring to him, but Eliezer was alluding to God. The governor then declared, "Since I have been acknowledged by you to be right and since I have been thinking that it is not possible for your academies to go astray with such idle matters, you are consequently acquitted and free to go."

After Rabbi Eliezer left, he was greatly distressed that he had been arrested for heresy. His disciples came to his home to comfort him but he would not be comforted. Rabbi Akiba said to him, "My master, may I say something?" He replied, "Say it." Akiba then said, "My master, perhaps one of the Christian sectarians expounded something in your presence and it pleased you." He responded, "By heaven! You have reminded me of something. Once I was walking up the upper market of Sepphoris when there came toward me a man by the name of Jacob of Kfar Sekhaniah, one of the disciples of Jesus ben Pantiri, who told me something in his name. He said, 'It is written in your Torah, *You shall not bring the fee of a whore . . . into the house of the Lord your God* (Deuteronomy 23:19). But may such money be used for the purpose of building a latrine for the high priest?' I made no reply. He then said to me, 'Thus was I taught by my master, *For they were amassed from fees of harlotry,/And they shall become harlots' fees again* (Micah 1:7)—they have come from a place of filth, let them go to a place of filth.' This pleased me and, therefore, I was arrested for heresy. For I transgressed that which is written in the Torah, *Keep yourself far away from her*—that means sectarianism—*Do not come near the doorway of her house* (Proverbs 5:8)—that means the ruling power."[121]

Rabbi Eliezer said, "Be diligent to learn the Torah and know how to answer a heretic." The whole universe is maintained only for the sake of the Torah.[122]

When Rabbi Eliezer took ill his disciples came to visit him. They asked him, "Our master, teach us the ways of life that we may merit life in the world to come." He said to them, "Be careful about the honor of your colleagues and when you pray, know before Whom you pray and restrain your children from needless recitation but place them between the knees of learned teachers. In this way you will merit life in the world to come."[123]

Rabbah bar Bar Hana said that when Rabbi Eliezer fell sick, his disciples entered his home to visit him. He said to them, "There is a fierce anger abroad in the world." They began to weep but Rabbi Akiba laughed. "Why are you laughing?" they asked him. "Why do you weep?" he retorted. They replied, "When the Torah scroll is in anguish shall we not weep?" He explained, "For that very reason I laugh. When I saw that my master's wine did not turn sour, his store of honey not rancid, his flax not smitten, nor his oil putrefied, I thought that, heavens forfend, my master had received his reward in this world, but now when I see my master lying in pain, I am happy—knowing that he will have his reward in the world to come." Rabbi Eliezer then said to him, "Akiba, have I overlooked anything in all the Torah?" He answered him, "Our master, you have taught us, *For there is not one good man on earth who does what is best and doesn't err* (Ecclesiastes 7:20)."[124]

When Rabbi Eliezer took ill, four scholars came to visit him: Rabbi Tarfon, Rabbi Joshua, Rabbi Eleazar ben Azariah, and Rabbi Akiba. Rabbi Tarfon was moved to say, "You are more valuable to the Jewish people than the rain, for the rain is of value in this world but you, my master, benefit us in this world and the next." Whereupon Rabbi Joshua said, "You are more valuable to Israel than the revolutions of the sun, for the sun is needed for this world, but my master, for this world and for the world to come." Then Rabbi Eliezer ben Azariah spoke and said, "You are more valuable to Israel than one's father and mother, for they train a child for this world but my master, for both this world and the next." Rabbi Akiba then said, "Suffering is valuable." Rabbi Eliezer then said, "Hold me up that I may hear the words of Akiba my disciple who said that suffering is precious," and he asked him, "Akiba, how do you know that?" He answered, "I interpret a scriptural text, *Manasseh was twelve years old when he became king, and he reigned fifty-five years in Jerusalem . . . he did much that was displeasing to the Lord . . .* (2 Kings 21:1 and the verses following) and it is again written, *These too are proverbs of Solomon, which the men of King Hezekiah of Judah copied* (Proverbs 25:1). Now would King Hezekiah have taught the entire world without teaching Torah to his son Manasseh? But all the trouble he took with him and all the labor he spent upon him did not make a decent person of him. What did? Suffering. As it is said, *The Lord spoke to Manasseh and his people, but they would not heed. So the Lord brought against them the officers of the army of the king of Assyria, who took Manasseh captive in manacles, bound him in fetters, and led him off to Babylon* (2 Chronicles 33:10–11). And it is further written, *In his distress, he entreated the Lord his God and humbled himself greatly before the God of his fathers. He prayed to Him, and He granted his prayer, heard his plea, and returned him to Jerusalem to his kingdom. Then Manasseh knew that the Lord alone was God* (2 Chronicles 12–13). So you learn how precious is suffering!"[125]

When Rabbi Eliezer was very ill, Rabbi Akiba and his colleagues went to visit him. He was seated in his canopied four-poster bed while they sat in his living room. It was the eve of the Sabbath and his son Hyrcanus went in to him to remove his *tefillin*. But his father rebuked him and he returned upset. "I believe," he told the visitors, "that my father's mind is deranged." But Rabbi Eliezer called out, "My mind is clear but it is his mind that is deranged. For he put off kindling the Sabbath lamp, for which one may incur the penalty of death at the hand of heaven, while he busied himself with the *tefillin*, the wearing of which on the Sabbath violates only a rabbinic prohibition." The sages, seeing that Rabbi Eliezer's mind was clear, entered his room and sat down at a distance of four cubits from him. "Why have you come?" he asked them. "To study the Torah," they replied. "And why have you not visited me more often?" "We had not time," they answered. He then said of them, "I shall be surprised if they die a natural death." Rabbi Akiba asked him, "And what will my death be?" and he replied, "Yours will be the most cruel of all." Rabbi Eliezer then put his two arms over his chest and exclaimed, "Alas, for these two arms of mine that have been like two scrolls of the Torah that are wrapped up. Much Torah have I studied and much have I taught. Much Torah have I learned, yet I have only skimmed from the knowledge of my teachers as much as a dog can lap from the sea. Much Torah have I taught but my disciples have taken from me as much as a painting stick withdraws from its tube. Moreover, I have studied three hundred laws on the subject of a deep bright spot—in connection with leprosy—yet no man has ever asked me about them. In addition, I have studied three hundred or, as some say, three thousand, laws about the planting of cucumbers (by magical means) and no man, except for Akiba ben Joseph, ever questioned me about them. For it once happened that he and I were walking together along a road when he said to me, 'My master, teach me about the magical planting of cucumbers.' I spoke one utterance and the whole field about us was filled with cucumbers. Then he said to me, 'Master, you have taught me how to plant them but now teach me how to harvest them.' I said something, and all the cucumbers came together in one place."

His visitors then asked him, "What is the law pertaining to a ball, a shoemaker's last, an amulet, a leather bag containing pearls, and a small weight?" He answered, "They can become unclean, and if unclean, they are restored to their cleanness just as they are." Then they asked him, "What of a shoe that is still on the last?" He replied, "It is clean," and as he said this last word, his soul departed. They said, "It is obvious that our master is clean." Rabbi Joshua arose and exclaimed, "The excommunication vow is annulled, the vow is annulled!"

After the Sabbath Rabbi Akiba set out and met his master's bier as it proceeded from Caesarea to Lydda. At once he tore his garments, plucked his hair, and beat his flesh until the blood spilled upon the ground. He wept and cried, "Woe is me! I grieve for you, my master. Woe is me! I mourn for you, my teacher who left all his generation orphaned!" The mourners lined up about the bier and Rabbi Akiba commenced his funeral address, "My father, my father! Israel's chariots and horsemen! I have many coins, but no money changer to take them."[126]

Rabbi Joshua kissed the stone on which Rabbi Eliezer used to sit while teaching his students and he said, "This stone represents Sinai and he who sat on it, the Ark of the Covenant."[127]

When Rabbi Eliezer, the disciple of Rabban Johanan ben Zakkai, lay dying, he gave the order, "Clear out the house of objects that will receive uncleanness when I die and prepare a throne for Rabban Johanan ben Zakkai." And there are those who say that just as his master had seen Hezekiah in a vision, so too did Rabbi Eliezer see Hezekiah in a vision.[128]

When Rabbi Eliezer died the glory of the Torah ceased. When he died a scroll of the Torah was concealed.[129]

As long as Rabbi Eliezer lived, the people would act according to his decisions. When he died, they wanted to act according to the decisions of Rabbi Joshua. But the sages told them that since they followed Rabbi Eliezer during his lifetime, they should do so after his death as well. Hence his teachings were *like nails fixed* (Ecclesiastes 12:11).[130]

3
Rabbi Joshua ben Hananiah

Once, as Rabban Johanan ben Zakkai was leaving Jerusalem, Rabbi Joshua followed after him and looked back at the Temple in ruins. "Woe unto us," Rabbi Joshua cried, "that this, the place where the transgressions of Israel were atoned for, is laid waste!" "My son," Rabban Johanan said to him, "do not grieve. We have another source of atonement as effective as this. And what is it? It is acts of loving-kindness, as it is said, *For I desire goodness, not sacrifice* (Hosea 6:6)."[1]

If one is invited to another's home, whatever the host tells him to do, he must do. The story is told of Rabbi Simon ben Antipatros, that he would ask many guests to come and stay with him. He would urge them to eat and drink and, at first, they would swear by the Torah that they would not, but later they did. When the time came for them to leave, he would whip them! The matter came to the attention of Rabban Johanan ben Zakkai and the sages and they were made angry by it. They said, "Who will go and investigate it for us?" Rabbi Joshua spoke up and said, "I will go and see how he conducts himself."

He went and found Rabbi Simon at the entrance of his house and greeted him, "Peace be upon you, Master." The other replied, "Peace be upon you, Master and Teacher." Rabbi Joshua said, "I need someplace to stay." The other answered, "Lodge here in peace." They sat down and were engaged in the study of Torah until evening. The next morning Rabbi Joshua said to his host, "Master, I should like to go to the bathhouse." He replied, "As you wish." Rabbi Joshua was then afraid that his host would smite him on his thighs—but nothing happened. After he returned they ate and drank and Rabbi Joshua asked, "Who will accompany me on my way back?" His host said, "I will." Rabbi

Joshua was thinking to himself, "What can I report to the sages who sent me to investigate?" He turned to look back and Rabbi Simon asked him, "Master, why did you turn to look behind you?" He answered, "I have something to ask you. Why did you whip the other guests who stayed with you but me you did not?" He said to him, "Master, you are a great sage and you have good manners. The other people who stay with me I usually urge to eat, but they vow by the Torah not to eat and then they eat and break their vow. I have heard from the mouth of the sages that whoever vows by the Torah and then breaks his vow is to be given forty lashes." Rabbi Joshua told him, "May heaven bless you for what you have done. By your life and by the life of your head, when someone behaves in this way, give him forty lashes on your account and another forty on account of the sages who sent me!" Rabbi Joshua returned and reported to the sages what he had witnessed while he was with Simon ben Antipatros.[2]

Rabbi Judah bar Pazzi in the name of Rabbi Jose ben Rabbi Judah said that there were three who put forward their teaching—on the subject of the Work of Creation—before their master: Rabbi Joshua before Rabban Johanan ben Zakkai, Rabbi Akiba before Rabbi Joshua, and Hananiah ben Hakinai before Rabbi Akiba. After that time their knowledge became unclear.[3]

Rabbi Joshua ben Hananiah said, "When we were engaged in rejoicing at the libation procession our eyes did not see sleep. How so? The first hour of the morning was devoted to the daily morning sacrifice, from there to the daily morning prayers, then to the additional sacrifice, afterward to the additional prayers, then to the house of study, afterward eating and drinking, then to the afternoon prayers, followed by the daily evening sacrifice and finally to the celebration of the libation procession, which went on to the morning."[4]

Rabbi Joshua married the daughter of a *kohen* and later did not feel well. He said, "Is Aaron not satisfied that I have attached myself to his posterity or my *kohen* father-in-law, that he now has a son-in-law like me?"[5]

The rabbis taught that when the Second Temple was destroyed many became ascetics, committing themselves not to eat meat and not to drink wine. Rabbi Joshua met them and said, "My sons, why do you not eat meat or drink wine?" They answered, "Shall we eat meat, which used to be brought as an offering on the altar as a sacrifice, now that the altar is no more?

Shall we drink wine, which used to be poured on the altar as a libation, but now no longer?" He said to them, "If so, then we should not eat bread because the meal offerings have ceased." They retorted, "Indeed, and we can manage with fruit." To which he replied, "We should not eat fruit because there is no more offering of firstfruits. Nor should we drink water because the ceremony of pouring water on the altar during the Feast of Tabernacles has ceased." They were silent. He then said to them, "My sons, come and listen to me. Not to mourn at all is impossible because the blow has fallen. But to mourn overly much is also impossible because we should not impose a decree on the community that the majority find unbearable, as it is written, *You are suffering from a curse, yet you go on defrauding Me— the whole nation of you* (Malachi 3:9)."[6]

Rabbi Joshua used to say, "A pious fool, a clever knave, an ascetic woman, and the sufferings of the Pharisees destroy the world."[7]

Rabbi Simon ben Gamaliel quoted Rabbi Joshua as having said, "Since the day that the Temple was destroyed there has been no day without its curse, the dew has not fallen to the good of the crops, and the fruit has lost its taste."[8]

We have learned in a *baraita* that after the death of Rabban Gamaliel, Rabbi Joshua sought to set aside his decisions. Rabbi Johanan ben Nuri arose and said, "As I see it, the body follows the head. During all the days of Rabban Gamaliel we agreed with his decisions and now you seek to annul them? We do not listen to you! For the law has already been determined in accordance with Rabban Gamaliel." And there was no person there who differed at all.[9]

The verse reads, *Justice, justice shall you pursue* (Deuteronomy 16:20). That may be interpreted to mean, Go after the sages to an academy of learning . . . for example, after Rabbi Joshua to Pekiin.[10]

Let all persons be regarded by you as potential robbers, but show them the respect that you would give Rabban Gamaliel. The story is told about Rabbi Joshua, who extended hospitality to all, that once a certain man called upon him early in the morning. He gave him food and drink and when night came took him up to the loft to sleep and then removed the ladder. What did the man do? In the middle of the night he got up, collected all the items of value in the loft and wrapped them in his cloak. He started to go down—thinking the ladder was still there—fell and broke his collarbone. When morning came, Rabbi Joshua rose early and found him where he had fallen. He said to him, "You empty-headed person! Do all persons behave as you do?" He replied, "Master, I did not know that you had removed the ladder from under me." Rabbi Joshua retorted, "Empty head! Do you not know that already yesterday—from the moment you arrived—we were suspicious of you?" Hence Rabbi Joshua said that all men should be in your eyes as robbers, but show them the respect you would show Rabban Gamaliel.[11]

The prophet said, *How welcome on the mountains are the footsteps of the herald announcing happiness* (Isaiah 52:7). Rabbi Joshua asked, "Why of all things in creation are the mountains to be so distinguished in that the herald announcing happiness is to appear upon them first? Because the fathers of the world are mountains, metaphorically speaking, as they are addressed in the verse, *Hear, you mountains, the case of the Lord—You firm foundations of the earth!* (Micah 6:2). And why does the herald announcing happiness appear first to the fathers of the world? Because when Israel was banished, the fathers of the world assembled with the mothers of the world and appeared before the Holy One and gave voice to a great lament. At once from the heavens above, the Holy One, responding to them, asked, '*Why should My beloved be in My House* (Jeremiah 11:15)? Why have My beloved given voice to so great a lament, as if for the dead, in My House?' They answered Him frankly, 'Master of the Universe, wherein have our children sinned that You should have done such a thing as to banish them?' He replied, '*They have executed so many vile designs* (Jeremiah 11:15) by seeking to disguise circumcision, which was the mark of holiness on their flesh.' Therefore they have been condemned to banishment. The fathers then asked Him, 'Master of the Universe, is it possible that you will forget them in their exile among the peoples of the world?' He answered, 'By My great name I swear that I shall not forget them among the peoples of the world, but instead I will restore them to their place, as is said, *And there is hope for your future, declares the Lord: Your children shall return to their country*' (Jeremiah 31:17). So the Holy One comforted the fathers, and they went and lay down again in their graves." Because the fathers spoke up on Israel's behalf, when he who brings good tidings of the redemption comes, he will first come to the graves in the Cave of Makhpelah. And who will be the ones bringing the good tidings? "They will be," said Rabbi Joshua, "the descendants of Jonadab son of Rechab, who will be the first with good tidings to Israel, for it is said, *There shall never cease to be a man of the line of Jonadab son of Rechab standing before Me* (Jeremiah 35:19)."[12]

Rabbi Eliezer said that if Israel repents, they will be redeemed; if not, they will not be redeemed. Rabbi Joshua said to him, "If Israel does not repent, they will not be redeemed, but the Holy One, blessed be He, will set up a king over them whose decrees will be as cruel as Haman's. They will then repent and He will bring them back to the right path." But we have learned elsewhere in another *baraita* that Rabbi Eliezer said that if Israel repents, they will be redeemed, as it is written, *Turn back, O rebellious children, I will heal your afflictions* (Jeremiah 3:22). Rabbi Joshua said to him, "But is it not written, *You were sold for no price,/And shall be redeemed without money* (Isaiah 52:3)? *You were sold for no price*—for idolatry; *and shall be redeemed without money*—without repentance and good deeds." To which Rabbi Eliezer replied, "But is it not written, *Turn back to Me and I will turn back to you* (Malachi 3:7)?" Rabbi Joshua retorted, "But is it not written, *I will take you, one from a town and two from a clan, and bring you to Zion* (Jeremiah 3:14)?" Rabbi Eliezer answered, "It is written, *In returning and rest shall you be saved* (Isaiah 30:15)." Rabbi Joshua responded, "But is it not written, *Thus said the Lord,/The Redeemer of Israel, his Holy One,/To the despised being,/To the abhorred nation,/To the slave of rulers:/Kings shall see and stand up; Nobles, and they shall prostrate themselves* (Isaiah 49:7)?" Rabbi Eliezer countered, But is it not written, *If you return, O Israel—declares the Lord—if you return to Me* (Jeremiah 4:1)?" Rabbi Joshua replied, "But is it not written elsewhere, *Then I heard the man dressed in linen, who was above the water of the river, swear by the Ever-Living One as he lifted his right hand and his left hand to heaven: 'For a time, times, and half a time; and when the breaking of the power of the holy people comes to an end, then shall all these things be fulfilled'* (Daniel 12:7)?" At this Rabbi Eliezer remained silent.[13]

Rabbi Joshua said, "Know how great is the power of repentance. Come and see from Manasseh, son of Hezekiah, who practiced many more abominations than all the nations. He sacrificed his son by fire to Baal outside Jerusalem, was involved in betting on flying doves, and brought offerings to all the host of heaven. The leaders of the troops of the king of Babylon came and they seized him by the hair of his head and brought him to Babylon. They put him in a pan over a fire and there he called upon all the various gods to whom he had sacrificed but not one of them answered him or saved him. He then thought, 'I will call on the God of my fathers with all my heart and perhaps He will perform for me the wonders He did for my father.' He prayed to the God of his fathers with all his heart and He heard his supplication, as it is said, *He prayed to Him and He granted his prayer, and returned him to Jerusalem to his kingdom. Then Manasseh knew that the Lord alone was God* (2 Chronicles 33:13). In that hour Manasseh said, 'There is judgment and there is a Judge.' "[14]

The verse reads, *Let the wicked be in Sheol,/all the nations who ignore God!* (Psalms 9:18). Rabbi Eliezer taught that none of the nations have a portion in the world to come. But Rabbi Joshua replied, "If the verse said, '*Let the wicked be in Sheol* and *all the nations*' and no more, you would have taught well. But what of the words *who ignore God*? You must admit that with these qualifying words the verse refers only to the wicked among the nations of the earth."[15]

These are the words of Rabban Gamaliel: "Minors who are children of the wicked of the Lord of Israel have no share in the world to come, as it is said, *For lo! That day is at hand, burning like an oven. All the arrogant and all the doers of evil shall be straw* (Malachi 3:19)."

But Rabbi Joshua said, "They do enter into the world to come. For later the verse reads, *The Lord protects the simple* (Psalms 116:6) and further, *Hew down the tree and destroy it, but leave the stump with its roots in the ground* (Daniel 4:20)."

Rabban Gamaliel then asked him, "How shall I interpret, *And leave of them neither stock nor boughs* (Malachi 3:19)?" Rabbi Joshua replied, "The meaning is that the Omnipresent will not leave for them the merit of a single religious duty or the remnant of a religious duty or for their fathers for all time."[16]

Rabbi Joshua ben Hananiah said, "When the wind goes forth into the world, the Holy One, blessed be He, reduces its violence by means of the mountains and breaks its force by means of the hills, saying to it, 'Take care that you do not harm My creatures.' " Why does He act so? *For a wind becomes faint before Me* (Isaiah 57:16). For what purpose does He break the force of the wind? For the sake of *And the souls I have made* (Isaiah 57:16).[17]

Rabbi Joshua said, "The evil eye, the inclination to do evil, and hatred of one's fellow human beings drive a person out of the world."[18]

He said, "A woman wants a *kab* of food with sexual satisfaction more than nine *kabs* with abstinence."[19]

Rabbi Joshua said, "Take a wife in your youth and take a wife in your old age. Beget children in your youth and beget children in your old age. Do not say, 'I shall not take a wife,' but marry her and have sons and daughters and increase the number of your offspring on earth because you do not know how many will remain with you or *if they are equally good* (Ecclesiastes 11:6), as it is stated, *Sow your seed in the morning* (Ecclesiastes 11:6)."

He used to say, "If you have given a *perutah* to a poor man in the morning and another poor man comes to you in the evening, give to him also because you do not know whether both acts of charity will remain with you or whether *they are equally good* (Ecclesiastes 11:6), as it is stated, *Sow your seed in the morning* (Ecclesiastes 11:6)."[20]

Rabbi Joshua taught, "A word is worth a *sela* but silence two *selas*. Let your words be like precious stones."[21]

He said, "He who learns a tradition but does not work on it is like a man who sows seed but does not harvest. And he who learns Torah and forgets it is like a woman who bears a child and buries it."

Solomon sought the source of wisdom. Rabbi Joshua said that it came from the head, Rabbi Eliezer said from the heart.[22]

If a person studied only two laws in the morning and two more in the evening, and in between was busy all day at his work, it is accounted to him as though he had fulfilled the whole Torah. This is the teaching of Rabbi Joshua ben Hananiah.[23]

Rabbi Joshua was asked, "Why is it that when a male is born he comes forth with his face downward, while a female comes forth with her face turned upward?" He answered, "The male looks toward the place of his creation—the earth—while the female looks toward the place of her creation—the rib." "And why must a woman use perfume, but a man does not need it?" He replied, "Man was created from the earth and the earth never putrefies, but Eve was created from a bone and if you leave meat unsalted for three days, it goes bad at once." The questions continued, "And why does a woman have a higher-pitched voice, but not a man?" "I shall give you an illustration," he said. "If you fill a pot with meat it does not make any sound as it cooks. But as soon as you put a bone into the pot, the sound of the sizzling begins to spread." "And why is a man easily appeased but not so a woman?" "Man was created from the earth," he answered, "and when you pour a drop of water upon it, it immediately absorbs the water. But Eve was created from a bone which, even if it soaked in water many days, does not become saturated." "And why does the man make demands upon the woman, whereas the woman does not make demands upon the man?" He replied, "This may be compared to a man who loses something. He seeks what he has lost, but the lost article does not seek him." "And why does a man deposit sperm within a woman, while a woman does not deposit sperm within a man?" He answered, "It is like a man who has an article in his hand and seeks a reliable person with whom he may deposit it." "Why does a man go out bareheaded while a woman goes out with her head covered?" He explained, "She is like a person who has done wrong and is embarrassed among people. Therefore she goes out with her head covered." "Why do women walk in front of the corpse at a funeral?" He said, "Because they brought death into the world, they therefore walk in front of the corpse, as it is written, *He is brought to the grave. . . . Everyone follows behind him,/Innumerable are those who precede him* (Job 21:32–33)." "And why was the practice of menstruation given to her?" He replied, "Because Eve shed the blood of Adam by causing death, therefore the practice of menstruation was given her." "And why was the precept of separating the dough given to woman?" He answered, "Because she corrupted Adam, who was the choice dough of the world, therefore the precept of separating the dough was given her." "And why was the *mitzvah* of kindling the Sabbath lights given to her?" He explained, "Because she extinguished the light of Adam's soul, therefore the *mitzvah* of the Sabbath lights was given to her."[24]

It was asked of Rabbi Joshua, "At what time may a father teach his son Greek?" He answered, "Let him teach it to him at a time when it is neither day nor night, for it has been written, *Let not this Book of the Teaching cease from your lips, but recite it day and night* (Joshua 1:8)."

Rabbi Joshua also said, "A father should not even take time to teach his son a craft lest he cause his son to neglect the words of the Torah, of which it is said, *Choose life* (Deuteronomy 30:19)."[25]

On the verse, *Then the Lord said to Moses, "Why do you cry out to Me . . .?"* (Exodus 14:15), Rabbi Joshua said, "It is like a king's friend who was concerned about a matter and came crying to the king. The king said, 'Why do you cry? You have only to decree and I will perform it.' God said the same to Moses, '*Why do you cry out to Me?* Speak, and I will do whatever you ask.' " God said to Moses, "All that Israel has to do is to go forward. Therefore let their feet step forward from the dry land to the sea and you will see the miracles that I shall perform for them."[26]

Rabbi Joshua said that the ten plagues with which the Egyptians were smitten in Egypt were wrought with one finger, for it says, *And the magicians said to Pharaoh, "This is the finger of God!"* (Exodus 8:15). But at the sea they were smitten with fifty plagues, for it says, *And when Israel saw the wondrous power* [literally, *hand*] (Exodus 14:31). There are five fingers to one hand and five times ten are fifty. You will likewise find that Job was also smitten with fifty plagues, for it says, *Pity me, pity me! You are my friends;/For the hand of God has struck me* (Job 19:21).[27]

Rabbi Joshua interpreted the verse, *Then I accounted those who died long since more fortunate than those who are still living* (Ecclesiastes 4:2) as referring to Israel when the people stood before Mount Sinai. Since they had participated in the making of the Golden Calf, Moses left no piece of ground on the mountain upon which he did not prostrate himself to beg mercy for Israel, but he was not answered. Five destroying angels attached themselves to him for the purpose of punishing Israel with annihilation. They were *Ketzef* (Wrath), *Mashhit* (Destruction), *Hashmed* (Annihilation), *Af* (Anger), and *Hemah* (Fury). Moses was immediately afraid of them. So what did he do? He invoked the deeds of the patriarchs and said to God, *Remember Your servants, Abraham, Isaac, and Jacob* (Exodus 32:13). The Holy One, blessed be He, answered him, "Moses, what claims have the patriarchs against Me? If I come to examine them, I have grievances against them—against Abraham for saying, *Oh, Lord God, how shall I know that I am to possess it?* (Genesis 15:8); against Isaac, as it is written, *Isaac favored Esau* (Genesis 25:28), whereas I hated him, as it is written, *I have rejected Esau* (Malachi 1:3); against Jacob, for saying, *My way is hid from the Lord* (Isaiah 40:27)." However, when Moses said, *You swore to them by Your Self* (Exodus 32:13), the Holy One, blessed be He, was filled with compassion for them, as it is stated, *And the Lord renounced the punishment He had planned to bring upon His people* (Exodus 32:14). At once three of the destroying angels left and two remained, *Af* and *Hemah*, as it is written, *For I was in dread of Af and Hemah* (Deuteronomy 9:19). Moses said to God, "Lord of the Universe, can I alone stand up against the two of them? You take on one and I the other," as it is written, *Rise, O Lord, against* Your *Af* (Psalms 7:7). How do we know that Moses stood up against the angel named *Hemah*? For it is stated, *He would have destroyed them had not Moses His chosen one confronted Him in the breach to avert His Hemah* (Psalms 106:23). It is with regard to all this that the verse declares, *Then I accounted those who died long since more fortunate than those who are still living* (Ecclesiastes 4:2), that is, more fortunate than I, Moses, and my contemporaries.[28]

There is a controversy among the *tannaim* with regard to the verse, *Jethro priest of Midian . . . heard* (Exodus 18:1). The question debated by the rabbis was, What news did he hear that he came and was converted to Judaism? Rabbi Joshua said that he heard of the victory in the battle against the Amalekites, since this is immediately preceded by *And Joshua overwhelmed the people of Amalek with the sword* (Exodus 17:13). Rabbi Eleazar of Modiim said that he had heard of the giving of the Torah and so he came. For when the Torah was given to Israel the sound traveled from one end of the earth to the other and all the pagan kings were seized with tremblings in their palaces, and they were moved to song, as it is said, *While in his palace all say "Glory!"* (Psalms 29:9). They all gathered together to ask the wicked Balaam, "What is this tumultuous noise we have heard? Perhaps a flood is coming upon the world, for it says, *The Lord sat enthroned at the Flood;/the Lord sits enthroned, king forever* (Psalms 29:10)." He replied, "The Holy One, blessed be He, has already sworn that He will not bring another flood upon the earth." "Perhaps," they suggested, "He will not bring a flood of water but He will bring a flood of fire, as it is said, *For with fire will the Lord contend* (Isaiah 66:16)." He answered, "He has already sworn that He will not destroy all flesh." "Then what is the sound of this overpowering noise that we have heard?" they asked. He said, "God has a precious treasure in His storehouse, hidden by Him, for a time equaling nine hundred and seventy-four generations before the world was created and He wanted to give it to His children, as it is said, *The Lord will give strength to His people* (Psalms 29:11)." Then at once they all exclaimed, *The Lord will bless His people with peace* (Psalms

29:11). Rabbi Eleazar said that Jethro had heard about the dividing of the Red Sea, and so he came, for it is said, *When all the kings of the Amorites . . . heard how the Lord had dried up the waters of the Jordan for the sake of the Israelites . . .* (Joshua 5:1). And Rahab the harlot also said to Joshua's spies, *For we have heard how the Lord had dried up the waters of the Red Sea* (Joshua 2:10).[29]

Commenting on the verse, *Now Moses . . . drove the flock into the wilderness* (Exodus 3:1), Rabbi Joshua said, "Why did he go with them to the wilderness? Because he foresaw that the Israelites would be exalted from the wilderness, as it is said, *Who is this that comes up from the wilderness?* (Song of Songs 3:6). For from the wilderness they had manna, the quails, the well, the Tabernacle, the *Shekhinah*, priesthood, a kingdom, and clouds of glory."[30]

The verse *And may God Almighty grant you mercy* (Genesis 43:14) is related to the verse *Blessed is the man whom You chastise, O Lord* (Psalms 94:12). How is the man blessed? Rabbi Joshua said, "If chastisements come upon you, you shall still be able to labor in the Torah. These are chastisements of love. But if you are not able to labor in the Torah, they are chastisements of punishment."[31]

When did Job flourish? Rabbi Joshua said that he lived during the time of Ahasuerus, in connection with whom the verse says, *Let beautiful young virgins be sought out for Your Majesty* (Esther 2:2), while it is written, *Nowhere in the land were women as beautiful as Job's daughters to be found* (Job 42:15).[32]

Rabbi Joshua said, "There is no death worse than death by hunger, as it is said, *Better off were the slain of the sword/Than those slain by famine* (Lamentations 4:9).[33]

Two students of Rabbi Joshua ben Hananiah changed their clothing to avoid detection during a time of persecution. They were accosted by a certain soldier who was an apostate. He said to them, "If you are sons of the Torah, you should be ready to give up your lives for its sake. While if you are not its children, why should you be killed for it?" "We are its children and we are ready to give up our lives for its sake but it is not usual for a person to commit suicide." He said to them, "I have three questions to ask you. If you answer them, good, but if not, I will finish you off." He asked first, "One verse says, *The Lord stands up to plead a cause,/He rises to judge peoples* (Isaiah 3:13), whereas another verse says, *For there I will sit in judgment/Over all the nations round about* (Joel 4:12). They answered him, "When the Holy One, blessed be He, judges Israel, He does so standing so that He shortens the trial and grants concessions. But when He judges the peoples of the world, He judges them sitting so that He prolongs the trial and searches out every detail." He said to them, "Your master, Rabbi Joshua, did not interpret the matter so. According to him both verses apply to the peoples of the world whom the Holy One, blessed be He, judges while sitting, prolonging the hearing, searching out every detail. Then afterward, He rises and becomes their adversary in inflicting punishment upon them."

Next he asked, "What is the meaning of the verse, *He who tills his land will have food in plenty,/But he who pursues vanities will have poverty in plenty* (Proverbs 28:19)?" They replied, "Better off is he who rents one field, plows it, fertilizes it, and weeds it than he who rents a number of fields and neglects them." He told them, "That is not the way your teacher Rabbi Joshua expounded it, but rather this way—He who serves God until the day of his death will be sated with His bread, the bread of the next world, *but he who pursues vanities will have poverty in plenty*—this refers to the heathen who follow after vanities, after the worship of idols."

Finally he asked them, "What is the meaning of *Have no fear, for it is another boy for you* (Genesis 35:17)?" They replied, "A woman in labor pain is calmed this way by being told, 'Have no fear, for you are giving birth to a boy.' " He said to them, "Your teacher, Rabbi Joshua, did not explain it that way, but with every tribal ancestor a twin sister was born."[34]

Commenting on the verse *Awesome as bannered hosts* (Song of Songs 6:10), Rabbi Joshua said, "It is like the fear inspired by earthly powers, such as generals and commanders and field marshals."[35]

Rabbi Joshua said, "Elijah will come not to cleanse nor to defile families, but to remove those who have come to power through force and to bring near those who have been cast afar by force." Rabbi Simon said, "To resolve the controversies among the sages." The rabbis say, "Neither to remove nor to bring near, but to make peace in the world."[36]

Rabbi Joshua said, "Great is peace, for when Israel declared at Sinai, *All that the Lord has spoken we will faithfully do* (Exodus 24:7), the Holy One, blessed be He, rejoiced in them, gave them His Torah, and blessed them with peace, as it is said, *The Lord will give strength to His people; the Lord will bless His people with peace* (Psalms 29:11)."

He said, "Great is peace for the divine covenant concluded with the priests was made with the word 'peace,' as it is stated, *Behold, I give unto them My covenant of peace* (Numbers 25:12)."

Again he said, "Great is peace for it is given as a blessing to the living and the dead. Whence to the living? It is stated, *And Jethro said to Moses, Go in peace'* (Exodus 4:18). And whence to the dead? It is stated, *You shall go to your fathers in peace* (Genesis 15:15)."

Rabbi Joshua also said, "The prophet is called 'messenger of the Lord' and the priest is called 'messenger of the Lord.' The prophet is so called, as it is stated, *And Haggai, the Lord's messenger, fulfilling the Lord's mission, spoke to the people* (Haggai 1:13). The priest is also called 'the messenger of the Lord,' as it is stated, *For the lips of a priest guard knowledge,/And men seek rulings from his mouth;/For he is a messenger of the Lord of Hosts* (Malachi 2:7). Lest you think that this applies even to a priest who is an ignoramus, the verse declares, *And men seek rulings from his mouth* (Malachi 2:7)."[37]

Aquila, the convert to Judaism, asked Rabbi Eliezer, "Is the love that the Holy One, blessed be He, feels toward the convert shown only in the grant of food and clothing, as it is said, . . . *and befriends the stranger, providing him with food and clothing* (Deuteronomy 10:18)? I have so many peacocks and pheasants that even my slaves take no notice of them!" He answered him, "Is the matter so insignificant in your eyes, one that our father Jacob asked for at the very beginning, as it is said, . . . *and gives me bread to eat and clothing to wear* (Genesis 28:20)? Is that something so trivial?"

He went to Rabbi Joshua and asked him the same question. He replied, "The meaning is that a proselyte who has become converted for the sake of heaven is worthy that his daughters marry into the priesthood. The word 'bread' signifies the showbread, and 'clothing' refers to the priestly vestments."

His disciples criticized this statement and said to him, "Is then that for which the patriarch begged so unimportant in your eyes, as it is said, . . . *and gives me bread to eat and clothing to wear* (Genesis 28:20)? So why do you put him off with an unsubstantial answer?" Rabbi Joshua then began to speak more persuasively to Aquila and told him, "The word 'bread' means the Torah, as it is stated, *Come, eat My bread* (Proverbs 9:5) and 'clothing' signifies glory, as it is stated, *Through Me Kings reign* (Proverbs 8:15)." Hence, *Better a patient spirit than a haughty spirit* (Proverbs 7:8) — better is the patience that Rabbi Joshua showed with Aquila the convert than the impatience displayed by Rabbi Eliezer. Otherwise, he might have returned to his former paganism.[38]

In explaining the verse *Bless the Lord, O my soul;/O Lord, my God, You are very great* (Psalms 104:1), Rabbi Berekhiah said in the name of Rabbi Eleazar and also in the name of Rabbi Joshua, "You were great in the world before the world was created. But after You created the world, it is written, *You are very great.* You were great before the Children of Israel went out of Egypt. But after the children of Israel left Egypt, it is written, *You are very great.* You were great before the prophets spoke your praise. But after the prophets spoke Your praise, *You are very great.*"[39]

A certain Gentile asked Rabbi Joshua a question, "You have festivals and we have festivals. We do not rejoice when you do and you do not rejoice when we do. When then do we both rejoice together?" Rabbi Joshua answered, "When the rain falls. And what is the proof? *The meadows are clothed with flocks* (Psalms 65:14) — what follows: *Raise a shout for God, all the earth* (Psalms 66:2) — not priests, Levites, or Israelites is written here but *all the earth.*"[40]

Rabbi Johanan on the first day of the festival of Tabernacles would recite the blessing, "Blessed are You, O Lord our God, King of the Universe, who has sanctified us with His commandments and has commanded us concerning the taking of the *lulav.*" But on the other days of the festival he ended with "Concerning the commandment of the elders." But Rabbi Joshua recited each day the blessing, "Concerning the taking of the *lulav.*" Rabbi Joshua did not agree with Rabbi Johanan that, according to the Torah, the *lulav* is obligatory only on the first day of the festival since the verse says, *On the first day you shall take the product of goodly trees, branches of palm trees . . .* (Leviticus 23:40). On all the remaining days the obligation has only the force of rabbinic authority. Rabbi Simon ben Halafta said that Rabbi Joshua actually agreed with Rabbi Johanan, and the reason he acted differently was because it is written, *The sayings of the wise are like goads. . . . They were given by one Shepherd* (Ecclesiastes 12:11); that is, the words of the Torah and the words of the sages have been given by the same Shepherd.[41]

The verse reads, *He shall wave the sheaf before the Lord* (Leviticus 23:11). How did the priest wave it? Rabbi Hama ben Ukba in the name of Rabbi Joshua ben Hananiah said, "He moved it forward and backward, upward and downward; forward and backward to symbolize that the waving of the sheaf was in honor of Him to whom the whole world belongs; upward and downward to symbolize that it was in honor of Him to whom belong the regions on high and the regions below."[42]

The people in Lod decreed a fast during Hanukkah. Rabbi Eliezer went and told Rabbi Joshua, who washed—which is not to be done on a fast—and he said to the people, "Go and observe a fast as a penalty for having fasted."[43]

Rabbi Joshua said, " 'Because I have given you many laws,' declared God, 'therefore have I given you much reward and have exhorted you with regard to all the commandments, which are your life, for the verse says, *Whoever keeps the commandment shall know no evil* (Ecclesiastes 8:5). And so in the case of every matter dealt with in this scriptural portion, such as the murder of a human being, the goring of an ox, the setting afire of someone's field, I have written its punishment and reward side by side.' It may be compared to a king who constructed two paths, one full of thorns, briars, and thistles, and the other with spices. The blind walk on the bad road, so that the thorns add injury upon injury, but those who see walk on the good road with the result that both they and the clothes they wear become scented. So too God laid out two roads, one for the righteous and one for the wicked. He who has no eyes walks in the way of the wicked and stumbles and cannot keep his footing, like the wicked Balaam who was driven from the world, and like Doeg and Ahithophel who were removed from life, and like Gehazi who departed from the world empty-handed. The righteous, however, who walk in their integrity, acquire a blessing, and so do their children after them, for the verse states, *The righteous man lives blamelessly;/ Happy are his children who come after him* (Proverbs 20:7)."[44]

Rabbi Dosa ben Harkinas once saw Rabbi Joshua and spoke this verse about him: *"To whom would he give instruction? . . . To those newly weaned from milk"* (Isaiah 28:9). He continued, "I recall that his mother would bring his crib into the study hall so that his ears would become acclimated to the words of Torah."[45]

Rabbi Joshua said, "If all the seas were ink and all the reeds growing by lakes were pens and heaven and earth writing sheets and all human beings scribes, it still would not be sufficient for the writing down of the words of Torah that I have studied, and what I have abstracted from it amounts to no more than the ocean would lose of its water if an eyeliner pencil were dipped in it."[46]

The story is told about Rabbi Joshua ben Hananiah that he went to Rome and he was told that a boy from Jerusalem was being kept in prison for immoral purposes. He had beautiful eyes, a handsome face, and his locks were curled. Rabbi Joshua went to look into the matter. When he came to the gate of the prison, he called out, "*Who was it who gave Jacob over to despoilment/And Israel to plunderers* (Isaiah 42:24)?" The boy answered, "*Surely, the Lord against whom they sinned/In whose ways they would not walk/And whose teaching they would not obey* (Isaiah 42:24)." Rabbi Joshua's eyes filled with tears and he exclaimed, "I swear that I shall not move from this place until I redeem this child for whatever price they ask for him." They say that he did not move from there until he redeemed him for a large sum of money. He sent him to the Land of Israel and it did not take much time before that child became a teacher in Israel. And who was he? Rabbi Ishmael ben Elisha.[47]

When Rabbi Eliezer, Rabbi Joshua, and Rabban Gamaliel went to Rome, they were at a certain place in the city and saw some children making little piles of dirt. They said, "Children in the Land of Israel play this way and they say, 'This is heave offering,' and 'That is tithe.' It is likely that there are Jews here." They went into a nearby house and were received there. When they sat down to eat, they noticed that before a dish was brought to them it would first be taken into a small room, and they wondered whether they might be eating from sacrifices offered to the dead.

They said to their host, "Why is it that no dish is served us that is not first brought into a small room?" He replied, "I have a very old father and he has vowed that he will never come out of that small room until he sees the sages of Israel."

They said to him, "Go and tell him, 'Come out to them now, for they are here.' " He at once came out to them and they asked him, "Why have you been doing this?" He answered, "Pray for my son, for he has not fathered a child." Rabbi Eliezer said to Rabbi Joshua, "Now, Joshua ben Hananiah, let us see what you will do." He said to them, "Bring me flax seeds," and they brought him flax seeds. He appeared to sow the seeds and scatter them on the table; he appeared to bring the seed up; he appeared to take hold of it until he drew up a woman, holding on to her tresses. He said to her, "Release this man from any magic you have done to him." She replied, "I shall not release my spell." He told her, "If you do not do it, I shall make known your secrets of magic." She answered, "I cannot do it, for the magical materials have been cast into the sea."

Rabbi Joshua uttered a command that the sea release the magic materials and they came up. They all prayed for their host, and his was the merit of fathering a son who became Rabbi Judah ben Batyra.

They said in later years, "If we had gone to Rome only for the purpose of producing that righteous man, it would have been enough for us."

Rabbi Joshua ben Hananiah said, "I can take cucumbers and pumpkins and turn them into rams and hosts of rams and they, in turn, will produce still more."[48]

The Romans asked Rabbi Joshua ben Hananiah, "How do we know that the Holy One, blessed be He, will resurrect the dead and that He knows what will happen in the future?" He answered, "Both may be deduced from this verse: *The Lord said to Moses: You are soon to lie with your fathers and rise up again* (Deuteronomy 31:16)." "But," they said, "perhaps *and rise up again* belongs to the second half of the verse, *and this people will rise up again, and go astray after the alien gods in their midst?*" He replied, "Then at least you have the answer to one of your questions, that He knows what will take place in the future!"[49]

Hadrian—may his bones rot!—asked Rabbi Joshua ben Hananiah, "From what part of the dead body will the Holy One, blessed be He, cause man to blossom forth in the future?" "From the nut of the spinal column," he answered. "How do you know that?" the emperor asked. "Bring me one and I shall prove it to you," he replied. When he got it, he threw it into a fire, but it was not consumed. He put it into water, but it did not dissolve. He ground it between millstones, but it was not crushed. He set it on an anvil and struck it with a hammer. The anvil split and the hammer broke, but it remained intact.[50]

The Roman emperor asked Rabbi Joshua ben Hananiah, "Why is it that your cooking for the Sabbath has such a good smell?" Rabbi Joshua replied, "We have a special spice called Sabbath that we put into it and therefore it smells so good."

Whereupon the emperor said, "Let me have some of it." But Rabbi Joshua answered, "It works only for those who observe the Sabbath."[51]

Hadrian—may his bones rot!—asked Rabbi Joshua ben Hananiah, "How did the Holy One, blessed be He, create the world?" He answered, "He took six balls, four for the four corners of the universe, one for above and one for below." "Is that actually possible?" asked the emperor. Rabbi Joshua then led him into a small room and said, "Stretch out your hands to east, west, north, and south. Even so was the work of Creation to the Lord."[52]

The emperor said to Rabbi Joshua ben Hananiah, "I want to see your God." Rabbi Joshua replied, "That is impossible." The emperor insisted, "You must show Him to me." The rabbi had the emperor go out of doors with him, the season being summer, in the month of *Tammuz*. He said to the emperor, "Look at the sun." "I cannot," answered the emperor. Then Rabbi Joshua retorted, "If you cannot even look at the sun, which is but one of the servants of the Holy One, blessed be He, how shall you look at the Holy One Himself?"[53]

The emperor once said to Rabbi Joshua ben Hananiah, "Your God is compared to a lion, for it is written, *A lion has roared,/Who can but fear?/My Lord God has spoken,/Who can but prophesy?* (Amos 3:8). But what is the greatness of this? A horseman can kill a lion!" Rabbi Joshua replied, "He has been compared not to the ordinary lion but to the lion of Be-Ilai." "It is my will," declared the emperor, "that you show it to me." He said, "That is impossible." "I affirm," the emperor insisted, "that I will see it." Rabbi Joshua prayed and the lion set out from its place. When it was four hundred parasangs distant it roared once, and all the pregnant women miscarried and the walls of Rome fell. When it was three hundred parasangs distant it roared again and the molar and incisor teeth of men fell out. Even the emperor himself fell from his throne to the ground. "I beg you," he implored of Rabbi Joshua, "pray that it return to its place." He prayed, and the animal returned to its place.[54]

On another occasion the emperor said to Rabbi Joshua ben Hananiah, "I should like to prepare a banquet for your God." He told him, "You cannot do it." "Why not?" "Because He has too large a number of attendants." "Indeed," the emperor stated, "I will do it." "Then," replied Rabbi Joshua, "go and set it up on the spacious lands of Rebita." The emperor spent the six months of warm weather making preparations when a tempest came up and swept everything into the sea. He then used the six months of cold weather in making preparations when rain fell and washed everything into the sea. "What is the meaning of this?" asked the emperor. Rabbi Joshua answered, "They are but the sweepers and sprinklers that march before Him!" "In that case," said the emperor, "I cannot do it!"[55]

Once the daughter of the emperor, looking at Rabbi Joshua ben Hananiah, exclaimed, "O, such glorious wisdom in so ugly a container!" He said to her, "My daughter, in what kind of containers does your father, the emperor, store his wine?" She replied, "In earthenware containers." He said, "Every ordinary person keeps his wine in earthenware containers, but your father—he does too?" She asked, "In what else then?" He answered, "You people, who are so important, should store your wine in containers of gold and silver." She went and told her father, who then had his wine poured into gold and silver containers, and it spoiled. The emperor asked his daughter, "Who gave you this advice?" She replied, "Rabbi Joshua ben Hananiah." He was sent for and the emperor asked him, "Why did you tell her this?" Rabbi Joshua said, "As she spoke to me, so did I speak to her." "But," the emperor persisted, "are there not handsome men who are scholars?" Rabbi Joshua replied, "If they were not handsome, they would be still greater scholars."[56]

The emperor's daughter once said to Rabbi Joshua ben Hananiah, "Your God is a carpenter, for it is written, *He sets the rafters of His lofts in the waters* (Psalms 104:3). Ask Him to make a spool for me." He replied, "Very well." He prayed for her and she was smitten with leprosy. She was then taken away to the open square in Rome and given a spool. (For it was the practice in Rome that whenever people were struck with leprosy they were taken to the open square, given a spool and skeins to wind, in order that people might see them and be moved to pray for their recovery.) One day Rabbi Joshua passed through the open square of Rome and he saw her sitting there, winding the skeins onto her spool. He exclaimed, "What a beautiful spool my God has give you!" She said, "I beg you, ask your God to take back what He has given me." He replied, "Our God grants a request, but having given it, He never takes it back."[57]

Hadrian—may his bones rot!—asked Rabbi Joshua ben Hananiah, "Do you maintain that every day the Holy One, blessed be He, creates a band of new angels who give voice to a new song before Him and then leave?" "Yes," he replied. "Where, then, do they go?" the emperor inquired. "To the place where they were created," was the answer. "And where were they created?" "From the river of fire," Rabbi Joshua told him. "And what is the nature of this river of fire?" the emperor wanted to know. Rabbi Joshua answered, "It is like the river Jordan, which does not cease flowing night or day." "What is the source of the river of fire?" the emperor inquired. Rabbi Joshua responded, "The perspiration of the *Hayyot*, caused by their bearing God's throne." The emperor's adviser said to him, "But the Jordan flows only by day and not by night." "Was I not watching the river at Bet Peor and saw that it flows by night just as it does by day?" the emperor retorted.[58]

When Rabbi Joshua ben Hananiah was standing in the presence of the emperor, a sectarian showed him by signs, "A people from whom God has turned away His face." Rabbi Joshua showed him by signs, "His hand is still stretched over us to protect us." The emperor asked Rabbi Joshua ben Hananiah, "What did he show you by signs?" He answered, "A people from whom God has turned away His face." "And what did you show him by signs?" "Thus and thus," he replied. Then the emperor asked the sectarian, "What did you show him?" He responded, "A people from whom God has turned away His face." "And he," the emperor inquired, "What did he show you?" The sectarian said, "I do not know." The emperor declared, "A man who does not know what is shown him in sign language dares to use sign language in the presence of the king!" They took the sectarian away and executed him.[59]

The emperor Hadrian said to Rabbi Joshua, "How great is the sheep that preserves itself among seventy wolves!" He answered him, "Great is the shepherd who rescues her and crushes them before her," and so is it written, *No weapon formed against you shall succeed* (Isaiah 54:17).[60]

The accursed Hadrian asked Rabbi Joshua ben Hananiah, "It is written in the Torah, *A land where you may eat food without stint, where you will lack nothing* (Deuteronomy 8:9). Are you able then to bring me three things if I ask for them?" "What are they?" he inquired. He replied, "Pepper, pheasants, and silk." He brought him pepper from Nizhana, pheasants from Sidon—others say from Akhbrin—and silk from Gush Halav.[61]

Hadrian—may his bones crumble!—questioned Rabbi Joshua ben Hananiah, "Am I not better than your teacher Moses?" "Why do you say that?" asked Rabbi Joshua. "Because I am alive and he is dead and it is written, *Even a live dog is better than a dead lion* (Ecclesiastes 9:4)." Rabbi Joshua retorted, "Can you issue a decree that no one shall kindle fire for three days?" The emperor answered, "Certainly I can," and he so commanded. In the evening of that day they both went up to the roof of the palace, and in the distance they saw smoke rising. Rabbi Joshua asked, "What is this?" He replied, "One of my officers is ill and the physician went in to visit him and told him that he could not be restored to health until he had warm water to drink." To which Rabbi Joshua rejoined, "(May he give up the ghost!) While you are alive, your order is neglected, whereas when our teacher Moses decreed for us, *You shall kindle no fire throughout your settlements on the Sabbath day* (Exodus 35:3), no Jew has ever kindled a fire on the Sabbath from his days on and his order has not been neglected through all these years until now, and yet you say, 'I am better than he!' "[62]

Hadrian—may his bones crumble!—thought of a problem for Rabbi Joshua ben Hananiah and said to him, "The Holy One, blessed be He, bestowed a great privilege upon the nations of the world when he gave five of the Ten Commandments to Israel and five to the nations of the world. In the first five commandments, which the Holy One, blessed be He, gave to Israel, His name is associated with the commandments, so that if the Jews sin, God raises a cry against them. But in the second five commandments—those he gave to the nations of the world—His name is not associated with them, so that when the nations of the world sin, He raises no cry against them."

Rabbi Joshua said in response, "Come and walk about the squares of the city with me." In every place where Rabbi Joshua took him, Hadrian saw a statue of himself. In each place Rabbi Joshua asked, "This object—what is it?" The emperor replied, "It is a statue of me." Finally Rabbi Joshua drew him along and took him to a privy, where he said to him, "My lord king, I see that you are the ruler everywhere in this city but in this place you are not." The emperor asked, "Why not?" Rabbi Joshua replied, "Because in every place I saw a statue of you but in this place there is none." Hadrian answered, "And you are a sage among the Jews! Would that be an honor due a king that a statue of him be set up in a place that is loathsome, a place that is repulsive, a place that is filthy?" Rabbi Joshua retorted, "Do not your ears hear what your mouth is saying? Would it redound to the glory of the Holy One, blessed be He, to have His name associated with murderers, with adulterers, with thieves?"

The emperor dismissed Rabbi Joshua, who then left. After the emperor went away, Rabbi Joshua's students said to him, "Master, you thrust him off with a broken reed of an answer, but what explanation will you give us?" Rabbi Joshua answered, "The manner of giving the Torah's Ten Commandments came into the mind of the Holy One, blessed be He, in the following way, and this is the way they were given. At first God went to the descendants of Esau and asked them, 'Will you accept the Torah?' They said right to His face, 'Master of the Universe, what is written in it?' He said, *You shall not murder* (Exodus 20:13). They replied, 'But this goes against our grain. Our father taught us to rely only upon the sword because he was told, *Yet by your sword you shall live* (Genesis 27:40). We cannot accept the Torah.'

"He then went to the descendants of Ammon and Moab and asked them, 'Will you accept the Torah?' They said right to His face, 'Master of the Universe, what is written in it?' He said, *You shall not commit adultery* (Exodus 20:13). They replied, 'But our very origins are in adultery, for it is written, *Thus the two daughters of Lot came to be with child by their father* (Genesis 19:36). We cannot accept the Torah.'

"Then He went to the descendants of Ishmael and asked them, 'Will you accept the Torah?' They said right to His face, 'Master of the Universe, what is written in it?' He said, *'You shall not steal.'* They answered, 'It is our very nature to live off that which is stolen and that which is obtained by assault. Of our ancestor Ishmael it is written, *He shall be a wild ass of a man;/His hand against everyone,/And everyone's hand against him* (Genesis 16:12). We cannot accept the Torah.'

"At long last He came to Israel. They said at once, '*All that the Lord has spoken we will faithfully do* (Exodus 24:7).'

"As soon as the Holy One, blessed be He, saw Israel's resolve and that they wished to accept the Torah with love and affection, with fear and reverence, with awe and trembling, He said, '*I the Lord am your God*' (Exodus 20:2)."[63]

A king of one of the nations of the world asked Rabbi Joshua ben Hananiah, "Is it not written in your Torah, *Yea, all His ways are just* (Deuteronomy 32:4)? How can all His ways be just when we see before our very eyes that He injures those who are without sin or blame, like the small number of persons who are born with some defect—blind or limping or deaf or dumb. They are as yet without sin—is this not an injustice?" Rabbi Joshua said to him, "Indeed, He has brought injury upon the good people among them in order to increase their reward in the world to come. As for the impious among them—and He knows who among them will be godless, walking in the way of evil and not good, and without faith—therefore He has caused them to be afflicted even before they were born. If you desire, I shall prove this to you. Give me a thousand gold coins and send with me two reliable men in whom you can place your trust." The king gave him what he asked for and commanded two of his men to go with him. They and the rabbi, with the gold coins in his possession, went on their way until they encountered a man blind from the day he left his mother's womb. Rabbi Joshua said to him, "Let me tell you that the king has sentenced me to death and I am giving you these thousand gold *dinars* that I hold, for safekeeping with you. If I be saved from the king's power, you will return them to me; and if, heaven forfend, I die, they will be yours as a gift." The blind man stretched out his hand and took the *dinars* from Rabbi Joshua while the two men of the king looked on. They all went on their way. After some time had elapsed Rabbi Joshua went back to the blind man and told him, "Be good enough to return the money I left with you, for the Holy One, blessed be He, rescued me from the king. I shall reward you for your trouble." But the blind man replied, "What you say has never happened. You left nothing with me and I have nothing of yours!" Rabbi Joshua said to him, "If that is what you say, come with me to the king and he will judge between you and me." So the two went off to the king, and Rabbi Joshua pleaded his case before him. The king said to him, "Bring proof of your claim," and Rabbi Joshua brought the two trustworthy men who testified that the blind man had received one thousand *dinars* from Rabbi Joshua. The blind man responded, "My lord king, this is not true for he has never given me anything, and they all are telling lies about me." The king grew angry at the blind man and ordered that he be hung. As he was being led to the gallows a man came up to him and whispered in his ear, "I saw your wife with another fellow. She was laughing with him and telling him, 'Wait until my blind husband dies; I shall marry you and together you and I will spend the thousand *dinars*.' " When the blind man heard his words, he cried out loudly, "Let me go! Let me go and I shall bring the thousand *dinars*." They freed him and he went and brought back the *dinars*. Rabbi Joshua ben Hananiah admonished him, "You wicked person! All this you did to me and I gave you the money in the presence of reliable witnesses. What would you have done had I given it to you without witnesses present! Without doubt, your Creator, in making you blind at birth, acted rightly and justly because He knew how evil your actions would be!" The king spoke up and said to Rabbi Joshua, "It is certainly true that your God is righteous and His judgment is righteous and in His ways there is no injustice. He is one and there is none like Him."[64]

In the days of Rabbi Joshua ben Hananiah, the Roman state agreed that the Temple could be rebuilt. Pappus and Lulianus set up tables from Acco as far as Antioch to provide those who came up from the Exile with all their needs. Then the Samaritans went to the emperor to warn him, *"Now be it known to the king that if this city is rebuilt and the walls completed, they will not pay tribute, poll tax, or land tax (Ezra 4:13)."* "Yet what can I do?" said he, "since I have already granted the permission." "Send an order that they must change its location or enlarge it by five cubits or diminish it by five cubits and then they will withdraw from it of their own accord." A crowd of Jews had gathered in the valley of Bet Rimmon and when the royal dispatches arrived, they burst into weeping and wanted to rebel against the imperial government. Some of them said that a sage should come and pacify the people. They suggested that Rabbi Joshua ben Hananiah should come, for he is a master of the Torah. So he came to speak and he told them this fable: "A lion killed an animal and ate it but a bone stuck in his throat. He proclaimed, 'I will reward anyone who removes it.' An Egyptian heron, which has a long beak, came and pulled it out, then demanded its reward. 'Go,' the lion replied, 'you will be able to brag that you entered the lion's mouth in peace and came out of it in peace.' Even so, let us be satisfied that we entered into negotiations with this people in peace and have emerged in peace."[65]

King Ptolemy asked the elders in Rome, "In how many days did the Holy One, blessed be He, create the world?" "In six days," they replied. "And since then Gehenna has been burning for the wicked," he exclaimed, "woe to the world for the judgments it must render!"[66]

A philosopher asked Rabbi Joshua ben Hananiah, "Is there a day when all the world is of one mind and all the nations worship before the Holy One, blessed be He?" Rabbi Joshua ben Hananiah answered, "There is one such day when all rejoice as one." "What day is that?" came back the question. Rabbi Joshua replied, "When the rains have held back and all the world is troubled because of it; then the day comes when the rains fall, and as a result, all the world rejoices and glorifies the Holy One, blessed be He, as it is said, *All the nations You have made will come to bow down before You, O Lord, and they will pay honor to Your name* (Psalms 86:9). Pay honor when? *For You are great and perform wonders* (Psalms 86:10). The wonders are the rains, as in *who performs great deeds which cannot be fathomed,/Wondrous things without number/Who gives rains to the earth* (Job 5:9–10). For this, *Praise the Lord, all you nations* (Psalms 117:1).[67]

A certain philosopher wanted to know how long it takes for a serpent to bear its young. When he saw snakes copulating he took them and placed them in a barrel and fed them until they bore. When the sages visited Rome he asked them how long it takes for a serpent to bear. Rabban Gamaliel turned pale and was unable to answer him. Later Rabbi Joshua met him and seeing his wan face, asked him, "Why is your face so pale?" "I was asked a question," he answered, "and I could not answer it." "And what was it?" "After how long does a serpent bear?" "After seven years," Rabbi Joshua told him. "How do you know that?" he inquired. Rabbi Joshua answered, "Because the dog, which is a wild beast, bears after fifty days, while it is written, *More cursed shall you be than all cattle and all the wild beasts* (Genesis 3:14) — hence, just as the cattle are seven times more accursed than the beast, so is the serpent seven times more accursed than the cattle!" In the evening Rabban Gamaliel went and told the answer to the philosopher, who began to beat his head against the wall, crying out, "All that for which I labored for seven years this man has come and offered to me on the end of a cane!"[68]

The emperor once asked Rabbi Joshua ben Hananiah, "How long is the period of gestation and birth of a serpent?" He told him, "Seven years." "But did not the wise men of Athens couple a male serpent with a female and she gave birth in three years?" Rabbi Joshua replied, "The female serpent in question had already been pregnant for four years." "But," the emperor continued, "did they not have sexual contact—and a female beast, once pregnant, does not permit it?" Rabbi Joshua answered, "Serpents have sexual intercourse the same way as human beings—having sexual contact even after pregnancy." "But," the emperor persisted, "are not the sages of Athens wise men—they must have discovered the facts about the serpent." Rabbi Joshua said, "We are wiser than they." "If so," remarked the emperor, "go and best them in questions and answers and bring them to me." Rabbi Joshua asked him, "How many are these wise men of Athens?" "Sixty men." The rabbi then said to him, "Have a ship with sixty rooms made for me, each room containing sixty cushions." The emperor had this done for him.

When Rabbi Joshua reached Athens, he went to a slaughter-house. There he found a man dressing an animal and he asked him, "Is your head for sale?" The man said, "Yes." "For how much?" asked Rabbi Joshua. The man answered, "For half a *zuz*." He gave him the money and said to him, "Give me your head." The man gave him an animal's head. Rabbi Joshua exclaimed, "Did I tell you the head of an animal? I said, 'Your head!' " Rabbi Joshua then said to him, "If you wish me to bother you no more, walk in front of me and show me the door of the school of the wise men of Athens." The man replied, "I am afraid because they put to death anyone who points them out." Rabbi Joshua then suggested, "Carry a bundle of reeds and when you reach the place, set it down as if to rest." It happened that way and Rabbi Joshua found that there were guards both outside the school and inside. If the wise men saw that someone had entered their school, they would kill the outside guards, and if someone was able to leave, they would kill the inside guards. Rabbi Joshua reversed the sole and heel of his shoes, leaving tracks, and they killed the inside guards. He then made tracks going to the door with his shoes in normal position and the outside guards were killed. He was thus able to enter, and he found the younger wise men sitting higher up and the elders below. He thought, "If I first extend greetings to the elders, then the young men will kill me, claiming that they are more important, for they sit higher up. And if I extend greetings to the young men first, then the elders will kill me, arguing that they are older and the others mere youngsters."

Rabbi Joshua then said to all, "Peace to you." They asked

him, "What are you doing here?" He answered, "I am a sage of the Jews and I desire to learn wisdom from you." "If so," they said, "we shall ask you some questions." He replied, "I agree, and if you defeat me then do to me whatever you wish. But if I defeat you, break bread with me on the ship." They asked him, "If a man wanted to marry a woman and consent was not given to him, does it make sense for him to seek a woman of even higher birth?" He took a peg and tried to push it into the stone wall and it would not go in, and then he tried to insert it higher up on the wall where there was a space between the stones and the peg went in. He then said, "In your case also it may happen that the second woman is his destined one." They asked again, "If a man lends money and later must seize his debt by force, is it to be expected that he should lend again?" He answered, "A man goes into a forest and cuts his first load of wood, but he cannot lift it. He keeps on cutting until someone comes along and helps him lift his bundle."

They said to him, "Tell us some stories." He began, "There was a mule that gave birth and around its neck there was a document in which was written, 'There is a claim against my father's house of one hundred thousand zuz.' " They asked him, "Can a mule give birth?" He replied, "This is one of those stories." They asked again, "When salt becomes unsavory, with what is it salted?" He answered, "With the afterbirth of a mule." "And is there such a thing as an afterbirth of a mule?" "And can salt become unsavory?" he retorted.

The wise men of Athens asked again, "Build a house in the sky." By his pronouncing the divine Name he suspended himself in midair between heaven and earth. He then called to them, "Bring me up bricks and clay from down there." They asked, "And is it possible to do that?" He retorted, "And is it possible to build a house between heaven and earth?"

They asked him, "Where is the center of the world?" He raised his fingers and pointing in front of him said, "Here." They said to him, "How can you prove it?" He answered, "Bring ropes and measure!" They then demanded, "We have a pit in the field. Bring it into the town." He told them, "Knot ropes for me out of bran flour and I shall bring it in." They then said, "We have a broken millstone. Mend it." He took a part of it that was broken off, threw it to them and said, "Take out the threads for me like a weaver and I shall mend it." Again they asked, "With what can we cut a bed of knives?" He replied, "With the horns of a donkey." They asked, "But does a donkey have horns?" He retorted, "And is there a bed of knives?" They brought him two eggs and asked him, "Which egg is from the black clucking hen and which from the white?" He brought them two cheeses and asked them, "Which is from a black goat and which from a white?" "A chicken dead in its shell—where has the spirit gone?" "From wherever it came, there it went." They demanded of him, "Show us something whose value is not worth the loss it causes." He brought a mat of reeds and spread it out, but it was too wide and long to get through the door. He then told them, "Bring a rake and a pickax and break down the door! That is an example of something whose value is not worth the loss it causes."

They gave up, and he brought them one by one to the ship, each to his separate room. When each one saw the sixty cushions, he thought that all would be coming to his room. Rabbi Joshua ordered the captain to set sail. Just before they left, Rabbi Joshua took some earth from their native soil. When they reached the straits, they filled a container with its water. When they arrived, they were presented to the emperor. He saw that they were depressed—far from home as they were—and he said, "These are not the same people." Rabbi Joshua therefore took some of the earth from their country and threw it at them. At once they grew haughty toward the emperor. He then said to Rabbi Joshua, "Do with them as you like." He brought the water that the Athenians had taken from the straits and poured it into a hole in the ground. He said to them, "Fill this hole with other water, and then you may leave." They tried to fill the hole by pouring in more water but as quickly as they did, the water from the straits would absorb it. They kept on filling until their shoulder joints became dislocated and they perished.[69]

The people of Alexandria asked Rabbi Joshua twelve questions, three concerning Jewish law, three about *aggadah*, three hypothetical questions, and three pertaining to proper conduct. The three matters of *aggadah* were the following. One verse reads, *For it is not My desire that anyone shall die* (Ezekiel 18:32), but another verse says, . . . *the Lord was resolved that they should die* (1 Samuel 2:25). He answered that the former verse refers to those who have repented, while the second verse refers to those who have not. They asked again about one verse that reads . . . *who* shows no favors and takes no bribe (Deuteronomy 10:17), while another verse states, *The Lord bestow His favor upon you* (Numbers 6:26). He replied that the first verse refers to the time before the heavenly decree has been passed, the second verse to the time after it has been passed. The third question was, one verse says, *For the Lord has chosen Zion* (Psalms 132:13), but another verse declares, *This city has aroused My anger and My wrath from the day it was built until this day* (Jeremiah 32:31). Rabbi Joshua explained that the first verse speaks of the time before Solomon married the daughter of Pharaoh while the second verse speaks of the time after that.

Three questions were hypothetical. They first asked, "Does Lot's wife impart ritual impurity?" He answered that a dead body does impart impurity but not a pillar of salt. Again he was asked, "Did the son of the Shunamite whom Elisha brought back to life impart ritual impurity?" He replied that only a dead body imparts impurity but not a living man. Then he was asked, "After the resurrection of the dead, would they need ritual purification with the ashes of the Red Heifer?" To this question he responded, "At that time we shall consider the question." Another version of this answer was, "At that time Moses will be among those resurrected. Let then Moses decide!"

Three questions pertained to human conduct. They asked first, "What should a person do to become wise?" He told them, "Let him engage more in study and less in business." To which they retorted, "Have not many done so, but it did not help them any." So he added, "Let them pray for compassion from Him who is the source of all wisdom," as it is said, *For the Lord grants wisdom;/Knowledge and discernment are by His decree* (Proverbs 2:6). Second, they asked, "What should a person do in order to become rich?" He answered, "Let him spend more time in business and deal with integrity." "But many are doing that," they spoke up, "and it has not been to any avail." To this he said, "Let them pray for compassion from Him who is the source of all wealth, as it is said, *Silver is Mine and gold is Mine—says the Lord of Hosts* (Haggai 2:8). Third, they asked, "What should a man do in order to have male children?" He replied, "Let him marry a woman who is suitable for him and conduct himself with modesty during marital intercourse." "But," they interposed, "many are doing that but it has not helped them." He rejoined, "Let them pray for compassion from Him who is the source of all children, as is it said, *Sons are the provision of the Lord; the fruit of the womb, His reward* (Psalms 127:3).[70]

When Rabbi Eliezer and Rabbi Joshua were young and the Temple was still standing in Jerusalem, they went on pilgrimage to the holy place. It was the eve of Yom Kippur, the day was hot, and as they were walking on the Temple mount they saw an angel coming toward them and in his hand was a white pressed tunic bright as the sun, but missing the border around its neck opening. They said to each other that this tunic must belong to one of them. They approached the angel and asked him to which one of them did the tunic belong. He answered, "Your tunics are better and more honorable than this one. This one belongs to a certain man in Ashkelon whose name is Joseph the gardener." They parted, and after the holidays they went to Ashkelon. The people of the town heard about their coming and went out to greet them. Each of the townspeople invited the sages to stay in his home but they declined and said that they wished to be the guests of Joseph the gardener. Several people accompanied them to his home, and from the distance they saw him at work in his garden collecting the chaff. They came up to him, exchanged greetings, and the sages told Joseph that they would like to be his guests. He said, "You left the rich men and the property owners and came to me! The Holy One, blessed be He, knows that all I have in my home are two loaves of bread." They replied that whatever he had would suffice and they would bother him for nothing else. He set the loaves before them and they ate bread, drank water, and then recited grace. They said to him, "You see that of all the people of your town we have come to you, so tell us about your life."

He said to them, "My masters, you can see my poverty and misery, and I have no work other than the gardening that you saw me do." They told him, "Even so, tell us whether you have been doing this since your youth." He replied, "My masters, if you really want to know about my affairs, I shall reveal everything to you. My father, of blessed memory, was one of the important men of this town, and he was one of the richest as well. After he died I lost that wealth and the men of the town hated me and drove me out. I left and built this house and planted this garden, seeding it with vegetables. I sell whatever I harvest, giving half the money to the poor, and with the other half I feed my family and myself."

They said to him, "Know that the Holy One, blessed be He, will greatly increase your reward for we have seen a white pressed tunic in the hand of an angel who told us that it was yours but it was missing the border for its neck opening. Therefore we have come to let you know and to inform you that the Holy One, blessed be He, will be good to you. Perhaps you will increase your good deeds." The man blessed them and praised them and they departed.

Joseph's wife then said to him, "I heard what the sages of Israel told you about the missing border of your tunic, so now try [through good deeds] to complete it." He said to her, "You speak like one of the noble women! But you know my poverty and my misery and I have nothing with which to perform any good deed." She replied, "Listen to me, my lord, and take my advice so that it will turn out well for you. Now take me out to the market and sell me into slavery and give the money you will get for me to the poor. Perhaps you will then complete your tunic." He told her, "I fear that whoever will buy you will treat you badly and will rape you and then I shall lose the entire tunic." She answered, "I swear to you by faith in heaven that such a disaster will not befall me ever." So he listened to her counsel, sold her into slavery, and gave the money as charity to the poor. Her new owner saw that she was beautiful and he tried to overcome her but he could not. He put her in charge of his treasure house and gave her his keys but she told him, "I am not fit to be your housekeeper." Her master became very angry. His fury burned within him, and he handed her over to the shepherd of his flocks, ordering him to subdue her, to seduce her, to rape her. The shepherd took her and every day tempted her and beat her badly but he could not succeed. He embittered her life with heavy labor and with every kind of difficulty, but she continued to resist. Some time passed and her husband sought her out. She was bitter in spirit and instead of her former lofty position, now there was calamity; instead of her former festive garments, she now was clothed in sackcloth. Her husband had disguised himself, and now he asked her, "Would you like me to purchase you from your owner and marry you, so rescuing you from your misfortune?" She answered, "Sir, it cannot be, because I am already married." He continued to try to persuade her but she would not listen to him. She firmly told him, "No!" When he saw this, it became crystal clear to him that she had not violated her oath or broken her covenant with him. He removed the veil from his face. She recognized him and they kissed and embraced each other and both burst into weeping. Their cry for help ascended to God and there was heard a voice announcing, "Your tunic is now complete, but the tunic of your wife is even finer than yours. Go to such-and-such a place and you will find much money that your father once hid there." He went to that place and he found money, gold, precious jewels, and pearls in great abundance. He liberated his wife from slavery and he continued to give charity and to perform kindnesses all the days of his life.[71]

The verse reads, *He reserves sound wisdom for the upright, He is a shield for those that live blamelessly* (Proverbs 2:7). Rabbi Eliezer asked Rabbi Joshua, "What is the meaning of this verse?" Rabbi Joshua answered, "My son, from the time a human being is formed in the womb of his mother, the Torah that he is to learn is reserved for him, and that is why Scripture says, *He reserves sound wisdom for the upright.* As for the second part of the verse, *He is a shield for those that live blamelessly,* just as a shield protects a person, so Torah protects all who study it, and that is why Scripture says, *He is a shield for those that live blamelessly.*[72]

The verse reads, *For the lips of a forbidden woman drip honey; her mouth is smoother than oil. In the end she is bitter as wormwood, sharp as a two-edged sword* (Proverbs 5:3). Rabbi Eliezer asked Rabbi Joshua, "Master, what does this term, *two-edged sword,* mean?" He replied, "My son, just as the sword cuts both ways, so does the promiscuous woman destroy a man's life both in this world and in the world to come."[73]

The students of Rabbi Joshua asked him, "Master, which is greater, repentance or charity?" He replied, "Repentance is greater than charity, for sometimes one gives charity to a person who does not deserve it, whereas repentance is offered by the penitent himself." They spoke up, "But Master, have we not already found that charity (*tzedakah*, literally, 'righteousness') is greater than repentance, since Scripture says concerning Abraham, *And because he put his trust in the Lord, He reckoned it to him for righteousness* (Genesis 15:6)? And elsewhere it says, *It will therefore be to our righteousness* (*tzedakah*) (Deuteronomy 6:25). Not only that, but David explained it by saying, *Your righteousness* (*tzeda-*

kah) is like the high mountains; Your justice like the great deep; man and beast You deliver, O Lord (Psalms 36:7)."[74]

The verse reads, *A scoundrel, an evil man lives by crooked speech* (Proverbs 6:12)—these are the evil-tongued whom God likens to idolaters. Why so? Because informing is as vicious as idolatry. Rabbi Joshua said that God compared them rather to murderers, for informing is as vicious as spilling blood. About murderers it is written, *Whoever sheds the blood of man,/By man shall his blood be shed* (Genesis 9:6). So too here, when the informer goes out and denounces another person to the government, it is the same as if he had spilled his blood.[75]

Rabbi Eliezer asked Rabbi Joshua, "Master, what is the meaning of the verse, *Without leaders, officers, or rulers* (Proverbs 6:7)?" Rabbi Joshua replied, "My son, the ant has neither king, nor overseer, nor ruler to make her wise, rather her wisdom comes from within her. God continued His rebuke and said, 'And you wicked ones, should you not have learned from her? But you held on to your laziness and your foolishness and failed to repent!' "[76]

Scripture states: *Thus said the Lord God: I am going to open your graves and lift you out of the graves, O My people, and bring you to the land of Israel* (Ezekiel 37:12). Rabbi Eliezer asked Rabbi Joshua, "What is this verse talking about?" Rabbi Joshua replied, "About those who die outside the Land of Israel." Rabbi Eliezer then asked, "And what does it say about those who die in the Land of Israel?" Rabbi Joshua answered, "Their land will atone for them, as it is said, *The land of His people makes expiation* (Deuteronomy 32:43)." Rabbi Eliezer asked, "What about the righteous? If they have sinned, will the land atone for them as well?" Rabbi Joshua replied, "My son, if it atones for the wicked, is it not an inference from the minor to the major that it will certainly atone for the righteous? Come and see what Solomon has said in his wisdom, that the righteous will not leave this world until the Omnipresent has forgiven them all their sins, as it is said, *The Lord will not let the righteous go hungry*—meaning, that he will depart to the next world free of sin; *but He denies the wicked what they crave* (Proverbs 10:3)—for He thrusts them away for Judgment Day."[77]

Rabbi Eliezer asked Rabbi Joshua, "What is the meaning of *Assuredly, the evil man will not escape* (Proverbs 11:21)?" Rabbi Joshua replied, "Although one hand is nourished the same as the other, if a person performs a *mitzvah* with one hand and transgresses with the other, the one hand cannot atone for the other. Why is that? Because *Assuredly, the evil one will not escape.* If a person negotiates a deal between himself and another and he swears an oath with his mouth but annuls it in his heart, would you say that he will go unpunished? It cannot be, for Scripture says . . . *will not escape.* It is said here *The evil man will not escape,* and it is said in the Ten Commandments, *For the Lord will not let escape he who swears falsely by His name* (Exodus 20:7). Just as the commandment there concerns a false oath, so the commandment here must refer to a false oath." Rabbi Eliezer retorted, "Not so, for the end of the verse states specifically, *But the offspring of the righteous will be safe* (Proverbs 11:21). If you see a righteous man of good ancestry, you may rest assured that he will not quickly sin. Why not? Because he will think about the consequences and will say, 'I had better suppress my evil inclination for the moment so as not to lose my reward in the world to come in the same moment.' So he is saved from the torment of Gehenna. Therefore it is said, *But the offspring of the righteous will be safe.* The wicked person, however, will not reason in the same way, but instead he will go to the prostitute and swear an oath to pay her fee so that he may satisfy his lustful inclination, but later he will violate his oath. The Holy Spirit will speak to him and say, 'O wicked one, it is not enough for you that you have committed a transgression but you also had to invoke My name for your lies! By your life, you shall not go unpunished by the torment of Gehenna!' "[78]

Rabbi Eliezer asked Rabbi Joshua, "Master, what should a person do to be saved from the torment of Gehenna?" Rabbi Joshua answered, "Let him go and perform good deeds."[79]

Rabbi Eliezer and Rabbi Joshua differed on the interpretation of the verse, *Train a child in the way he ought to go, he will not swerve from it even in old age* (Proverbs 22:6). Rabbi Eliezer said, "If you educate your child in words of Torah while he is yet young, he will continually grow up in accord with them, as it is said, *He will not swerve from them even in old age.* It is like the tendril of a vine— if you do not train it when it is still young and moist, once it dries out you will be unable to do so." Rabbi Joshua said, *"Train a child in the way he ought to go*—why?—*he will not swerve from it even in old age.* It is like an ox that has not been taught when young to plow; later it is too difficult for it to learn how."[80]

Rabbi Eliezer asked Rabbi Joshua, "Master, when was the second set of tablets given to Israel?" Rabbi Joshua answered,

"On the Day of Atonement." Rabbi Eliezer asked, "Where is the proof?" Rabbi Joshua replied, "Just as it took forty days for the first set, so did it take forty days for the second set. Go and count from the day when the first set was broken until the following Day of Atonement and you will see that it was eighty days—forty and forty. The first forty Moses waited on earth and the second forty he went up to heaven and came down again."

Rabbi Eliezer asked, "Master, what is the meaning of the verse, *You have sowed much and brought in little; you eat without being satisfied; you drink without getting your fill; you clothe yourselves, but no one gets warm; and who earns anything earns it for a leaky purse* (Haggai 1:6)?" Rabbi Joshua answered, "*You have sowed much and brought in little*—since the end of the *omer*; *you eat without being satisfied*—since the end of the showbread; *you drink without getting your fill*—since the end of the libations; *you clothe yourselves, but no one gets warm*—since the end of the garments of the high priesthood; *and he who earns anything earns it for a leaky purse*—since the end of the *shekel* payments."[81]

The story is told that once Rabbi Johanan ben Beroka and Rabbi Eleazar Hisma went to greet Rabbi Joshua at Pekiin and he asked them, "What thing new was taught today at the academy?" They replied, "Master, we are your disciples and it is your water that we drink." He retorted, "Even so, it is impossible that nothing new was said at the academy. Whose Sabbath was it?" They answered, "It was the Sabbath of Rabbi Eleazar ben Azariah." "And what was his subject today?" They replied, "He dealt with the portion of *Hakhel*." He asked, "And how did he expound it?" They said, "The text reads, *Gather the people—men, women, children* (Deuteronomy 31:12). Now the men came to learn and the women to listen, but what reason was there for the children to come? The explanation is that they came so that those who brought them might receive their reward." He said to them, "You had this precious pearl in your hands and you wished to deprive me of it!"

He made a further exposition, this time on the verses *You have affirmed this day that the Lord is your God* (Deuteronomy 26:17) *And the Lord has affirmed this day that you are . . . His treasured people* (Deuteronomy 26:18): "The Holy One, blessed be He, said to Israel, 'You have made Me the only object of your love in the world, as it is written, *Hear, O Israel! The Lord is our God, the Lord alone* (Deuteronomy 6:4). I, on my part, will make you the only object of My love in the world, as it is said, *And who is like Your people, Israel, a unique nation on earth* (2 Samuel 7:23).' "

He also opened a discourse on the text, *The sayings of the wise are like goads, like nails fixed in prodding sticks. They were given by one Shepherd* (Ecclesiastes 12:11). "Why were the words of the Torah compared to goads? In order to tell you that just as goads direct the cow along the furrows in order to bring life to the world, so the words of Torah direct those who study them away from the paths of death to the paths of life. And should you assume that just as a nail contracts but does not expand, so too the words of Torah contract, but do not expand, Scripture states *fixed* (literally 'planted'), to teach that just as a plant is fruitful and multiplies, so too are the words of Torah fruitful and they multiply. *Prodding sticks* (literally 'masters in collections') applies to the scholars, who sit in groups and study the Torah, some declaring a thing ritually unclean, others declaring it ritually clean; some pronouncing a thing forbidden, others pronouncing it permitted; some disqualifying an object, others upholding its fitness. How can I study Torah under such circumstances? Scripture states, *They were given by one Shepherd*. One God has given them, one leader has uttered them at the command of the Lord of all creation, blessed be He, as it is said, *God spoke all these words* (Exodus 20:1). Do you then make your ear like a funnel and acquire for yourself a heart that can understand the words of those who declare a thing ritually clean and of those who call it unclean, the words of those who forbid and of those who permit, the words of those who disqualify and of those who uphold its fitness."

Rabbi Joshua then spoke to them in these words: "Blessed is the generation in whose midst is Rabbi Eleazar ben Azariah for such a generation can never be called orphaned."[82]

Rabbi Joshua ben Hananiah remarked, "No one has ever gotten the better of me except a woman, a little boy, and a little girl. What was the incident involving the woman? I was once staying at an inn where the woman made beans for me. On that first day I ate them all and left nothing. On the second day I ate and left nothing. On the third day she spoiled the beans with too much salt and as soon as I tasted them, I pulled back my hand. She said, 'Rabbi, why did you withdraw your hand from the food?' I told her that I had already eaten earlier in the day. To which she said, 'Why did you then not withdraw your hand from the bread? Rabbi, perhaps you have left over the beans today as *pe'ah* because you did not do so yesterday and the day before, and have not the sages declared that nothing is to be left in the pot, but *pe'ah* is to be left on the plate!'

"What was the incident with the little girl? Once I was going on my way and there was a path cutting across a field and I took it. A little girl called out to me, 'My Master, are you not walking across a private field?' I replied, 'No, I am walking along a well-trodden path.' She retorted, 'Robbers like you have trodden it down!'

"What was the incident with the boy? Once I was going on my way when I saw this boy who was sitting at the crossroads. I said to him, 'My son, which road shall we take to the city?' He answered, 'This one is long but short and that one is short but long.' I went along the one that was short but long. When I approached the city the road was blocked by gardens and orchards. I went back and asked the boy, 'Did you not tell me that this was short?' He replied, 'My Master, did I not tell you that it was short but also long?' I kissed him on his head and said to him, 'Happy are you, O Israel, in that all of you are wise, from your elders to your little ones!' "[83]

Once Rabbi Joshua was going along his way when he met a child holding a covered dish. He asked, "What do you have in that covered dish?" The child replied, "If my mother wanted you to know, she would not have told me to cover it." He proceeded on his way and met another child, whom he asked, "What is the water of the city like?" The child answered, "Why worry? Garlic and onions are plentiful." When he entered the city, he met a little girl standing at the well and filling her pitcher. He said to her, "Give me some water to drink." She replied, "For both you and your donkey." When he had finished drinking and was turning to leave, he said to her, "My daughter, you have acted like Rebekah." She retorted, "I have acted like Rebekah, but you have not acted like Eliezer!"[84]

The emperor once asked Rabbi Joshua ben Hananiah, "Why did you not come to the meeting place of the scholars?" He replied, "The snowy mountain (his hoary head) is surrounded by ice (his white beard), the dogs no longer bark (his voice cannot be heard), and the grinders no longer grind (his teeth have fallen out)."[85]

When the soul of Rabbi Joshua ben Hananiah was about to go to its rest, the rabbis said to him, "Who will defend us against the heretics?" He replied, *"Counsel is perished from the children, their wisdom is vanished* (Jeremiah 49:7). As soon as counsel perishes from the children—that is, the children of Israel—the wisdom of the peoples of the world vanishes. Or I may derive it from here: *And* [Esau] *said, Let us start on our journey, and I will proceed at your pace* (Genesis 33:12)."[86]

When Rabbi Joshua died, goodness departed from the world. When he died, men of counsel and reflection were no more.[87]

4

Rabbi Eleazar ben Azariah

Of Rabbi Eleazar ben Azariah it was said that he was wise, rich, and tenth in descent from Ezra.[1]

There was a certain garden from which Rabbi Eleazar ben Azariah used to receive the first tithe. Rabbi Akiba went and changed its gate so that it faced a cemetery. Seeing this, Rabbi Eleazar remarked, "Akiba with his shepherd's bag but I have enough on which to live!"[2]

Rav, and according to others, Rabbi Judah in the name of Rav, said that thirteen thousand calves were the yearly tithe of Rabbi Eleazar ben Azariah's herds.[3]

Rabbi Eleazar ben Azariah's cow used to go out—on the Sabbath—with a strap between its horns to which the sages took exception.[4]

Once Rabbi Eleazar ben Azariah and Rabbi Akiba were traveling on a ship. The latter built a *sukkah* on the ship's bow but a wind came up and blew it off the ship. Rabbi Eleazar said to his colleague, "Akiba, where is your *sukkah* now?"[5]

In this fashion did Rabbi Eleazar ben Azariah interpret the verse, *For on this day atonement shall be made for you to cleanse you of all your sins; you shall be clean before the Lord* (Leviticus 16:30)—"for transgressions between a person and the Lord the Day of Atonement atones. But for transgressions between one human being and another, the Day of Atonement atones only if the person asks forgiveness of the one whom he has wronged."[6]

Rabbi Mattiah ben Heresh asked Rabbi Eleazar ben Azariah in Rome, "Have you heard of the four kinds of atonement that Rabbi Ishmael expounded?" He replied, "There are three, with repentance connected with each. If a person transgresses a positive commandment and does repentance at once, before he leaves the place he is already forgiven, as it is said, *Turn back, O rebellious children,/I will heal your afflictions* (Jeremiah 3:22). If a person violates a negative commandment and then does repentance, his repentance causes the suspension of any punishment and the next Yom Kippur effects atonement, as it is said, *For on this day atonement shall be made for you to cleanse you of all your sins* (Leviticus 16:30). If a person commits a wrong, the punishment for which is extirpation or death by order of the court but the person does repentance, then that repentance and Yom Kippur suspend the punishment and suffering completes the process, as it is said, *I will punish their transgression with the rod,/Their iniquity with plagues* (Psalms 89:33). But if the person has been guilty of profaning God's Name, then repentance has no power to suspend punishment, nor Yom Kippur to effect atonement nor suffering to complete it, but all of them together suspend punishment and only death completes the process, as it is said, *Then the Lord of Hosts revealed Himself to my ears:/'This iniquity shall never be forgiven you/Until you die,' said my Lord God of Hosts* (Isaiah 22:14)."[7]

The verse reads, . . . *I planted vineyards* (Ecclesiastes 2:4). This refers to the rows of disciples who sat in rows as in a vineyard; as we have learned—this exposition was made by Rabbi Eleazar ben Azariah in the presence of the sages in the vineyard of Jabneh. Was it then in a vineyard? Surely not, but it was so called only because the disciples sat in rows as in a vineyard.[8]

The verse reads, *Now the man knew his wife Eve, and she conceived and bore Cain* (Genesis 4:1). Rabbi Eleazar ben Azariah said, "Three wonders were performed on that day: on that day Adam and Eve were created, on that day they had sexual intercourse, and on that very day they produced offspring."[9]

The verse reads . . . *For you alone have I found righteous* (Genesis 7:1). Rabbi Eleazar ben Azariah said, "We find that only a part of a person's good qualities may be spoken of in his presence, but not all of them. They may be told only when he is not present. For in Noah's presence Scripture says, *For you alone have I found righteous,* but when he is not present, the verse reads, *Noah was a righteous man; he was blameless in his age* (Genesis 6:9)."[10]

The verse reads, *When Isaac was old and his eyes were too dim to see* (Genesis 27:1). Rabbi Eleazar ben Azariah said, "*Too dim to see*—to see the evil of that wicked man [his son Esau]. The Holy

One, blessed be He, said, 'Shall Isaac go into the marketplace and people will say, "Here is the father of that scoundrel!" Rather will I make his eyes dim, so that he shall stay at home.' "[11]

The verse reads, *I will drive them out before you little by little . . . I will not drive them out before you in a single year, lest the land become desolate and the wild beasts multiply to your hurt* (Exodus 23:30 and 29). Rabbi Eleazar ben Azariah said, "Should not the question be asked that if the people of Israel is righteous, why should there be fear of wild beasts? Is it not true that if they be righteous, they need not fear wild beasts, as it is said, *For you will have a pact with the rocks in the field,/And the beasts of the field will be your allies* (Job 5:23). Should you ask, why then did Joshua go to all that trouble—to conquer the land quickly so that wild beasts not multiply—the answer is because Israel had sinned and that is why it was decreed for them that *I will drive them out before you little by little . . . lest the wild beasts multiply.*"[12]

Rabbi Abba said, "All agree that when Israel was liberated from Egypt that it was at night, as it is said, *. . . For in the month of Abib, at night, that the Lord your God freed you from Egypt* (Deuteronomy 16:1). And when they departed from Egypt all agree that it was during the day, as it is said, *It was on the morrow of the Passover offering that the Israelites started out boldly* (Numbers 33:3). The sages differed only about the "hurry" cited in Exodus 12:11. Rabbi Eleazar thought that the hurry was that of the Egyptians and Rabbi Akiba thought that the hurry was that of the Israelites."[13]

An interpretation of the word *ba-kosharot* (Psalms 68:7) was given by Rabbi Eleazar ben Azariah: there were both weeping and singing at the Exodus. The Egyptians wept because they had been despoiled, for the Israelites had emptied their houses, as it is said, *They stripped the Egyptians* (Exodus 12:36). The Israelites, however, sang because they were carting away the spoil of their enemies.[14]

Rabbi Eleazar ben Azariah said, "Moses broke the first set of tablets only because he was commanded to do so by the Almighty, as it is said, *. . . that Moses displayed before all Israel* (Deuteronomy 34:12). As everywhere else he acted on the command of God, so here too, he acted on the command of God."[15]

The verse in Numbers (29:35) reads, *On the eighth day you shall hold a solemn assembly.* Ecclesiastes (11:2), however, reads,

Distribute portions to seven and also to eight. As to what the two numbers mean, Rabbi Eleazar, Rabbi Nehemiah, and Rabbi Joshua differed. Rabbi Eleazar said, "The words, *Distribute portions to seven* contain an allusion to the Sabbath, of which it is written, *And the seventh time* (1 Kings 18:44). The words, *and also to eight* contain an allusion to the eight days of circumcision, of which it is written, *Elijah . . . put his face between his knees* (1 Kings 18:42). These two verses intimate that Elijah said to the Holy One, blessed be He, 'Master of the Universe, even if the Israelites have performed no commandments other than the Sabbath and circumcision, the merit of these two is sufficient for You to send down rain because of them.'"

Rabbi Nehemiah stated, "The words, *Distribute portions to seven*, refer to the generation that Moses circumcised, the seventh generation from Abraham. The Holy One, blessed be He, said to Joshua, 'The master of Israel, Moses, circumcised them in the eighth, as it is said, *At that time the Lord said to Joshua, "Make flint knives and proceed with a second circumcision of the Israelites"* (Joshua 5:2), and bring them into the covenant.' The words 'a second circumcision' imply that God was saying, 'Circumcise them a second time; you will not have to do it a third time, for from now on they will perform the rite of circumcision for themselves.'"

Rabbi Joshua maintained that the words *Distribute portions to seven* refer to the seven days of Passover. The words *and also to eight* allude to the eight festival days made up by the seven days of the Feast of Tabernacles and the Eighth Day Festival that comes immediately afterward. The words *and also* mean that we entreat You because of Pentecost, New Year's Day, and the Day of Atonement as well as because of the other festival days to *Distribute portions.*[16]

Rabbi Eleazar ben Azariah said, "Where there is no Torah, there is no right conduct; where there is no right conduct, there is no Torah. Where there is no wisdom, there is no piety; where there is no piety, there is no wisdom. Where there is no perception, there is no knowledge; where there is no knowledge, there is no perception. Where there is no bread, there is no Torah; where there is no Torah, there is no bread."

He used to say, "He whose wisdom exceeds his deeds, to what may he be compared? To a tree whose branches are many but whose roots are few. A wind comes along and uproots it and overturns it, as it is said, *He shall be like a tamarisk in the desert,/Which does not sense the coming of good:/It is set in the scorched places of the wilderness,/In a barren land without inhabitant* (Jeremiah 17:6). But he whose deeds exceed his wisdom, to what is he likened? To a tree whose branches are few but whose roots are many. Then if even all the winds of the world come along and blow against it, they cannot stir it from its place, as it is said, *He shall be like a tree planted by waters,/Sending forth its roots by a stream:/It does not sense the coming of heat,/Its leaves are ever fresh;/It has no care in a year of droughts,/It does not cease to yield fruit* (Jeremiah 17:8)."[17]

Rabbi Eleazar ben Azariah said, "The Torah taught right conduct. If a person of Israel has ten pounds of silver, let him eat vegetables in a pot. If he has twenty pounds, let him eat vegetables in a stewing pot. If he has thirty, let him eat a pound of meat each week. If he has fifty, he may have as much as a pound of meat a day. And why all this? In order to conserve the goods of Israelites." Rabbi Eleazar ben Shammua said that when he be in a position to purchase a pound of meat per week, let him first consult with the members of his family before he acts. And how do we know this? Because it is written, . . . *and you say, "I shall eat some meat"* (Deuteronomy 12:20). Therefore, Moses warned and gave them this sign that they should not eat or drink too much.[18]

Resh Lakish said in the name of Rabbi Eleazar ben Azariah, "A man must not make a distinction among his children, for on account of the coat of many colors made by our ancestor Jacob for Joseph, . . . *they hated him* (Genesis 37:4)."[19]

Rabbi Eleazar ben Azariah said, "Woe unto us on the Day of Judgment and woe unto us on the day of rebuke. Joseph was mere flesh and blood, yet when he rebuked his brothers, they could not withstand his rebuke. How much less will the human being of flesh and blood be able to withstand the rebuke of the Holy One, blessed be He, who is Judge and Prosecutor, who sits on the throne of judgment and judges every single person!"[20]

Rabbi Eleazar ben Azariah said, "The entire Torah is based on justice. God purposely gave the laws after having given the Ten Commandments to teach the world that He punishes those who transgress the laws. He did not destroy Sodom until after it had perverted justice, for it says, . . . *arrogance! She had plenty of bread and untroubled tranquillity; yet she did not support the poor and the needy* (Ezekiel 16:49). Jerusalem also was not sent into exile until after she had perverted justice, for it says, *They do not judge the case of the orphan,/And the widow's cause never reaches them* (Isaiah 1:23)."[21]

Rabbi Eleazar ben Azariah said that anyone who refrains from procreation is as though he had shed blood and had also diminished the divine image. What is the proof? *Whoever sheds the blood of man,/By man shall his blood be shed* (Genesis 9:6). Why? *For in His image/Did God make man* (Genesis 9:6). And that is followed by *Be fertile, then, and increase* (Genesis 9:7).[22]

Rabbi Eleazar ben Azariah said, "The foreskin is repulsive for the word is used with reference to wicked people, as it is written, *For all these nations are uncircumcised* (Jeremiah 9:25)."[23]

Rabbi Shizvi quoted Rabbi Eleazar ben Azariah as having said, "A person's earning a livelihood is as difficult as the splitting of the Red Sea, as it is said, *The prisoner struggles to be loosed,/He is not cut down and slain,/And he shall not want for food* (Isaiah 51:14), and the verse following reads, *For I the Lord your God—/Who stirs up the sea into roaring waves* (Isaiah 51:15)."[24]

Rabbi Eleazar ben Azariah said, "A person's excretory organs—when blocked—become as painful as the day of death and as difficult to resolve as the dividing of the Red Sea, for it is said, *The prisoner struggles to be loosed . . .* (Isaiah 51:14)." And that is followed by *For I the Lord your God—/Who stir up the sea into roaring waves* (Isaiah 51:15).[25]

Rabbi Sheshet quoted Rabbi Eleazar ben Azariah as having said that he who speaks slander of another and he who gives false testimony about another deserve to be thrown to the dogs, as it is said . . . *you shall cast it to the dogs* (Exodus 22:30) and the next verse reads *You must not carry false rumors; you shall not join hands with the guilty to act as a malicious witness* (Exodus 23:1).[26]

Again Rabbi Sheshet quoted Rabbi Eleazar ben Azariah as having said that the person who despises the festivals is as though he were engaged in idolatry, for it is said, *You shall not make molten gods for yourselves* (Exodus 34:17) and the next verse reads, *You shall observe the Feast of Unleavened Bread* (Exodus 34:18).[27]

Rabbi Sheshet quoted Rabbi Eleazar ben Azariah further as having said, "I could excuse all the Israelite world from judgment from the day of the destruction of the Temple until the present time, for it is said, *Therefore,/Listen to this, unhappy one,/Who are drunk, but not with wine!* (Isaiah 51:21)."[28]

Rabbi Shizvi quoted Rabbi Eleazar ben Azariah as having

said, "What is the exposition of the text, *A negligent man never has game to roast* (Proverbs 12:27)? It means that he who is negligent will not live long nor will he enjoy length of days."[29]

Rabbi Eleazar ben Azariah said, "If you see a generation to whom the words of the Torah are dear, *Your springs will gush forth/In streams in the public squares* (Proverbs 5:16). If not, *They will be yours alone,/Others having no part with you* (Proverbs 5:17)."[30]

The elders came to Rabbi Dosa ben Harkinas . . . He saw among them Rabbi Eleazar ben Azariah and with respect to him he recited the verses, *"I have been young and am now old,/but I have never seen a righteous man abandoned,/or his children seeking bread./He is always generous and lends,/and his children are held blessed* (Psalms 37:25–26). I know him to be in the tenth generation of his family from Ezra. His eyes are like those of Ezra."[31]

When Rabbi Eleazar, Rabbi Joshua, and Rabbi Akiba went to bathe in the hot baths of Tiberias, a sectarian saw them. He mumbled his formulas of magic, and they were held fast and could not move in the arched chamber of the bathhouse (where there were idolatrous statues). Rabbi Eleazar said to Rabbi Joshua, "Now Joshua ben Hanina, see what you can do."

When the sectarian tried to leave, Rabbi Joshua uttered his incantations of magic, and the doorway of the bathhouse seized the sectarian and held him fast. Whoever went in had to give him a knock to push by and whoever went out had to give him a knock to get out. He said to them, "Undo whatever you have done and let me go."

They said to him, "Release us and we shall release you." They released one another.[32]

Once Rabbi Eleazar ben Azariah and Rabbi Ishmael were staying in the same place. The former was reclining and the latter was sitting upright. When the time came to recite the morning *Shema*, Rabbi Eleazar ben Azariah sat up and Rabbi Ishmael reclined. Whereupon Rabbi Eleazar said to Rabbi Ishmael, "What you are doing is like the case of a man in the marketplace who was asked, 'Why do you wear your beard so long?' He replied, 'It is in protest against the destroyers who cut their beards short, and for no other reason.' I who was reclining sat up to recite the *Shema* properly. But you, you were already upright, and you reclined for no other reason than to protest what I did!"

Rabbi Ishmael replied, "Eleazar, you sat upright in accordance with the words of the school of Shammai, whose opinion it was that one should be upright while reciting the *Shema*. I reclined to show my agreement with the school of Hillel that maintained that one may be in any position while reciting the *Shema*."

An alternate explanation had it that Ishmael replied, "I reclined so that the students should not observe me upright and therefore conclude that the law follows the opinion of the school of Shammai."[33]

Rabbi Eleazar ben Azariah and Rabbi Eleazar of Modiim were struggling with the meaning of the verse, *At that time, they shall call Jerusalem "Throne of the Lord"* (Jeremiah 3:17). Rabbi Eleazar ben Azariah asked Rabbi Eleazar of Modiim, "Can Jerusalem hold so many people as will crowd into it when it becomes His throne?" His colleague replied, "The Holy One will say to Jerusalem, 'Extend yourself, enlarge yourself, receive your multitudes—*enlarge the site of your tent, extend the size of your dwelling* (Isaiah 54:2).' "[34]

Shortly before Rabbi Eleazar ben Azariah died, his disciples came to visit him. They sat before him and they asked him, "Master, teach us the right ways of life." He said to them, "My sons, what can I teach you? Go and let each of you be concerned for the honor of his colleague. And when you stand up to pray, know before Whom you stand and pray, for on that account you will be worthy to enter into the life of the World to Come."[35]

When Rabbi Eleazar ben Azariah died, great wealth ceased among the sages. When Rabbi Eleazar ben Azariah died, the crown of wisdom ceased, for *the crown of the wise is their wealth* (Proverbs 14:24).[36]

5

Rabbi Eleazar ben Arakh

Rabbi Johanan ben Zakkai said to his five disciples, "Go and see which is the right way to which a person should cleave." Rabbi Eliezer replied, "A liberal eye." Rabbi Joshua said, "A good friend." Rabbi Jose answered, "A good neighbor." Rabbi Simon said, "Foreseeing the future." Rabbi Eleazar replied, "A good heart." Whereupon Rabbi Johanan ben Zakkai said, "I prefer the answer of Rabbi Eleazar ben Arakh, for in his words your words are included."

He said to them, "Go and see which is the evil way that a person should shun." Rabbi Eliezer replied, "A grudging eye." Rabbi Joshua answered, "A bad friend." Rabbi Jose said, "A bad neighbor." Rabbi Simon replied, "Borrowing and not repaying, for he who borrows from another person is as one who borrows from God, as it is said, *The wicked man borrows and does not repay;/the righteous is generous and keeps giving* (Psalms 37:21)." Rabbi Eleazar answered, "Meanheartedness." Whereupon Rabbi Johanan ben Zakkai said to them, "I prefer the answer of Rabbi Eleazar ben Arakh, for in his words your words are included."[1]

Rabbi Eleazar said, "Be conscientious in the study of Torah and know how to answer the unbeliever; know in whose presence you labor and who is your Employer who will pay you your reward for your labor."[2]

When the son of Rabban Johanan ben Zakkai died, his disciples came in to comfort him. Rabbi Eliezer said, "Adam had a son who died, yet he permitted himself to be comforted. And how do we know that? It is said, *Adam knew his wife again* (Genesis 4:25). So may you too find comfort." Rabbi Johanan said to him, "Is it not enough that I am grieving for my own loss that you must remind me of Adam's grief?"

Rabbi Joshua entered and said to him, "With your permission, may I say something to you?" "Speak," he told him. Rabbi Joshua said, "Job had sons and daughters, all of whom died in one day and he permitted himself to be comforted. How do we know that to be so? For it is said, *The Lord has given, and the Lord has taken away; blessed be the name of the Lord* (Job 1:21)." Rabbi Johanan said to him, "Is it not enough that I am grieving for my own loss that you must remind me of Job's grief?"

Rabbi Jose entered and sat down before him and said, "Master, with your permission may I say something to you?" He said, "Speak." Rabbi Jose said, "Aaron had two grown sons, both of whom died on the same day, yet he permitted himself to be comforted. And how do we know that to be so? For it is said, *And Aaron was silent* (Leviticus 10:3). Silence means consolation, so may you too be comforted." Rabban Johanan replied, "Is it not enough that I am grieving for my own loss that you must remind me of Aaron's grief?"

Rabbi Simon came in and said to him, "Master, with your permission, may I say something to you?" "Speak," he replied. Rabbi Simon said, "King David had a son who died, yet he permitted himself to be comforted. May you too, therefore, be comforted. And how do we know that David was comforted? For it is said, *David consoled his wife Bathsheba; he went to her and lay with her. She bore a son and she named him Solomon* (2 Samuel 12:24). You, Master, may you too be comforted."

Rabban Johanan responded, "Is it not enough that I am grieving for my own loss that you must remind me of King David's grief?"

Rabbi Eleazar ben Arakh entered and as soon as Rabban Johanan saw him, he said to his servant, "Take my clothing and prepare to follow me to the bathhouse for he is a great man and I shall be unable to resist him." Rabbi Eleazar sat down before him and said to him, "I shall tell you a parable as to what this may be compared. To a man with whom the king had left an object in his care. Every day the man would cry out, 'Woe unto me! When shall I be relieved in peace of this trust given me?' You too, my Master, had a son. He studied the Torah, the prophets, and the holy Writings. He studied Mishnah, *Halakhah*, *Aggadah*, and he departed from the world without sin. You should feel comforted in the knowledge that you have returned the trust given you unimpaired."[3]

The story is told about Rabban Johanan ben Zakkai that once he was riding out of Jerusalem on a donkey and Rabbi Eleazar ben Arakh was directing the donkey from behind. Rabbi Eleazar said, "Master, teach me a chapter about the Work of the Chariot." He replied, "My son, have I not taught you that the Chariot should not be studied with an individual unless he be a sage who understands it on his own?" To which Rabbi Eleazar said, "Master, permit me to say before you something that you have taught me." Rabban Johanan ben Zakkai answered, "Speak," and at once Rabban Johanan descended from the donkey, wrapped his garment around him, and sat on a stone under an olive tree. Rabbi Eleazar asked, "My Master, why did you dismount from the donkey?" The answer came, "Is it possible that you should be expounding about the Work of the Chariot—with the result being that the Divine Presence will attend, with the ministering angels accompanying us—and I should be sitting on a donkey?" At once Rabbi Eleazar ben Arakh began expounding about the Work of the Chariot. Fire from heaven struck and singed all the trees in the field and the trees broke into song. Which song did they sing? *Praise the Lord, O you who are on earth,/all sea monsters and ocean depths,/all mountains and hills,/all fruit trees and cedars,/He has exalted the horn of His people/for the glory of all His faithful ones,/Israel, the people close to him. Hallelujah* (Psalms 148:7, 9, 14). Even an angel answered from the midst of the fire, saying, "According to the words of Rabbi Eleazar ben Arakh is the Work of the Chariot!" Rabban Johanan ben Zakkai rose to his feet and kissed him on his head and said, "Blessed be the Lord, the God of Israel, who has given to Abraham our father a son who knows how to understand, to research, and to expound the Work of the Chariot like Eleazar ben Arakh! There are those who expound well but do not practice well, there are those who practice well but do not expound well, but you, Eleazar ben Arakh, you expound well and you practice well. Blessed are you, Abraham our father, in that Eleazar ben Arakh is your descendant!"

Now when these things were told to Rabbi Joshua, he and Rabbi Jose the priest were setting out on a journey. They said, "Let us also expound on the Work of the Chariot," so Rabbi Joshua began to expound. Now the day was that of the summer solstice but the heavens became overcast and a kind of rainbow appeared in the clouds. The ministering angels assembled and came to watch as though it were the entertainment given a bridegroom and bride. Rabbi Jose left to tell Rabban Johanan ben Zakkai what had happened. The latter said, "Blessed are you and blessed is she who bore you, and blessed are my eyes that witnessed this. Moreover, in a dream I saw that you and I were reclining on Mount Sinai when a heavenly voice was sent to us to say, "Ascend heavenward, ascend heavenward! Here there are great banqueting chambers and fine dining couches prepared for you. You, your disciples, and your disciples' disciples are designated for the third heavenly class."

This corresponds to that which has been said, *In Your presence is perfect joy* (Psalms 16:11). There are seven classes of righteous in the time to come.[4]

The reason all people sought the counsel of a teacher like Rabbi Eleazar ben Arakh was that when he gave counsel it turned out well. People would say to him, "You are a prophet!" and he would answer, "I am neither a prophet nor the son of a prophet, but I have a tradition from my masters that all counsel given in God's name turns out well."[5]

When Rabban Johanan ben Zakkai died, his disciples went to Jabneh, all except Rabbi Eleazar ben Arakh. He joined his wife at Emmaus, a place of good water and with a beautiful view. He waited for the others to come to him, but they did not come. Since they did not, he wanted to go to them, but his wife would not let him. She said, "Who needs them?" He answered, "They need me." To which she replied, "In the case of a vessel containing food, with mice about, which goes to which? Do the mice go to the vessel or does the vessel go to the mice?" He listened to her and he stayed there until he had forgotten his learning. Some time later the others came to him and asked, "Which is better to eat together with a relish, wheat bread or barley bread?" He was unable to answer.[6]

6

Rabbi Dosa ben Harkinas

In the days of Rabbi Dosa ben Harkinas it was declared in his name that it was permitted for a man to marry the co-wife of his daughter. It was difficult for the sages publicly to forbid such a thing because he was old, a great scholar, and since he had become blind, he no longer came to the academy. Among themselves they asked, "Who volunteers to go and tell him of our disagreement?" Rabbi Joshua said, "I shall go." "Who else?" Rabbi Eleazar ben Azariah agreed. "And who else?" Rabbi Akiba volunteered. They went to Rabbi Dosa's home and waited at the door, where his servant saw them. She told Rabbi Dosa, "Rabbi, the sages of Israel have come to you." He said, "Have them enter," and they did so. He took hold of Rabbi Joshua and had him sit on a gilded couch. The latter spoke up. "My Master, tell your other student to sit down." "Who is that?" he inquired. The response was "Rabbi Eleazar ben Azariah." Rabbi Dosa asked, "Does then our friend Azariah have a son?" and he applied to him this verse. *I have been young and am now old,/but I have never seen a righteous man abandoned,/or his children seeking bread* (Psalms 37:25). He then took hold of Rabbi Eleazar and seated him on a gilded couch. Whereupon the latter said to him, "My Master, tell your other student to be seated." Rabbi Dosa asked, "And who is he?" He responded, "Akiba ben Joseph." Rabbi Dosa exclaimed, "Are you that Akiba ben Joseph whose name reaches from one end of the world to the other? Sit down, my son, and may there be many like you in Israel." He applied to him this verse. *A good name is better than fragrant oil* (Ecclesiastes 7:1).

They began to pepper him with questions about the law until finally they came to the question about a man marrying his daughter's co-wife. "What is the law in such a case?" they asked.

He answered, "With regard to this matter there is a difference of opinion between the school of Shammai and the school of Hillel." "And according to which one is the law decided?" they asked again. He replied, "According to the school of Hillel." They stated, "But it has been quoted in your name that the law is in accordance with the school of Shammai." He asked them, "How did you hear it? In the name of Dosa or in the name of Ben Harkinas?" They answered, "We swear that we heard it quoted in the name of Ben Harkinas." He explained, "I have a younger brother. He is the firstborn of Satan and his name is Jonathan. He is a disciple of the school of Shammai, and be careful with him lest he overwhelm you with many laws, for he can cite three hundred proofs that it is permitted for a man to marry the co-wife of his daughter. But I call heaven and earth to witness that upon this mortar-shaped seat did the prophet Haggai sit as he decided these three issues: the co-wife of one's daughter is forbidden in marriage; Jews who live in the lands of Ammon and Moab must give the tithe to the poor in the Sabbatical year; and we may accept candidates for conversion to Judaism from the Cardinians and the Palmyreans."

We have also learned that when they had entered Rabbi Dosa's home, they came in through one entrance but when they left, it was through three separate doors. Rabbi Akiba was met by that Jonathan who asked him questions that he was unable to answer. Jonathan then asked him, "Are you that Akiba whose name extends from one end of the world to the other? Happy may you be that you have attained this, but in reality you have not even reached the status of an oxen shepherd!" To which Rabbi Akiba responded, "Not even to the status of a shepherd of sheep!"[1]

Rabbi Dosa ben Harkinas said, "Late morning sleep, midday wine, frivolous childish talk, and frequenting the gathering places of the ignorant—these undermine a person's life."[2]

7

Rabbi Samuel the Small

Once it happened that the elders gathered in the upper chamber of the house of Gedaya in Jericho when a heavenly voice spoke out and said, "There are among you two who are worthy of receiving the Holy Spirit, and Hillel the Elder is one of them." They all then looked at Samuel the Small.

Again the elders assembled in the upper chamber at Jabneh when a heavenly voice spoke out and said, "There are among you two who are worthy of receiving the Holy Spirit, and Samuel the Small is one of them." They all then looked at Rabbi Eliezer ben Hyrcanus, and they rejoiced that their opinion was in agreement with that of God.[1]

Samuel the Small said, "Do not rejoice when your enemy falls, and when he stumbles let not your heart be glad."[2]

Abba Isi ben Johanan quoted Samuel the Small as having said that this world is likened to a person's eyeball: the white of the eye corresponds to the ocean that surrounds the entire world; the iris to the populated area of the world; the pupil of the eye to Jerusalem; the face in the pupil to the Temple. May it be rebuilt speedily in our days and in the days of all Israel, Amen.[3]

Samuel the Small was asked, "What is the meaning of *All the upright in heart shall follow it* (Psalms 94:15)?" He answered, "The reward of the upright follows upon their death, as it is said, *All the upright in heart shall follow it*; but the reward of the wicked is paid them here and now, as it is said, *God . . . requites with destruction those who reject Him—never slow with those who reject Him, but requiting them instantly* (Deuteronomy 7:10)."[4]

The question was asked of Samuel the Small, "What is the meaning of *Sometimes a good man perishes in spite of his goodness* (Ecclesiastes 7:15)?" He replied, "It is revealed and known to the

One who issued a command and the world came into being that a righteous person will at some time in the future cease being righteous. Therefore, the Holy One, blessed be He, decides, 'While he is still in a state of righteousness I will remove him from this world.' Hence it is said, *Sometimes a good man perishes despite his goodness*—that is, while he is still in his state of goodness. *And sometimes a wicked one endures in spite of his wickedness* (Ecclesiastes 7:15). For as long as a person lives, the Holy One, blessed be He, hopes that he will repent; but once he dies, all hope for him is lost, as it is said, *At death the hopes of a wicked man are doomed* (Proverbs 11:7)—that is, hopes for his repentance."[5]

Samuel the Small once ordered a fast day—rain had not fallen for a long time—and rain came down before sunrise. People thought that they should praise the congregation that had prayed for the rain, but Samuel the Small said to them, "I shall tell you a parable. It is like a slave entreating his master for some gift. The master tells his retainers, 'Give it to him. I do not care to listen to his voice any further.' "

Again it happened that Samuel the Small decreed that the people should fast because of a lack of rain. The rains came after sunset. People thought that the congregation merited praise, for their prayers had been answered so quickly. Samuel the Small spoke up, "It is not that the congregation deserves praise, for I shall tell you a parable. It is like a slave who was begging for a gift from his master. The latter tells his staff, 'Wait until he feels crushed and is sorrowful and then give it to him.' "

When then does Samuel the Small think a congregation deserves praise? If when the congregation in its prayers recites, "He causes the wind to blow," and immediately a wind springs up; or when a congregation in its prayers recites, "He causes the rain to fall," and at once the rain commences to come down.[6]

Samuel the Small fell ill with dropsy. He cried out, "Master of the Universe, who can determine which sin of mine caused this!" And he recovered.[7]

When Samuel the Small lay dying, he uttered this prophecy: Simon and Ishmael will meet their death by the sword, their colleagues will die violently, the people will be plundered, and great troubles will follow afterward.[8]

When he died, Rabban Gamaliel and Rabbi Eleazar ben Azariah eulogized him. "For such a person it is fitting to weep," they said, "for such a man, it is fitting to mourn. Kings die and leave their crowns to their sons. Samuel the Small took all the precious things in the world with him and departed."

The people mourned and said, "O pious one, O modest soul, worthy disciple of Hillel!" Since Samuel the Small left no son, they placed his key and his writing tablet in his coffin.[9]

═══ 8 ═══
Lesser Luminaries

Rabbi Hanina ben Gamaliel II

The story is told that Rabbi Hanina ben Gamaliel was reading the following verse in Kabul: . . . *Reuben went and lay with Bilhah, his father's concubine. . . . Now the sons of Jacob were twelve in number* (Genesis 35:22), and he said to the translator, "Translate only the latter part of the verse."[1]

Rabbi Joshua ben Hyrcanus

Rabbi Joshua ben Hyrcanus declared that Job served God only out of love, as it is written, *Though he slay me, yet will I hope in Him* (Job 13:15). But yet the matter is in doubt as to whether the text means *I will hope* or *I will not hope*. However, another verse reads, *Until I die I will maintain my integrity* (Job 27:5), and that teaches us that Job acted only from love.

But Rabbi Joshua (ben Hananiah) said, "O Rabban Johanan ben Zakkai, would that someone would roll away the dust from off your eyes for you used to interpret Scripture all the days of your life to the effect that Job served God only out of fear, as it is said, *That man* (Job) *was blameless and upright; he feared God and shunned evil* (Job 1:1). Now, your disciple's disciple, Joshua ben Hyrcanus, has taught that Job acted only out of love for God!"[2]

Plemo

Plemo used to say every day, "I defy Satan!" One day—it was on the eve of the Day of Atonement—Satan appeared to him in the guise of a poor man who came to his door. Plemo brought him a piece of bread. The poor man said to him, "On such a day as this when everyone is indoors, shall I be out of doors?" Plemo took him inside and gave him the bread. The poor man said, "On such a day as this everyone eats at the table, but I am alone." Plemo seated him at the table. Satan made his skin full of scabs and acted in a repulsive manner. Plemo told him to sit properly. The poor man—really Satan—asked for a cup of wine. When Plemo gave it to him, he coughed and spat up his sputum into the cup. Plemo rebuked him and he pretended to fall dead. The rumor began to circulate that Plemo had killed a man and he heard of it. He ran away and hid himself in a toilet outside the city. Satan ran after him and when he saw how distressed he was, he revealed himself to him and asked, "Why did you speak in the way you did—to defy Satan?" Whereupon Plemo asked him in return, "But how else should I speak?" Satan replied, "You should say, 'May the Compassionate One rebuke Satan!' "[3]

Rabbi Pappias

It was taught in the name of Rabbi Pappias that it was disgraceful that Hezekiah and his associates did not break into a song of thanksgiving until the earth itself broke into song, as it is said, *From the end of the earth/We hear singing: Glory to the righteous* (Isaiah 24:16). A similar verse reads, "Blessed be the Lord," Jethro said, "*who delivered you . . .*" (Exodus 18:10).

Again it was taught in the name of Rabbi Pappias that it was disgraceful that Moses and the six hundred thousand Israelites with him did not utter this blessing until Jethro came and said, "Blessed be the Lord . . ." (Exodus 18:10).[4]

Rabbi Pappias said, "The congregation of Israel praised the horses and chariots of Pharaoh, as it is said, *You made Your steeds tread the sea* (Habakkuk 3:15).[5]

Rabbi Jose ben Dormaskit

Once Rabbi Jose ben Dormaskit went to Lod to pay his respects to Rabbi Eliezer, who asked him, "What new thing happened in the academy today?" Rabbi Jose replied, "The sages voted and decided that those Jews who own fields in Ammon and Moab be required to set aside a tithe for the poor from crops raised in the seventh year." Rabbi Eliezer then said to Rabbi Jose, "Jose, stretch out your hands and lose your sight!" Rabbi Jose stretched out his hands and lost his sight.

But then Rabbi Eliezer wept and quoted, *The counsel of the Lord is for those who fear Him; to them He makes known His covenant* (Psalms 25:14), and he said to Rabbi Jose, "Go back to the academy and tell them, 'Have no fear as to the correctness of your decision, for I have a tradition from Rabban Johanan ben Zakkai who heard from his teacher who heard from his teacher that it is a law going back to Moses at Sinai that Jews who own fields in Ammon and Moab are required to set aside a tithe for the poor from crops raised in the seventh year.' " What was the reasoning for it? Because those who returned from Babylonia did not take back all the lands that had originally been conquered by their ancestors who had come up from Egypt and the original sanctity of such lands held only for that time and not for all time in the future. The authorities permitted such lands to remain outside the laws governing the areas of major Jewish settlement so that the poor might derive their support from such lands during the seventh year.

When Rabbi Eliezer calmed himself, he prayed, "May it be His will that Jose see again," and he did.[6]

Rabbi Jose ben Dormaskit said that the generation of the Flood cast their eyes up and down in order to satisfy their lust, as the verse reads, *the sons of God saw how beautiful the daughters of men were* (Genesis 6:2). Therefore, God opened up both the upper and the lower fountainheads in order to destroy them, as it is written, *All the fountains of the great deep burst apart* (Genesis 7:11).[7]

Rabbi Jose ben Dormaskit said, "Every time you show compassion to another, God will show compassion to you. But if you do not show mercy to another person, no one will show mercy to you. Abraham is an example. Because he obtained mercy for Abimelech, having prayed for him, Abraham received his reward immediately. Scripture states, *Abraham then prayed to God and God healed Abimelech and his wife* (Genesis 20:17). And what reward did Abraham receive? The wife of Abraham was remembered and she gave birth to a son, as the verse immediately after the story of Abimelech relates, *And the Lord remembered Sarah as He had promised, and the Lord did for Sarah as He had spoken* (Genesis 21:1)."[8]

9
Trajan

When Trajan was about to execute Pappus and his brother
Lulianus in Laodicea, he said to them, "If you are of the people
of Hananiah, Mishael, and Azariah, let your God come and
deliver you from my hands even as He delivered them from
Nebuchadnezzar." They replied, "Hananiah, Mishael, and
Azariah were righteous men and Nebuchadnezzar was a worthy
king and it was fitting that a miracle should take place through
them. We, however, are sinners against God and you are a
wicked king and are not worthy that a miracle should occur
through you. Moreover, because of our sins, we deserve death at
the hand of God and if you do not kill us, God has many other
agents of death. He has many lions, bears, leopards, snakes,
venomous serpents, and scorpions that will come and attack us.
The Holy One, blessed be He, has put us in your hands only that
He might exact vengeance for our blood from you." Nevertheless, he killed them. It is said that before he had moved from that
place a despatch against him arrived from Rome and his skull
was split open with clubs.[1]

Rabbi Aha longed to see the face of Rabbi Alexandri (who
had died). Rabbi Alexandri appeared to him in a dream and
revealed two things to him. One was that nobody had a place
nearer to the center of paradise than the slain of Laodicea—
blessed be He who removed the reproach of Lulianus and
Pappus! The second was that happy is he who comes to the next
world with his learning in his possession.[2]

The wife of Trajan—may his bones be pulverized!—gave
birth to a child on the ninth of Av while all the Jews were
mourning. The child died during Hanukkah and the Jews asked
each other, "Shall we celebrate the festival by kindling the lights

or not?" They decided to light them and risk the consequences. Some individuals slandered them to Trajan's wife, telling her, "When your child was born the Jews mourned, and when your child died they kindled lights!" She sent a message to her husband, "Instead of subjugating the barbarians, come and subdue the Jews who have rebelled against you." He boarded a ship and expected the voyage to take ten days, but the winds cut the journey to five. Upon his arrival he found Jews who were occupied with this verse, *The Lord will bring a nation against you from afar, from the end of the earth, which will swoop down like the eagle* (Deuteronomy 28:49). He said to them, "I am the eagle who planned to come in ten days, but the winds brought me in five!" He surrounded the men with his legions and slaughtered them. He then said to the women, "Surrender yourselves to my soldiers or I will do to you what I did to the men." They answered, "Do to the inferiors what you did to the superiors." He at once ordered his legions to surround them and massacred them, so that their blood mingled with that of the men and streamed to the coast and then into the sea, staining it as far as Cyprus. Whereupon the Holy Spirit cried out, *For these things do I weep* (Lamentations 1:16).[3]

The verse reads, *All around me He has built/Misery and hardship* (Lamentations 3:5). "Misery" refers to Vespasian and "hardship" to Trajan.

He is a lurking bear to me,/A lion in hiding (Lamentations 3:10). "A lurking bear" refers to Vespasian, "a lion in hiding" to Trajan.[4]

Rabbi Judah said, "Whoever has never seen the basilica synagogue of Alexandria in Egypt has never seen Jewish glory in his entire life. It was a large basilica with one colonnade inside another. Sometimes it held twice as many people as those who went forth from Egypt. Within it there were seventy golden thrones, one for each of the seventy elders, each throne worth twenty-five talents of gold, and there was a wooden platform in the center. The worshipers did not sit without any order, but the goldsmiths sat by themselves, the weavers by themselves, the workers in bronze by themselves, and the blacksmiths by themselves. Why was all this? So that when a stranger came, he could find his fellow craftsmen and so start to earn his livelihood."

And who destroyed it all? The evil Trajan.[5]

Notes

Chapter 1

1. According to the story found in *Gittin* 56b, Vespasian, then commanding the Roman troops besieging Jerusalem and later emperor of Rome, granted permission to Rabban Johanan ben Zakkai to establish an academy of learning in Jabneh. Upon the destruction of Jerusalem in 70 C.E. this academy became the seat of religious authority for the Jews. For more information about Rabban Johanan see my earlier book, *The Legends of the Rabbis*, volume 1 (Northvale, NJ, 1994), pp. 261–278. The teachers immediately after the destruction are placed in the second generation of *tannaim*. Rabban Gamaliel II is known also as Gamaliel of Jabneh, to distinguish him from his grandfather, Gamaliel I, who was Hillel's grandson and president of the Sanhedrin in the first century. The father of Rabban Gamaliel II was Rabban Simon ben Gamaliel who was active in Jerusalem during the last years of the Jewish state. In *Sanhedrin* 5a, the second part of the verse, Genesis 49:10, is interpreted as referring to the descendants of Hillel "who teach Torah to the people." Gamaliel II was perhaps the first head of the academy to bear the title *Nasi*, variously translated as "prince" or "patriarch," a title going back to biblical times. See Leviticus 4:22, Numbers 7:11ff. The term *Nasi*, in Ezekiel 40ff., is the title of the civil head of the Jewish people.

   The title was inherited by Gamaliel II's descendants succeeding him in the presidency of the academy. The holder of the title was recognized by the Roman authorities as the religious and civil head of the Jews. George Foot Moore in his *Judaism in the First Centuries of the Christian Era*, vol. 1 (Cambridge, 1950), p. 87, writes, "The older and younger contemporaries of Gamaliel II, and their disciples and successors in the next generation"—from about 80 to 140 C.E.—"are the fundamental authorities of normative Judaism as we know it in the literature which it has always esteemed authentic."

2. *Sanhedrin* 32b. Rabbi Judah ben Ilai's quotation of Rabban Gamaliel II is from *Tosefta Bava Kamma* 9:30 and *Yerushalmi Bava Kamma* 8:10 (6c). In *Sifre Deuteronomy* 96 and *Shabbat* 151b it is quoted in the name of Gamaliel III.

3. *Avot de-Rabbi Natan* (22:1) 26a-b. The first teaching here is also quoted in the name of Joshua ben Perahiah in *Pirkei Avot* 1:16.

4. *Berakhot* 17a. The rabbis here speak about the dignity of labor. The scholar is not superior to the farmer, even though the latter's learning be little. The statement is also directed against the arrogance to which scholars may sometimes succumb.

5. *Tosefta Berakhot* 2:6. There were two *tannaim* by the name of Eleazar

ben Zadok. The earlier one lived during the time of Gamaliel II; the second one belonged to the fourth generation of the *tannaim*, two generations later. The *Shema* is the basic creed of Judaism, recited daily during the morning and evening prayers and at bedtime: *Hear, O Israel! The Lord is our God, the Lord alone* (Deuteronomy 6:4). Others translate the Hebrew as . . . *The Lord our God, the Lord is one.* "The Prayer" or the *Shemoneh Esrei*, the Eighteen Benedictions (really nineteen) is recited three times daily—in the evening, morning, and afternoon prayers. Together with the *Shema*, it constitutes the heart of the service. Gamaliel II was the authority who fixed the public service and the order of the prayers. He had Simon ha-Pakuli edit "the Prayer" in its final form and made it a duty to recite "the Prayer" three times daily (*Megillah* 17b, *Berakhot* 28b). Rashi *ad loc.* explains that the name ha-Pakuli may mean "the cotton dealer."

The story about Rabban Gamaliel's insistence on reciting the bedtime *Shema* even on the first night following his marriage is from Mishnah *Berakhot* 2:5.

The story about the sons of Gamaliel is found in Mishnah *Berakhot* 1:1 and reflects the opinion of Gamaliel as opposed to Rabbi Eliezer who said that the *Shema* may be recited only until the end of "the first watch" (the third or fourth hour of the night, depending on whether the night is divided into four or three watches) and that of the sages who stated that the *Shema* may be recited only until midnight (Mishnah *Berakhot* 1:1).

The story about Gamaliel and his daughter is found in *Genesis Rabbah* 26:4.

6. *Berakhot* 4:3, *Numbers Rabbah* 18:21, and *Yerushalmi Taanit*, 2:2 (65c). See note 5. Among the heretics were those Judaeo-Christians who were following the new religion. They created difficulties for the Jews with the Roman authorities (*Tosefta* Hullin 2:24). They denounced the Jews to the Romans (*Rosh Hashanah* 18a). Although "the Prayer" is not aimed against non-Jews, it furnished ammunition for enemies of the Jews through the ages. The editing of this prayer is ascribed to Samuel the Little (*Berakhot* 28a, *Megillah* 17b). Rabban Gamaliel had asked him to do it.

7. *Tosefta Bava Kamma* 9:30 and *Yerushalmi Bava Kamma* 8:7 (6c). Also see *Shabbat* 151a. Rabbi Judah mentioned here is Rabbi Judah bar Ilai, a *tanna* of the fourth generation. Rabban Gamaliel recommends that a person be merciful to others despite the fact that his own conduct was not always so. But in his defense it may be said that when he was stern, it was in defense of the unity of the Jewish people under the recognized authority of the *Nasi*, the head of the academy. The destruction of the Jewish state by the Romans could have otherwise led to chaos and the disappearance of the Jews.

8. *Esther Rabbah Proem* 9, and introduction to Midrash *Abba Gurion*. Abba Urion is also called Abba Gurion of Sidon, a town in Phoenicia. A *tanna*, he is mentioned in *Kiddushin* 4:14. The saying beginning with "when the lesser person . . ." does not occur in *Esther Rabbah*, and it is inserted from the *Yalkut*. Evidently, corruption among judges appointed by the Romans was not uncommon. See next story. The text in *Esther Rabbah* ends by pointing to Ahasuerus as the "godless king." It would have been too dangerous to state that the "godless king" was the Roman emperor Domitian, who reigned from 81–96 C.E. See Tacitus, *The Annals of Imperial Rome* (New York, 1984), pp. 7 and 18.

9. *Shabbat* 116a and 116b. See also *Kallah* 1:10 (50b). It is unusual to have a *tanna* quoting from the Gospels as does Rabban Gamaliel here. See Matthew 5:17–18. Note that Acts 5:34 refers to "a Pharisee named Gamaliel,

a doctor of the law. . . ." Salo Baron, in *A Social and Religious History of the Jews*, vol. 2 (New York, 1937–1983), pp. 130–131 writes, "The reticence of the talmudic sages on the subject of the rising tide of Christianity has often attracted attention. The rare and glaringly inaccurate references of the Jewish teachers to Jesus reveal how little they were preoccupied with the new religion during the first century. Even where the rabbis quoted a passage from the Gospels, as in their satirical description of the corrupt Christian judge unmasked by Rabban Gamaliel II and his sister, they evidently knew it from hearsay only." Gedaliah Alon, in *The Jews in Their Land in the Talmudic Age*, vol. 1 (Jerusalem, 1980), p. 214, says that the "wise man"—*philosophos* in the text—"was probably a citizen learned in the law who no doubt had been authorized by the procurator to act as a judge even though he was a Christian, or a sympathizer with Christianity. It would also appear from this episode that government judges sometimes sought to apply Jewish law to cases affecting Jews." He uses as an illustration—"Rabbi Tarfon taught: In places where you find courts of the Gentiles, even though their judgments correspond to Jewish law, do not avail yourself of their services (*Gittin* 88b)." One of the greatest disciples of Rabban Johanan ben Zakkai, Rabbi Eliezer ben Hyrcanus, married Imma Shalom, the sister of Rabban Gamaliel (*Shabbat* 116a, *Bava Metzia* 59b). R. Travers Herford, in *Christianity in Talmud and Midrash* (Clifton, NJ: 1966), says that the judge was probably a Jewish Christian (p. 149).

10. *Avot de-Rabbi Natan* 28:4 (28a). Rome taxed the people in its colonies exorbitantly. Rabban Gamaliel is here criticizing the life of ease and luxury led by the upper classes that contributed to the disintegration of the Roman empire.

11. *Mekhilta d'Rabbi Simon bar Johai*, p. 151; Abba Judin of Sidon, the Phoenician town, was a student of Rabbi Judah ha-Nasi, redactor of the Mishnah. The ordinary person is encouraged to believe that his prayer for the redemption of Israel counts. As Alon explains our text in *The Jews in Their Land in the Talmudic Age* 2:527, not only the great or the saintly could think that their prayers were acceptable but "Every single person is a fit spokesman before the throne of Mercy. . . . The coming of the Messiah is in the hands of every man." The proof-text from Exodus, however, is weak because it refers to the outcry of the widow or the orphan (Exodus 22:21).

12. *Yerushalmi Bava Kamma* 4:4 (4a) and *Sifre on Deuteronomy*, 344. There are several differences between these sources. The Yerushalmi adds two more Jewish laws to which the officers take exception. The daughter of an Israelite should not serve as a midwife for a Gentile woman (the reason, she would be helping bring to birth a child for idolatry). But a Gentile woman may serve as a midwife for the daughter of an Israelite. The daughter of an Israelite should not suckle the child of a Gentile woman (for the same reason), but a Gentile woman may suckle the child of the daughter of an Israelite (see Mishnah *Avodah Zarah* 2:1). The second rule to which they objected was, "If the ox of an Israelite gored the ox of a Gentile, the owner is not culpable. But if the ox of a Gentile gored the ox of an Israelite, whether it was accounted harmless or an attested danger, the owner must pay full damages (Mishnah *Bava Kamma* 4:3)." The *Yerushalmi* passage ends, "Even so, they had not reached the Ladder of Tyre before they had forgotten everything they had learned." The Ladder of Tyre was a promontory near Tyre, a seaport of ancient Phoenicia, now Lebanon.

The *Sifre* source states that the two Roman officials "went to Rabban Gamaliel at Usha." But Usha was the locale of rabbinic synods and enactments during and after the Hadrianic persecutions. See *Ketubbot* 50a. It is possible that "Usha" in the text is a scribal error for Jabneh. See Louis Finkelstein, "Studies in Tannaitic Midrashim," *Proceedings of the American Academy for Jewish Research* 6 (1934–1935): 215. Another possibility, suggested by A. J. Baumgarten in "The Akiban Opposition," *Hebrew Union College Annual* 50 (1979): 196 n. 61, is that the correct reading is "R. Simon ben Gamaliel at Usha," meaning R. Simon ben Gamaliel II after the Bar Kokhba rebellion, when the Roman authorities were investigating the patriarchate that had failed to prevent the revolt. Saul Lieberman links this story with the fact that "Jewish courts existed in the Diaspora after the destruction of the Second Temple. These courts were recognized by the government . . . they were supposed to judge according to Jewish law. It is therefore natural to expect that the Roman government in Syria was interested in the fairness of Jewish civil law. A delegation was accordingly sent to the authoritative academy in Palestine to learn something about Jewish officials, for matters affecting Jews and Gentiles would have been brought to Roman courts. Hence the Roman delegates could legitimately feel that there was no moral obligation to reveal these unfair laws to the government." See S. Lieberman, "Achievements and Aspirations of Modern Jewish Scholarship," in *American Academy for Jewish Research Jubilee Volume* (Jerusalem, 1980), pp. 375–376. Lieberman believes that this visit of the Romans to Rabban Gamaliel took place before the Hadrianic persecution, when the rabbis trusted the Romans and had a more positive attitude toward Rome (see *Shabbat* 33b).

The *Sifre* source differs from the *Yerushalmi* again in saying that the Roman officials were ordered by the government to disguise themselves so that it would not be known that they are not Jews. Lieberman thinks that this is not part of the original story "Achievements and Aspirations," p. 173 n. 14).

With regard to the subject matter studied, see Louis Finkelstein, "Midras, Halakot we-Haggadot," in *Baer Jubilee Volume* (Jerusalem, 1961), pp. 28ff. Mishnah also includes Midrash. "Midras" here refers to the early single short explanations "Midras, Halakot," p. 32). *Halakhah* refers to oral traditions. The original curriculum was first the study of Bible, then simple explanation (*midrash*), then oral traditions (*halakhot*), followed by *aggadot* (nonlegal material).

The question of deceiving a Gentile is dealt with in *Tosefta Bava Kamma* 10:15 and *Yerushalmi Bava Kamma* 4:3. In *Bava Kamma* 113a Rabbi Akiba forbids it because of the duty to sanctify God's name. See *Shittah Mekubetzet ad loc.* Other sources conclude that both kinds of stolen property are forbidden.

This story is discussed in Baron, *A Social and Religious History of the Jews* 2:300–301 and 430 n. 10.

13. *Avodah Zarah* 3:4 and 44b, *Yerushalmi Avodah Zarah* 3:4 (42d). The ancient rabbis would use Roman baths. Herbert Danby, in his translation of *The Mishnah*, p. 440, suggests that the name of the Roman here may have originally been in the text, "Proklos the philosopher." Rabban Gamaliel demurred from answering the question while he was in the bath because it is not permitted to discuss matters of Torah while naked. The *Yerushalmi* version gives the patronymic as "ben Peloselos." Aphrodite was the Greek goddess of love and beauty identified by the Romans with Venus. She was supposed to have risen from the sea near the island of Cyprus. Her husband was Hephaestus (Vulcan) and she was attended by the Graces and Eros (Cupid).

14. *Midrash Tehillim* 103:5, *Hullin* 59b.

15. *Sanhedrin* 39a. The text, for the questioner of Rabban Gamaliel, has the word "Caesar" used as a cognomen for "Roman emperor." A variant reading is *kofer*, "one who denies God," or a pagan. Gamaliel visited Rome, and if the story is historically accurate, he may have met with the emperor. Others understand that the questioner of Gamaliel was the plenipotentiary of the Roman emperor, that is, the Roman procurator or governor of Judea. Instead of Gamaliel's daughter giving the answers, the Midrash *ha-Gadol*, p. 84, states that it was the daughter of the emperor. The Hebrew word translated here as "military commander" is *dukus* from the Latin *dux*, "a leader." The literal translation of the Hebrew is not "a wife to serve him" but "a female servant to serve him."

16. *Sanhedrin* 39a. *In re* Gamaliel speaking to the emperor, see note 15.

17. *Sanhedrin* 39a. See note 15.

18. *Sanhedrin* 39a. The emperor assumed that since the verse from Amos sets forth two verbs, there must also be two different subjects. See note 15.

19. *Sanhedrin* 39a. Cf. *Pirkei Avot* 3:7. Rashi *ad loc.* here explains that the servant was lightly struck. Others translate, "Struck him with a ladle." The servant was rebuked for letting the sun shine into the emperor's house, so warming it, undesirable in the Middle East.

20. *Mekhilta, ba-Hodesh*, chap. 6, *Avodah Zarah* 54b–55a, *Midrash Tanhuma Yitro*, 16. In *Avodah Zarah* 55a, the questioner is General Agrippa, explained by Rashi as really meaning a captain in the service of Agrippa II, who is regarded as the last Herodian king of Judea and who survived the fall of Jerusalem for several decades. About him Baron writes, ". . . the best accoutured Jewish soldiers were in the employ of Agrippa II who, styling himself Marcus Julius Agrippa, ruled over a predominantly pagan kingdom and was an outright Roman collaborationist" (*A Social and Religious History of the Jews* 2:91). The point of the parable is that the idol is a dead thing, so God does not wage war against it. The verses from Zephaniah are made to be questions instead of declarative sentences as they are in the prophet, and the story as told in the *Mekhilta* and Talmud require the translation as given.

The story in *Avodah Zarah* 55a has Rabban Gamaliel tell a different parable in answer to the question, Why should God be jealous of idols that are certainly inferior? "To what may the matter be compared? To a man who marries an additional wife. If the second wife be her superior, the first will not be jealous of her; but if she be her inferior, the first wife will be provoked to jealousy," because it is an affront to her that her husband chose an inferior woman to take her place in his affections. *Avodah Zarah* 54b relates that "philosophers asked the Elders in Rome" the questions in this story. Gamaliel went to Rome in 95 C.E. near the end of Domitian's reign with Rabbi Joshua ben Hananiah and Rabbi Akiba. Several of the preceding stories may be ascribed to that period.

21. *Numbers Rabbah* 12:4 and *Pesikta de Rav Kahana* 1:2.

22. *Sifre on Deuteronomy*, 351. The name Agnitus has been variously identified as a corruption of Atticus or Quintos or Quietus. Reuven Hammer, in *Sifre: A Tannaitic Commentary on the Book of Deuteronomy* (New Haven and London, 1986) p. 509 n. 7, says that the general is probably Marcus Antonius Julianus, procurator of Jordan at the time of the destruction of the Temple in 70 C.E. The answer of Gamaliel is contradicted by Rabbi Akiba, who holds that only one Torah was given, together with the methods of its interpretation, which made it possible to expound its text (*Sifre on Leviticus, Behukotai* 8, near end).

23. *Genesis Rabbah* 1:9. The Jewish belief with regard to Creation is that God created everything, there was no preexistent matter—*creatio ex nihilo*. The argument posed by the philosopher, who quoted the items mentioned in Genesis 1:2, would have challenged Jewish belief. His position was that Creation began with verse 3, with the creation of light. The first two verses of Genesis he takes to be an introduction, and therefore God has used eternal primeval matter with which He created the world.

24. *Midrash on Psalms* 10:8 and *Yevamot* 102b. The "philosopher" must have been a member of the new Judaeo-Christian sect who believed that "the wait for the Lord" had already culminated with the coming of Jesus. His Jewish background is evidenced by his knowledge of the Jewish laws of levirate marriage, the ceremony described in Deuteronomy 25:5–10; and also *Yevamot* 12:1. See Herford, *Christianity in Talmud and Midrash*, p. 235. The alleged rejection of the Jewish people refers to the destruction of the Temple by the Romans in 70 c.e. Levirate marriage is the biblical requirement that when a married man dies childless, his brother marry the widow. Should he refuse, the widow performs the rite of *halitzah*. The brother-in-law only submits to it. In the image drawn by the text God stands toward the Jewish people in the relationship of the brother-in-law to his sister-in-law. He cannot perform *halitzah* and His action, so to speak, is invalid. Therefore, the bond between Him and His people remains in force as they continue to seek Him.

25. *Soferim* 5:15 (37b), *Tosefta Shabbat*, 13:2–3, *Shabbat* 115a. The three sources have some variants. Rabbi Halafta, a *tanna* of the second generation, was an older contemporary of Rabban Gamaliel. The Targum or Aramaic translation of Job must have been an earlier work than the one we presently have. It is permitted to review what one has studied in Scripture on the Sabbath. Mishnah *Shabbat* 16:1 states that if a book of the Bible is written in Aramaic or in any other translation, it is saved in storage. Rabbi Judah ha-Nasi, three generations later, declared that it is not permissible to destroy such writings with one's own hands (see *Soferim* 5:15). The objection to a written translation of a biblical book as opposed to an oral one at that time was the concern that the same sanctity might be attached to it as to the Hebrew text. The *Tosefta* places the incident in Tiberias, where Rabban Gamaliel was seated at the table of Johanan ben Nezif. The reason for the suppression by Gamaliel I of the translation of the book of Job was the very fact of translation, yet Gamaliel II had another translation. See Ephraim E. Urbach, *The Sages—Their Concepts and Beliefs*, vol. 1 (Jerusalem, 1975), pp. 410–411.

26. *Sukkah* 41b, *Tosefta Sukkah* 2:11. The journey to Rome by Rabban Gamaliel and his colleagues—Rabbi Akiba was the youngest of them—was of great importance. W. Bacher, in *The Jewish Encyclopedia*, vol. 5 (New York, 1901–1906), p. 560, says the journey was undertaken in 95 c.e. toward the end of Domitian's reign, its purpose being "the prevention of a danger which threatened on the part of the cruel emperor." See later, story ending with note 29. The point of this story is that one does not discharge his obligation on Sukkot with a borrowed *lulav*, but here the case was not so. Saul Lieberman, in *Tosefta ki-fshutah*, vol 4 (New York, 1962), p. 867, explains: *sheh-nitnu be-matanah gemurah*, each rabbi gave the *lulav* to the next as an unqualified gift. The *Gemara* asks, Why does the text tell the high cost of the *lulav*? The answer is to let us know that the opportunity of fulfilling a religious duty was so precious to Rabban Gamaliel that he was ready to pay any price. Of course, he was a wealthy man. The Romans permitted him to retain his large landed estate, despite the likely implication of his father in the revolt against Rome. This was also true of Rabbi Eleazar ben Azariah and Rabbi Eliezer ben Hyr-

canus who also were allowed to keep their landed estates despite the fact that all Jewish land, as a reprisal for the revolt against Rome, 67–70 C.E., was declared to be the emperor's possession. See Baron, *A Social and Religious History of the Jews* 2:104–105. A *zuz* was one fourth of a shekel. The Tosefta says the price paid for the *lulav* was one golden *dinar*. For the commandment concerning the use of the *lulav* on the Feast of Tabernacles, see Leviticus 23:40.

Mishnat Rabbi Eliezer, p. 103, is the source for the symbolism of the four species.

27. *Horayot* 10a-b and *Berakhot* 28a. There is a bitter undertone in Rabbi Joshua's words to Rabban Gamaliel for his ignorance of the great difficulty of ordinary scholars in earning a living. Under the Roman rule of Judea the people suffered widespread poverty, but Rabban Gamaliel was a rich man, See Baron, *A Social and Religious History of the Jews* 1:262 *et seq.* Is it possible that the star that "rises once in seventy years" was Halley's comet that appears about every 75 years? It appeared in 1910 and again in 1985. The quoted biblical verse is from the advice given by the elders to Rehoboam, son of King Solomon. Rabbi Johanan ben Gudguda belonged to an earlier generation and the reference must be to Rabbi Johanan ben Nuri. Rabban Gamaliel appointed both him and Rabbi Eleazar Hisma as supervisors of students in the academy so that they could earn a living. Alon, in *The Jews in Their Land in the Talmudic Age*, p. 228, says that Gamaliel ordained the two men. They declined the first request because, being modest, they thought themselves undeserving of the honor. This sea journey is identified with the trip to Rome in 95 C.E.

28. *Tosefta Shabbat* 13:14, *Eruvin* 43a, *Yerushalmi Eruvin* 4:2 (21d), and Mishnah *Shabbat* 16:8 in a briefer version. The elders with whom Gamaliel sailed to Rome in 95 C.E. were Eleazar ben Azariah, Joshua ben Hananiah, and Akiba.

29. *Exodus Rabbah* 30:9. See similar story about Akiba and Turnus Rufus (Midrash *Tanhuma Ki Tissa*, 33). The word *min*, "sectarian," usually refers to an adherent of the then new Christian faith. By means of the winds and storms, he says, God carries on the Sabbath. The second answer to him is that since God's height fills the entire earth, He may carry throughout the earth on the Sabbath.

30. The story is from *Deuteronomy Rabbah* 2:24. Alon, in *The Jews in Their Land in the Talmudic Age* 1:125, writes, "It has been suggested that the senator is none other than the martyred Senator T. Flavius Clemens, whose wife was the noblewoman Domitilla." If so, this places Rabban Gamaliel in Rome in the year 95 C.E. Zecharias Frankel, in his *Darkhei ha-Mishnah* (Warsaw, 1923), p. 84 (second edition, p. 87), agrees with Alon that Rabban Gamaliel made two voyages to Rome, a suggestion rejected by Graetz, who also states that Flavius Clemens and his wife had become converts to Judaism. Clemens was sentenced to death by his cousin, the Emperor Domitian in 95 C.E. because of his conversion. See Heinrich H. Graetz, *History of the Jews*, vol. 2 (Philadelphia; 1891–1898), pp. 87–92. The term "God-fearing man" had a special meaning at that time—a man who had rejected paganism but had not fully accepted Judaism.

31. *Derekh Eretz Rabbah* 5:2 (56b) and *Kallah Rabbati*, chap. 7 (54a). Rabban Gamaliel was not to be grouped together with the others for he was the patriarch and the head of the academy, but the philosopher found a diplomatic solution.

32. *Sanhedrin* 90b. Again, the Hebrew *minim*, "sectarians," is a term generally used to describe the Judaeo-Christians. Herford, *Christianity in*

Talmud and Midrash, pp. 231–234, writes that "it is not unlikely that the *minim* put their question to R. Gamliel (*sic*) in Rome . . . in 95 C.E." "The doctrine of the resurrection of the dead was one of the most frequent subjects of controversy between Jews and *minim,*" Herford says. Both sides believed in resurrection. The difference lay in the fact that the Jews said it could be proven from their Scriptures while the Christians argued that resurrection was the result of the resurrection of Jesus (see John 14:19 and 1 Corinthians 15:20 *et seq.*). The proof from the Torah is based on a misreading of the verse since *and rise up* clearly belongs to the second half of the verse. This the sectarians quickly detect. Their rejoinder to the proof from Isaiah is that it prophesies one special occurrence wrought by Ezekiel (chap. 37). The proof from the Hagiographa is a rather farfetched interpretation of the verse from the Song of Songs, that since it is interpreted by the rabbis as a dialogue between God and the Jewish people, the last words of the verse refer to the dead whom God will cause to speak again. But the sectarians answer that the Hebrew word interpreted as "speak" really means "move," and movement of the lips takes place in the grave and belongs to this world, not the next. The *Gemara* supports this argument by quoting Rabbi Johanan that the lips of a person move in the grave when a *halakhah* he has taught is repeated in his name.

33. *Sanhedrin* 90b–91a. The talmudic word translated as "emperor" is "Kaisar," "Caesar," which may be understood as any emperor of Rome or perhaps his representative, the governor of Judea. The words "the sperm" are inserted by me to clarify the meaning of the text. The story about the return voyage comes from Mishnah *Eruvin* 4:1.

34. *Yerushalmi Sukkah* 3:8 (53d). See Leviticus 23:40 for the prescribed practice of waving the *lulav,* the palm branches. The people also waved their branches at the reading of Psalms 118:25. The traditional practice is to wave the branches at both points in the service. Rabbi Akiba was younger than the other two sages.

35. *Yerushalmi Sukkah* 2:10 (53b). This statement tells of the importance these rabbis attached to sleeping in the *sukkah* during the festival of Sukkot. See Leviticus 23:42 for the commandment to live in a booth during the festival.

36. *Sanhedrin* 104b and *Lamentations Rabbah* 1:2. The latter gives as a reason for Gamaliel's weeping his being reminded by the woman's crying of the destruction of the Temple by the Romans in 70 C.E. The same source tells that the son who died was an adult. Rabban Gamaliel, usually tough and blunt, could be tender too.

37. *Numbers Rabbah* 9:19. Cf. *Sotah* 28a.

38. *Numbers Rabbah* 9:31. The offering is brought by the husband of the woman suspected of adultery on her behalf. No oil is poured, no frankincense is placed upon the offering.

39. *Avot de-Rabbi Natan* 36:4 (31b). It would seem that Rabban Gamaliel is here expressing a favorable view concerning the future of the generation of the wilderness on their way to the Promised Land. He notes in the first verse that the lives of the parents and the lives of the children are prolonged because they did not sin in the wilderness, so the parents will endure and they will be deemed worthy of life in the hereafter because of their children. The second verse strengthens his point that the children's virtue will be credited to the parents. See the dispute between Rabbi Eliezer ben Hyrcanus and Rabbi Joshua ben Hananiah concerning the future of the generation of the wilderness [*Avot de-Rabbi Natan* 36:3 (31b)]. Rabbi Jose the Galilean

supports the view of Rabbi Eliezer and Rabban Gamaliel that of Rabbi Joshua (*Avot de-Rabbi Natan* 36:4).

40. *Eruvin* 64b, *Leviticus Rabbah* 37:3, *Tosefta Pisha* 2:15 and *Yerushalmi Avodah Zarah* 1:9 (40a). There are minor variations among the four sources. Acco was a Phoenician town on the Mediterranean coast. The Israeli city of Acre stands on or near its location. The name of Tabi is omitted from several of the sources that tell that Rabban Gamaliel was accompanied by Rabbi Ilai alone. Because the majority of the people using that road were non-Jews—it was probably in a part of ancient Palestine where few Jews lived—Rabban Gamaliel assumed that the loaf of bread in the road had been dropped by a non-Jew. The events of this story occurred soon after Passover. Rabban Gamaliel ruled that the leaven of a non-Jew is permitted after Passover and hence he could tell Mabgai, a Samaritan name (see *Makkot* 11a), to take it. Otherwise, if the leaven of a non-Jew were prohibited after Passover, all benefit from its use would be forbidden, including the giving of it as a gift— as Rabban Gamaliel does here. Aaron Hyman, in *Toldot tannaim ve-amoraim*, vol. 1 (London, 1910), p. 142, describes Rabbi Ilai as "a student of all the great sages of the academy at Jabneh in the time of Rabban Gamaliel." The Ladder of Tyre was a promontory south of the city of that name.

41. *Song of Songs Rabbah* 5:14, *Pesikta de-Rav Kahana* 11:22. At the beginning of the midrashic section the comment on *Adorned with sapphires* (Song of Songs 5:14) is that the study of Torah is as hard as sapphires and so wears down a man's strength. The scholar becomes physically weaker as his study of the Torah progresses.

42. *Tosefta Shabbat* 7:5. See also *Berakhot* 53a. Evidently Rabban Gamaliel had instructed the members of his household not to follow what he considered to be a superstitious pagan practice—the text reads "the ways of the Amorites." The ancients believed that when a person sneezed he was expelling the breath synonymous with life and therefore the moment was critical. Those nearby would at once respond with *marpei!*, "Healing!" A comparable practice today is the exclamation *Gesundheit!* or "God bless you!" or *La-briyut!* or *Assuta!* Saul Lieberman, in *Tosefta ki-fshutah*, vol. 3, *Shabbat* 7:7, p. 94, says that such a response to a sneeze is not an imitation of heathen practices, for "it is an ancient custom among Jews."

43. *Yerushalmi Niddah* 1:4 (49b). Rabban Gamaliel had a close and warm relationship with his servants and evidently instructed the members of his household to deal with them respectfully.

44. *Yerushalmi Niddah* 2:1 (49d) and *Leviticus Rabbah* 19:4. The wine was intended as *terumah*, "heave-offering," to be given to the priests that, if defiled by impurity, would become completely unusable. Rabban Gamaliel praised Tabita for being so punctilious in the observance of the laws of family purity and thereby saving the wine for its religiously ordained purpose.

45. *Yerushalmi Shevuot* 5:6 (36c) and *Yerushalmi Ketubbot* 3:10 (28a). See Exodus 21:27 for the commandment requiring the freeing of a slave whose tooth has been knocked out by his master. But the rabbis mandated testimony by at least two witnesses for the penalty to be effected. Jewish law prohibits a man from giving testimony against himself. "A man must not declare himself as wicked" (*Yevamot* 25b). Rabbi Joshua ben Hananiah, like Rabban Gamaliel, was a *tanna* of the second generation.

46. *Yerushalmi Sukkah* 2:1 (52d), *Sukkah* 20b. From this account it is learned that he who sleeps under a bed in a *sukkah* has not fulfilled the requirement to dwell in the *sukkah*, contrary to the opinion of Rabbi Judah ben Ilai, who maintains that he has.

47. *Yerushalmi Sukkah* 2:1 (52d), *Yerushalmi Eruvin* 10:1 (26a), *Mekhilta Pisha*, chap. 17, *Semahot* 1:12 (44a). The rabbis said that Jewish male slaves are not subject to the law of phylacteries.

48. Mishnah *Berakhot* 2:7, *Semahot* 1:11 (44a). Despite his reputation for sternness, Rabban Gamaliel had a warm relationship with his slave Tabi.

49. *Sifre on Deuteronomy* 16 (Louis Finkelstein [New York, 1969], p. 16). See *Horayot* 10a–b, where the reason for the appointment is discussed and see earlier, my note 27 and the story in the text that ends with that note. Rabban Gamaliel wanted the supervisors or proctors to maintain order and to discourage contentious arguments among the students. But being modest and self-effacing, his two appointees did not attempt to exercise any authority or to stand in front of the students and control their discussions. Alon, in *The Jews in Their Land in the Talmudic Age* 1:228, takes a different view of this incident. He states that the two scholars were not appointed as overseers at the Jabneh academy. They were elevated from the status of student to the rank of sage and to regular membership in the Sanhedrin. In other words he ordained them, and Alon concludes "that even in Rabban Gamaliel's day it was the Patriarch who effected ordination." My earlier story and note 27 tell of the poverty of the two scholars. It is narrated of Rabbi Johanan ben Nuri that he had to take charity, that he would go out into the fields with the gleaners in order to pick up his subsistence. See *Yerushalmi Peah* 8 (20d).

50. *Tosefta Pisha* 3:10. Leaven is burned on the morning of the fourteenth day of *Nisan*, the morning of the day before Passover. There were two scholars by the name of Rabbi Eleazar ben Zadok; the first was a member of the second generation of *tannaim*, the second, of the fourth generation (c. 140–c. 165 c.e.). Lod or Lydda was a city that, according to the Talmud (*Betzah* 5a), was in those times a day's journey from Jerusalem. During the Roman period its name was changed to Diapolis. After the destruction of Jerusalem it became renowned as a seat of Jewish learning, and its academy is mentioned often in talmudic literature. Rabbi Eliezer lived there (*Sanhedrin* 32b); Rabbi Tarfon taught there (*Bava Metzia* 49b); Rabbi Akiba was active there (*Rosh Hashanah* 1:6). The name Zonen is found in *Avodah Zarah* 55a where he engages in a conversation with Rabbi Akiba.

51. *Tosefta Pisha* 10:12. Concerning Lod, see previous note. Boethus ben Zeno or Zunin was a pious merchant nearly contemporaneous with Rabbi Akiba. He is mentioned in the Mishnah (*Bava Metzia* 5:3 and *Avodah Zarah* 5:2). Many names in the Talmud are Greek, Ezra often being translated as Boethus. To understand the use of the word "reclining" one must remember that the festive meal on the first night of Passover, the *Seder*, was, in its essence, comparable to a festive meal among the ancient Greeks and Romans. There was no dinner table for the entire company. Each person had a small table in front of him and he reclined on an elongated seat, somewhat like a small armless sofa. This practice was later changed as diners sat on chairs at one table. The origin of "reclining" or leaning was forgotten, and it became one of the Four Questions. On the Passover night the meal was eaten first, for the Paschal lamb had to be consumed before midnight. After the meal those present discussed the story of the Exodus from Egypt and the laws of Passover, and the *Haggadah* praises those who prolong such narration. It tells of five sages, Rabbis Eliezer, Joshua, Eleazar ben Azariah, Akiba, and Tarfon who engaged in this kind of discussion until their disciples interrupted them with the announcement that it was time for the morning prayers. The lifting of the *ka'arah*, the special plate with the symbolic food

upon it, near the start of the reading of the *Haggadah* today, is a reminder that at this point in ancient times the individual tables with the plates upon them were lifted and removed, a signal for the beginning of the narration (the *haggadah*).

Rabban Gamaliel figures prominently in the *Haggadah* read at the *Seder*. It is he who teaches the significance of the three principal symbols of the *Seder*: the roast bone (in ancient times the Paschal lamb), the *matzah*, and the bitter herbs.

52. *Tosefta Berakhot* 4:15. The discussion is about the *berakhah ahronah*, the blessing recited after eating food other than bread following a meal and the normal recital of grace. In the text of the Tosefta preceding our story Rabban Gamaliel requires the new recital of three blessings constituting the full grace after meals. The sages say only one blessing, an abbreviated grace, must be recited. See Mishnah *Berakhot* 6:8. Rabbi Akiba dared to differ with Rabban Gamaliel in that he followed the opinion of the majority, a procedure taught by Rabban Gamaliel himself! The area of the Jordan River valley where Jericho is located is famous for dates. Jericho is known in Hebrew as "The City of Dates."

53. *Mekhilta, Amalek*, chap. 3, *Kiddushin* 32b, *Sifre on Deuteronomy* 38. With regard to "reclining" at a festive meal see note 51. Midrash on Proverbs, chap. 9, tells a similar story but there it is Tabi, Rabban Gamaliel's slave, who was serving the guests.

54. *Makkot* 24a. Psalm 15 describes the qualities of a most admirable human being. Gamaliel thinks that all of the qualities must be embodied within such a person. Akiba answers that the practice of any one of the virtues suffices.

55. *Tosefta Kiddushin* 1:11. Under Roman occupation poverty and unemployment were widespread among the Jews of Judea, and Rabban Gamaliel sets forth in graphic terms the difference between having a trade and steady employment or the reverse. The first statement, that by Gamaliel directly, stresses the security and protection that a trade affords its possessor. The third statement quoted in the name of Gamaliel by Jose ben Eleazar is an elaboration of it. The second statement, that by Jose in the name of Gamaliel, also makes the point of the security a trade gives, but adds the thought that not having a trade makes one the object of people's stares and sympathy. Rabbi Jose without the patronymic is usually Jose ben Halafta, a *tanna* of the fourth generation whose locale of teaching was Sepphoris (see Rashi, *Zevahim* 58b, near end of the page). Another Rabbi Jose, found without a patronymic, is an *amora* quoted more often in the Palestinian Talmud. Jose ben Eleazar was the grandson of Rabbi Simon ben Johai and a *tanna* of the sixth and last generation. Hyman, in his *Toldot tannaim ve-amoraim* 2:720, top of first column, conjectures that therefore the Gamaliel in this text was the son of Rabbi Judah ha-Nasi and himself a *tanna* of the sixth generation, but usually when a *tanna* quotes the teaching of another, the latter is of an earlier generation.

56. *Yerushalmi Peah* 1:1 (2b). The Palestinian Talmud gives no answer to Gamaliel's question. Instead it asks how can Gamaliel quote a decision made by the sages at Usha after his death. The answer the Talmud gives is that Gamaliel's ruling that a person may not expend more than one fifth of what he owns for charity or other religious purposes was the accepted practice in his day but was forgotten after his death. The sages at Usha sometime later considered the subject independently and reached the same conclusion as did their predecessors. The Sanhedrin changed its seat several

times during the second century because of the turbulence of the times. It met in Usha in Galilee near Sepphoris, in Tiberias, and Shefar'am, the later seat of Judah ha-Nasi and the Sanhedrin. The synod at Usha was active, especially during the reign of Antoninus Pius after 140 C.E. It was convened by the sages who had studied under Rabbi Akiba. Yeshevav was a friend of Akiba and younger therefore than Gamaliel. See *Yevamot* 49a, *Ketubbot* 29a, *Kiddushin* 64a, 68a.

57. *Tosefta Bava Kamma* 7:2. The thief steals stealthily when no person sees. The robber holds up people or robs in full view. The thief is concerned about the opinion of human beings but not of God; the robber cares about neither. The Torah requires greater punishment for the thief (see Exodus 21:37 and 22:3). So Gamaliel's illustration here quoted by Meir, a *tanna* of the fourth generation, points to the man who invited the people but not the king as deserving of greater punishment than the man who invited neither, for the former valued the esteem of the people but not of the king, while the latter cared for neither.

58. *Yerushalmi Berakhot* 2:9 (19a) and *Yerushalmi Bava Batra* 5:2 (15a). Rabbi Abbahu was active during the second and third generations of *amoraim*. Both Joshua and Judah ben Pappos were contemporaries of Gamaliel II.

59. *Tosefta Eduyyot* 1:1. "The vineyard at Jabneh" was, of course, the academy there established by Rabban Johanan ben Zakkai at the time of the destruction of Jerusalem in 70 C.E. The Sanhedrin moved there, and Gamaliel II as patriarch presided over both. After the destruction of the Temple and Jerusalem by the Romans the rabbis were pessimistic about the Jewish future.

60. *Derekh Eretz Zutah* 10:1 (59a). The synagogue, literally "the house of assembly," is where scholars come to study and pray. Gablan was a highland district whose soil was richly fertile (see *Ketubbot* 112a). The Messiah will come when society is in ruins.

61. *Tosefta Mo'ed* 2:15. "The bench of the Gentiles" was the place where they did business on the Sabbath. Rabbi Akiba in the following passage states that it is permissible to take a seat near "the bench of the Gentiles" on the Sabbath. Perhaps it was legally allowed, but the custom was not to do so for appearances' sake.

62. *Tosefta Mikvaot* 6:3. Aquila was a non-Jew by birth who converted to Judaism and studied under Rabbi Akiba, Rabbi Eliezer ben Hyrcanus, and Rabbi Joshua ben Hananiah. See the article by Louis Ginzberg in the *Jewish Encyclopedia* 2:34–38. Joshua ben Kevusai was the son-in-law of Rabbi Akiba (see *Shabbat* 147a) and lived a long life until the days of Rabbi Judah ha-Nasi. Ashkelon on the sea was originally a Philistine town. Aquila refused to bathe in the ritual baths since he regarded Ashkelon as heathen territory and bathed in the sea instead. According to the first opinion, Gamaliel was not so particular, but according to Joshua ben Kevusai, Gamaliel agreed with Aquila and also bathed in the sea.

63. *Semahot* 5:17 (46a). Gamaliel ordered excommunication of even his own brother-in-law, Eliezer ben Hyrcanus (*Bava Metzia* 59b). See also the paragraph in the text after the next one.

64. *Pirkei de-Rabbi Eliezer*, chap. 51 (73b). The second story is from *Rosh Hashanah* 25a. The "parts" of the hour, *halakim*, are 4 minutes, $3\frac{1}{3}$ seconds. A eulogy, according to Jewish law, cannot be delivered on *Rosh Hodesh*, the New Moon, the first day of the Jewish month.

65. Mishnah *Rosh Hashanah* 1:6 for the bare story, *Yerushalmi Rosh Hashanah* 1:6 (57b) for the full story. Rabbi Akiba detained the witnesses at

Lod (Lydda) because so many witnesses were unnecessary and also to prevent an unnecessary violation of the Sabbath. Witnesses for the purpose of reporting the sighting of the New Moon may profane the Sabbath (Mishnah *Rosh Hashanah* 1:5) but here Rabbi Akiba thought they should not because there were more witnesses than were needed. Rabban Gamaliel admonishes him for detaining the witnesses because in the future they will not come, assuming that they will not be needed. Gir is probably Geder, and the name of the man was Shazpar. The "head of Gir" refers to the chairman or chief magistrate of the local governing body. See Alon, *The Jews in Their Land in the Talmudic Age* 1:180. Rabbi Judah the baker was a contemporary of Rabbi Akiba and was executed by the Roman authorities (see *Yerushalmi Hagigah*, beginning of second chapter).

66. Mishnah *Rosh Hashanah* 2:8–9, *Yerushalmi Rosh Hashanah* 2:5 (57c). Dosa ben Harkinas—in the Palestinian Talmud the patronymic is Arkinas— was an older contemporary of Gamaliel II. Although Johanan ben Nuri and Dosa both disagreed with Rabban Gamaliel here, they asserted that the decision of his court must be accepted and respected. Once the court has decided, that is the law, especially here in the matter of the calendar. Otherwise, chaos would ensue. Rabbi Joshua came to the same conclusion eventually and humbled himself before Gamaliel. The testimony of the second pair of witnesses refuted that of the first pair, for if the moon had been seen the night before as the first pair had said, it should have been even more visible on the next night. Gamaliel acted sternly and insisted that Joshua submit to his authority, but not out of arrogance. His fear was that the Jewish people's unity of the past might be shattered, with the result that the people would break into quarreling sects and eventually disappear. Heretofore, the Temple and Jerusalem served as magnets, drawing the people into a coherent unit. Now the Temple and Jerusalem, the Jewish capital, were destroyed and the Jewish state was no more, with Rome laying its oppressive and impoverishing hand upon the Jews. He saw the academy, Jewish law, and the Jewish court as the centripetal force to keep the people together. Hence his severity against Joshua.

67. *Bekhorot* 36a. Zadok was a *tanna* of priestly descent and the most influential personality in Gamaliel's tribunal, sitting always at his right hand (see *Yerushalmi Sanhedrin* 19c). When the animal slit its lip it created a blemish. A *haver* was a learned and pious man not open to suspicion. Joshua's affirmative answer meant that since Zadok was a *haver*, and there is a difference, he was not suspected of deliberately cutting the animal's lip and so creating a blemish, making it possible for a *kohen*, a priest, to eat the firstborn animal outside the Temple. Concerning Huzpit, see note 68. The original text here translated as "scholars" in the sentence, "Wait until the scholars come . . ." literally translated is "shield-bearers." Therefore it has been suggested that the term means armed guards who permitted entrance to the academy only by those approved by Rabban Gamaliel. See Shamai Kanter, *Rabban Gamaliel II: The Legal Traditions* (Ann Arbor, 1980), p. 100 and n. 70. The same term is used in the story following.

68. *Berakhot* 27b–28a, *Yerushalmi Berakhot* 4:1 (near end), *Yerushalmi Taanit* 4:1 (17a-b), *Tosefta Yadayim* 2:17–18. Huzpit was surnamed the *Meturgaman* or Translator-Interpreter and met his death as a martyr during the Hadrianic persecution. (See *Lamentations Rabbah* 2:4.) The *Meturgaman* explained the rabbi's lecture to the public. Huzpit was the "mouthpiece" of Rabban Gamaliel. He is mentioned once in the Mishnah in connection with the law of *prosbul* (*Shevuot* 10:6). With reference to the humiliation of Joshua

by Gamaliel previously, see the two preceding stories. To be deposed as head of the academy is also to be removed from the position of patriarch or *Nasi* and from serving as head of the court, although Louis Ginzberg says that Gamaliel was removed only from being head of the academy. Eleazar ben Azariah was younger than Gamaliel and Joshua but older than Akiba. His statement, "Behold I am like a seventy-year-old man" is familiar to the readers of the *Haggadah*. See also *Yerushalmi Berakhot* 1:6 (3d) and *Sifre on Deuteronomy*, 130. The teachers of Abba Joseph bar Dostai were Eleazar, Jose the Galilean, and Ben Azzai. Gamaliel was reproached before for not making himself familiar with the poverty of the rabbis and their difficulties in earning a living. See the story earlier ending with note 27. The indirect language of Joshua, referring to the ashes of the Red Heifer and the living waters of ritual purification (Numbers 19:17), was to serve notice on Eleazar that Gamaliel would resume his previous office and title and that Eleazar should step down. But Eleazar was given the honor of occasionally giving the lecture at the academy and also the position of *Av Bet Din*, the deputy head of the court. The Yerushalmi version has several differences: Eleazar ben Azariah is sixteen years of age, not eighteen; Akiba was saddened at not having been chosen to head the academy; Joshua's occupation is that of a needlemaker; the number of added benches was eighty, according to one authority, three hundred according to another, apart from those standing behind the benches; Eleazar ben Azariah is appointed *Av Bet Din*. However, the Babylonian Talmud's version is fuller. It should be noted that the prediction of Eleazar's wife was accurate. Simon ben Johai was a *tanna* of the fourth generation. Akiba's ancestry was slighted because he was supposedly a descendant of a family of converts to Judaism. One of his forebears, it was said, was Sisera, the general of Jabin, king of Hazor, who waged war against the people of Israel (Judges 4:2, *Berakhot* 27b).

69. *Semahot* 6:1 (46a). Bathing is forbidden during the seven-day period of mourning for one's parent, spouse, child, or sibling but if for hygienic reasons, it is permitted (*Yoreh Deah* 381:1, 2). See Isaac Klein, *A Guide to Jewish Religious Practice* (New York, 1979), p. 289.

70. *Ketubbot* 8b, *Tosefta Niddah* 9:17, *Mo'ed Katan* 27a. See also *Yerushalmi Berakhot* 3:1 (20b). Before Rabban Gamaliel fixed the simple funeral as the Jewish standard, burial expenses were high. For the wealthy, bodies were brought out on tall stately beds, ornamented and covered with rich coverlets. See *Mo'ed Katan* 27a-b. Josephus, *Antiquities* 17:8:3 and *Wars* 1:33:9, tells about Herod's extraordinary golden bier. Some scholars ascribe this passage to Gamaliel the Elder.

71. *Mo'ed Katan* 27a, *Yerushalmi Berakhot* 3:1 (20a). Overturning the bed for the seven-day period of mourning—except for the Sabbath—was the ancient practice symbolizing mourning by the family. Later the practice was to sit on the floor, still later on low stools or benches. Eliezer and Joshua differed as to when the mourning period was to begin as related in the text of the Talmud preceding this narrative. Eliezer's wife, Imma Shalom, was the sister of Gamaliel. When the family referred to Eliezer at the end of this story they called him not by name but by the title "Elder." In ancient times burials were often done in caves, some large enough for multiple burials in a series of vaults. The body was placed in a vault horizontally and a large stone was rolled upon the opening to serve as a cover. Example of such ancient caves may be seen in Israel today at Me'arat ha-Makhpelah in Hebron and at Bet Shearim.

72. *Tosefta Shabbat* 7:18. Funeral pyres were made for kings who died.

This text shows that the patriarchate was regarded as a kind of royalty.

73. *Sotah* 49b and *Bava Kamma* 83a. See introduction to *Greek in Jewish Palestine* (New York, 1942), by Saul Lieberman. He says that this practice of training many young Jews in Greek and Greek culture "was established in the beginning of the second century for the purpose of facilitating relations between the House of the Patriarch and the Roman government." The Talmud states that the members of the family of Gamaliel II were allowed to study Greek because they were "near to the kingdom," that is, near to governmental authority (*Bava Kamma* 83a).

74. *Megillah* 21a and *Yerushalmi Sotah* 9:16. A tribute to Rabban Gamaliel in rather extravagant terms. Some scholars refer this text to Gamaliel the Elder.

Chapter 2

1. *Avot de Rabbi Natan* 14:3 (23b–24a). *Pirkei Avot* 2:10–11 describes Eliezer ben Hyrcanus simply as "a cemented cistern that loses not a drop," Joshua ben Hananiah as "happy is she who gave birth to him," Jose the priest as "a pious man," the fourth disciple, Simon ben Netanel, instead of Ishmael ben Hananiah as "a fearer of sin," and Eleazar ben Arakh as "a spring flowing with ever-sustained vigor." Both sources agree on the portrayal of Eliezer ben Hyrcanus as a cemented cistern that retains everything poured into it—a picture of a scholar with a strong memory. Moreover, he was also greatly influenced by the teachings of the past, whose authority he would have liked to see govern the present. He was a conservative, a maverick right-winger, a xenophobe, and misogynist. He was a follower of the school of Shammai—frequently transmitting Shammaitic traditions—and like it, he would have restricted the grounds for divorce to adultery alone, while the rabbis generally were very liberal in this regard. It would appear from the text of *Bava Kamma* 84a that he also interprets "an eye for an eye" literally, as Louis Finkelstein states in his *The Pharisees*, pp. 720–724, but David Weiss-Halivni explains that the words there are not a declarative statement but a question and that Eliezer ben Hyrcanus also interprets "an eye for an eye" in terms of monetary payment (seminar led by Weiss-Halivni at The Jewish Theological Seminary on November 30, 1989). Ishmael ben Hananiah is described as "an oasis." But the word in the text is doubtful and some emend it to *arugah*, "a garden bed" or "grove," a term applied to a scholar in *Derekh Eretz Zuta* 1:2. Eliezer is often called "Eliezer the Great."

2. *Pirkei Avot* 2:12. In the first statement a higher value is placed on the accurate preservation of the Tradition; in the second, on the critical and original mind. Abba Saul was a contemporary of Rabbi Judah ha-Nasi of the fifth generation of *tannaim*. He had a different tradition pertaining to the statement of Johanan ben Zakkai.

3. This story is found in longer or shorter versions and with various differences in a number of sources: *Pirkei de-Rabbi Eliezer*, chaps. 1 and 2; *Genesis Rabbah* 42:1; Midrash *Tanhuma* 3:10; *Avot de-Rabbi Natan* (6:3) 20b–21a. See also *Yalkut Me'am Lo'ez* (The Torah Anthology), Exodus 3, vol. 6, pp. 9–12. As examples of differences in the story, Midrash *Tanhuma* states that the opportunity for Eliezer's flight to Jerusalem to study at the academy of Rabban Johanan came when his father and brothers had to flee from the forces of the Roman authorities with whom Hyrcanus had formerly had a

close connection. On the other hand, according to the story in *Pirkei de-Rabbi Eliezer*, it was the prophet Elijah who appeared to Eliezer and urged him to go to study with Rabban Johanan ben Zakkai in Jerusalem. Hyrcanus was a wealthy landowner whom the Romans favored by not seizing his property. Tosafot in *Shabbat* 104a s.v. *Amar lo* tries to soften the statement that Eliezer did not learn Torah until he was 28. It explains *de-lo asak ad she-naaseh gadol*, that he did not engage in the learning of Torah systematically until he became an adult. About the central importance in Jewish liturgy of the *Shema* and the *Prayer (Tefillah)* or the Eighteen Benedictions, see note 5. *In re* Ben Zizit Ha-Kasat, Nakdimon ben Guryon, and Ben Kalba Savua, see my earlier book, *The Legends of the Rabbis*, 1:329–330.

4. *Yerushalmi Avodah Zarah* 3:1 (42c), *Yerushalmi Sotah* 9:16 (24c), and *Yerushalmi Horayot* 3:5 (48c). The last-mentioned source, before telling the story as we have it, quotes Rabbi Jacob bar Idi in the name of Rabbi Joshua ben Levi, as saying that first the elders entered the upper room in the house of Gediya in Jericho, where a voice said to them, "There are among you two who are worthy to receive the Holy Spirit, and Hillel the Elder is one of them," and then they gazed upon Samuel the Small.

5. *Sanhedrin* 17b. Judah bar Ezekiel was an *amora* of the second generation, Rav, of the first. They lived during the early part of the third century. The term "the seventy languages" is an expression for the languages of the world, the various languages spoken by people. Betar was famous as the last stronghold of Bar Kokhba (134–135 C.E.). Simon the Temanite was the youngest of this group of four and hence sat on the ground below the level of the others.

6. *Pirkei Avot* 2:15, *Shabbat* 153a and 144a, *Ecclesiastes Rabbah* 7:14 and 9:8, *Avot de-Rabbi Natan* 15:4 (24b). A similar thought is found in *Ben Sira* 5:7. The first teaching here is akin to other rabbinic injunctions like not slandering another, not speaking ill of another, not embarrassing or humiliating another person in public. All these are based on the biblical commandment to love one's neighbor as oneself (Leviticus 19:18) or as Hillel rephrased it, "What is hateful to you, do not do to another person" (*Shabbat* 31a).

With regard to his second teaching, it should be noted that the rabbis spoke sharply against anger, going so far as to say: "He who is angry may be compared to an idol-worshiper (*Shabbat* 105b)."

Since a person does not know the date of his death, he should always be in a state of repentance for tomorrow he may die. In *Kohelet Rabbah* 7:14 Rabbi Eliezer is quoted as saying that three things may annul divine decrees: prayer, charity, and repentance.

It is good to be close to scholars so that one may learn from them but not closer than they permit. Perhaps Rabbi Eliezer here is reacting to the hostility of some of his colleagues who eventually excommunicated him or he may have taught this after his excommunication.

7. *Ketubbot* 50a.

8. *Sifre on Deuteronomy* 144 and *Sanhedrin* 32b. It is of interest to note that the court of Gamaliel II is not mentioned here as would be expected since Rabban Gamaliel II's court succeeded that of Rabban Johanan ben Zakkai. Perhaps it was because of the resentment felt against Gamaliel for having publicly humiliated three sages, for which he was temporarily removed from his position as head of the court. See the earlier account ending with note 66.

9. *Song of Songs Rabbah*, chap. 1. The word here translated as "oval" is *ris*, meaning "an arena," "a racing course."

10. *Kallah* 1:24 (51b). Rabbi Eliezer stresses the importance of respect

for one's teacher. Ben Azzai amplifies his teaching. The word *mishnah* here refers to the teachings of the oral law transmitted thus far. The Mishnah as we know it was not given its final redaction until almost a century later. The word *shas* here, of course, cannot be a reference to the Talmud, which was not edited until four centuries later. The word is an acronym for *shishah sedarim*, "six orders," a term referring to the six orders of the tractates of the Mishnah. Michael Higger, in his edition of *Mesikhtot Kallah* (New York, 1936), uses *talmud* in place of *shas* on the basis of variant manuscript readings. Telling one's blind teacher that night has come must also be done in a respectful manner. Simply to say that the sun has set would call attention to his blindness. However, to ask that he remove his phylacteries is a delicate and indirect way of saying it, for they are worn only during the day.

11. *Berakhot* 27b. Rashi *ad loc.* explains "whoever prays behind his teacher" as meaning that the student takes his position immediately behind that of his teacher, thus showing pride or arrogance. Tosafot offers another explanation—when the student bows in prayer it might appear that he is bowing in worship of his master, if he stands just behind him. To greet one's master, in the ordinary way, the way two friends might greet each other, is not the way to greet one's teacher. He should be greeted as one's master and teacher. To differ with the decisions of the school of one's teacher, according to one explanation, means to start an academy of one's own. To utter an opinion not heard from one's teacher, according to one explanation, means quoting an opinion in the name of one's teacher that he has not heard from him. But all in all this passage illustrates the conservative stance of Rabbi Eliezer.

12. *Leviticus Rabbah* 20:7. A *mil* equals 2,000 cubits or 1,121 meters or 1,226 yards.

13. *Yerushalmi Gittin* 1:2 (43a), *Yerushalmi Sheviit* 6:1 (36c), *Leviticus Rabbah* 20:6, *Midrash Tanhuma, Aharei. 6; Pesikta de-Rab Kahana,* 26:7; *Eruvin* 63a. In *Tanhuma* and *Eruvin* the period of time is not a week but a year. Imma Shalom was the sister of Rabban Gamaliel II. Rabbi Eliezer advocated the removal from any office of one who teaches the law in the presence of his own teacher (*Eruvin* 63a). In *Eruvin* and *Yerushalmi Sheviit* he said that the sons of Aaron the high priest met sudden death (Leviticus 10:2) because they taught the law in the presence of Moses their teacher. So too in *Leviticus Rabbah*.

14. *Yoma* 53b. See also Simon ben Johai later on the subject. The "him" who was ordered "brought to Babylon" by Nebuchadnezzar was the boy king of Judah named Jehoiachin. Eliezer says that among the "the precious vessels" of the Temple that accompanied him was the Ark of the Covenant. Therefore it was missing from the Second Temple built by the Jews after their return from Babylonian exile. See *Leviticus Rabbah* 20:5.

15. *Midrash on Psalms* 137:10. The two biblical translations are from the 1917 Jewish Publication Society's *The Holy Scriptures*, since their language fits the requirements of this midrashic text. The quotation from Psalms is puzzling because there it is the Edomites who are charged with uttering these words.

16. *Leviticus Rabbah* 4:1. Rabbi Eliezer interprets the verse as referring to the Babylonian conquest of Jerusalem, while Rabbi Joshua takes the verse to refer to the events at Mount Sinai. Eliezer uses a play on words to connect *ha-tavekh*, "the middle," with *hatokh*, "to cut," hence "to decide"—where the law was decided. The proverb says that incongruous things may be found in the same place. Zechariah and Uriah were prophets who were killed by the

people for rebuking them on account of their wrongdoing. For Zechariah see 2 Chronicles 24:20–21; for Uriah, see Jeremiah 26:20–23. See also my *Legends of the Rabbis* 1:167. Rabbi Joshua reads *haresha*, "wickedness," as *harshea*, hence "condemnation." He refers to the events described in Exodus 32:27 *et seq.*

17. Mishnah *Sotah* 9:15, *Yerushalmi Sotah* 9:16 (24c). A hyperbolic cry of despair—"Things are not like they used to be!" Rabbi Eliezer ben Hyrcanus is occasionally called Rabbi Eliezer "the Great" in rabbinic literature.

18. *Sefer Torah* 3:10 (62b), *Soferim* 3:13 (where the name is given as Rabbi Eleazar). Rule 10 in *Massekhet Sefer Torah* teaches that a Torah scroll may not be placed on a bed but if someone has done it, it is forbidden to sit on the bed because of the respect due the Torah scroll.

19. *Eruvin* 54b. Rabbi Judah was the son of Ilai, a fourth-generation *tanna*. His remark was inserted into the original text later.

20. *Kallah* 1:22. *In re* Rabbi Judah see the previous note. The "commandment" here is explained as the husband's marital duty.

21. *Kallah* 1:10 and *Kallah Rabbati* 1:15 (52a). The second question was asked of Imma Shalom with the expectation that perhaps its answer might also provide the answer to the first question. She uses the word "converse" as a euphemism for cohabit. The word within the brackets she did not say. They are to be inferred. Her manner of speech observes high standards of delicacy. The night is divided into three watches. Rabbi Eliezer cohabited with her only during the middle watch and not during the first or last watch, which are the normal periods for intercourse. He was concerned about other women coming to mind during the latter watches for during those periods women are to be found in the streets.

22. *Midrash Tanhuma, Beshallah* 21; *Sotah* 48b; *Mekhilta de-Rabbi Ishmael, Beshallah* 2. Eleazar here is the son of Azariah, a contemporary of Eliezer ben Hyrcanus. The rabbis here project their language and conceptions to the earlier days of Jeremiah. Rabbi Eliezer's statement about the importance of work is from *Avot-de-Rabbi Natan* (Version B), edited by Solomon Schechter, p. 44.

23. *Bava Batra* 121b, *Taanit* 31b, and *Lamentations Rabbah, Proems* 33. When the sun's rays are strong, as during the early part of the summer, they dry the wood. Insufficiently dried wood can harbor worms, and they make the wood unfit for the altar. Therefore, the felling of trees for the altar fires was discontinued from the fifteenth of *Av*.

24. *Avot de-Rabbi Natan*, chap. 6. The teaching of Rabbi Jose ben Joezer is from *Pirkei Avot* 1:4. Rabbi Eliezer left Jabneh, where he had studied under Rabban Johanan ben Zakkai and served in the Sanhedrin under Rabban Gamaliel II to establish his own academy at Lod or Lydda. Jose is an abbreviated form of Joseph. Zeredah is mentioned in Joshua 15:35. *In re* Jose ben Joezer see my *Legends of the Rabbis* 1:187–189. Rabbi Akiba was a student of Rabbi Eliezer.

25. *Pesikta de Rav Kahana* 4:7, *Pesikta Rabbati* 14:13, *Numbers Rabbah* 19:7, *Midrash Tanhuma* on *Hukkat* 8. Moses went up to heaven to receive the Ten Commandments and the Torah. *In re* the calf whose neck is to be broken, see Deuteronomy 21:1 ff. With regard to the Red Heifer see Numbers 19:2. The teaching of Rabbi Eliezer is found in Mishnah *Parah* 1:1. Rabbi Jose assumes that since that teaching is the first mishnah in the tractate that discusses the laws of the Red Heifer it shows that Rabbi Eliezer actually started his instruction with this teaching. The attempt to find a text proving that Rabbi Eliezer was a lineal descendant of Moses would argue that the

verse referring to Eliezer, the second son of Moses, should have read, "and the name of the second was Eliezer." But the text reads instead, *And the other was named Eliezer.* Rabbi Jose bar Hanina assumes therefore that the word *other* means Rabbi Eliezer who lived about 1,600 years later. Rabbi William G. Braude, in *Pesikta de-Rab Kahana* (Philadelphia, 1975), pp. 80–81, writes, "R. Jose bar R. Hanina's exegetical *tour de force* seems intended to indicate God's comforting of Moses for his disappointment in his immediate descendants. Moses, like God Himself, is understood to have meditated deeply on the Red Heifer as a means of purifying Israel. Thus, after Israel had defiled themselves with idolatry, Moses used the powder of the Golden Calf, an anticipation, as it were, of the use of the ash of the Red Heifer, to begin Israel's purification (see Exodus 32:20), for he was passionately concerned with the extirpation of idolatry. His remote descendant, R. Eliezer, likewise concerned, began his instruction in the Oral Law with regulations pertaining to the ash of the Red Heifer, in striking contrast to Moses' own children who, in their lack of concern for God's prohibition of idolatry, were a grievous disappointment to Moses. . . ." Rabbi Jose bar Hanina was an *amora* of the second generation. Rabbi Judah ha-Nasi, in his redaction of the Mishnah, placed a teaching of Rabbi Eliezer at the beginning of the first mishnah (*Berakhot* 1:1), the start of the Oral Law, to please Moses, the putative ancestor of Eliezer.

26. *Shabbat* 152b. The Throne of Glory is the throne of God. The quotation is from the conversation of Abigail with David.

27. *Pirkei de-Rabbi Eliezer*, ch. 33 (41a). On the analogy of the seeds see parallels in 1 Corinthians 15:36ff., *Ketubbot* 111b, and *Sanhedrin* 96b. As to whether the shrouds used at the burial will be the garments worn at the resurrection see *Genesis Rabbah* 96:6, *Shabbat* 114a, and *Semahot* 9.

28. *Pirkei de-Rabbi Eliezer*, chap. 51 (73b). After the coming of the Messiah there will be neither sin nor sickness nor misfortune. Even death will be no more. See *Genesis Rabbah* 26:6.

29. *Pirkei de-Rabbi Eliezer*, chap. 15 (17a). Rabbi Eliezer ben Hyrcanus was deemed worthy of being endowed with the Holy Spirit. See *Sanhedrin* 11a and *Yerushalmi Sotah*, end. On the two ways see *Genesis Rabbah* 21:5 and *Yoma* 38b. On Elijah in Jewish literature see *Jewish Encyclopedia* 5:122ff. and Solomon Schechter, *Aspects of Jewish Theology* (New York, 1909), p. 288. See also *Kiddushin* 70a, *Ruth Rabbah* 5:6, and *Seder Olam Rabbah*, 17. Samuel, like Elijah, tried to reconcile man and God. On Samuel in rabbinic literature see *Jewish Encyclopedia* 11:7. The verse, 1 Samuel 2:26, tells that Samuel grew in esteem and favor both with God and with men. His favor with God is the result of his righteousness, his favor with men the result of his love for his fellow human beings.

30. *Tosefta Sanhedrin* 13:2. Rabbi Joshua ben Hananiah was a contemporary of Rabbi Eliezer, *tannaim* of the second generation. See also Mishnah *Sanhedrin* 10:1. Whether there was salvation outside of Judaism was one of the concerns of the ancient sages for several generations before the Romans destroyed the Temple and Jerusalem in 70 C.E., and it continued to be discussed by them for generations afterward. Gedaliah Alon, in *The Jews in Their Land in the Talmudic Age* 2:558–559 writes, "It does appear that during the years between the Destruction and the Bar Kochba War, the moderate opinion represented by Rabbi Joshua gained more or less universal acceptance."

31. *Pesikta de-Rav Kahana* 24:2–4. See also *Yoma* 8:9. The word *mikveh*, from the Hebrew root meaning "to hope," means both "pool of hope" and

"pool of cleansing." In a parallel passage, Midrash on Psalms 4:9, the text continues "which of the two can go to the other—the pool of cleansing to the unclean person or the unclean person to the pool of cleansing? Obviously, the unclean person has to go to the pool of cleansing, let himself down, and immerse himself in it. So too must Israel go to the Holy One who will cleanse them." The prayer of Rabbi Eliezer that he recited after the daily *Amidah*—and the rabbis encouraged individual prayers after the *Amidah*—is found in *Yerushalmi Berakhot* 4:2 (7d). Baron, in his *Social and Religious History of the Jews* 2:120, says that "coming from a man as cantankerous . . . as he," this prayer is doubly significant.

32. *Pesikta de-Rav Kahana* 2:5. The new Jewish Publication Society (J.P.S.) translation of the second half of the verse is *Sin is a reproach to any people*. Rabbi Joshua gives voice to a theory accepted by the ancient rabbis, that Israel's sins are the cause of all the sorrows that befall it, a theory incorporated in the traditional festival *musaf* service in the prayer, *u-Mipnei hataeinu*.

The second paragraph on God loving the righteous is from the Midrash on Proverbs, chap. 13. The biblical proof-text does not actually refer to God. The first half of the verse is the familiar *He who spares the rod hates his son* (Proverbs 13:24). But the proof-text can be justified in that God is the father of all. The "nations" referred to here are the four nations of ancient times who were the great enemies of the Jewish people: Assyria, Babylonia, Greece, and Rome.

33. *Pesikta Rabbati* 25:2. Compare this with *Exodus Rabbah* 21:7. Rabbi Eliezer urges a person to live properly so that the accusing angels will not all join against him, when he will have no other recourse but to appeal for God's mercy, the compassion of the great Healer. Some interpret "physician" to mean human physicians. See *Ben Sira* 38:1.

34. *Yerushalmi Berakhot* 2:7, *Berakhot* 16b, *Semahot* 1:10 (44a). Earlier, citing Mishnah *Berakhot* 2:7, we pointed to the fact that Rabban Gamaliel II did accept condolences upon the death of his manservant Tabi. See story ending with note 48. But there Rabban Gamaliel explained that Tabi was a worthy person and unlike other slaves. In *Berakhot* 16b a formula is given that may be said to the person whose slave dies: "May the Omnipresent repair your loss." So the accepted tradition does not follow Rabbi Eliezer.

35. *Tosefta Berakhot*, chap. 3. See Michael Higger, *Aggadot ha-tannaim* (New York, 1929), p. 12. Other sages give their own versions of a "brief prayer." Rabbi Jose, a fourth-generation *tanna*, says: "Hear the voice of prayer of Your people Israel and speedily fulfill their request. Blessed be the One who hears prayers." Rabbi Eleazar ben Zadok, a second-generation *tanna* or another by the same name in the fourth generation, says: "Hear the sound of the cry of Your people Israel and quickly grant their request. Blessed be the One who hears prayer." Others said: "The needs of Your people are many and their knowledge scanty. May it be Your will, O Lord our God, that You answer all the needs of each one and grant each creature whatever he or she lacks. Blessed be the One who hears prayer."

36. *Tosefta Megillah* 3:34. See also Mishnah *Megillah* 4:10 where Rabbi Eliezer states that chapter 16 of Ezekiel should not be chosen as a prophetic reading for the Sabbath-morning service. Aramaic was the language commonly spoken by Jews during Rabbi Eliezer's time rather than Hebrew. So *Tosefta Megillah* 3:31 reads, "There are passages of Scripture that are read and translated, some read and not translated, others not read and not translated." Evidently Rabbi Eliezer felt that this verse should not be read because it casts

shame on Jerusalem and he was angry that it had been read. He could be brusque.

37. *Midrash on Psalms* 105:10. The literal translation of the verse is *He led them out.* . . . The verses Psalms 105:10–11 speak of the Exodus from Egypt.

38. *Midrash on Psalms* 22:12. Rabbi Joshua ben Hananiah was a contemporary of Rabbi Eliezer.

39. *Pesikta de-Rav Kahana* 3:16, *Midrash on Psalms* 9:9, *Mekhilta, Amalek*, chap. 2. Whenever "hand" is mentioned in Scriptures the reference is to the right hand. See *Zevahim* 24a.

40. *Sifre on Deuteronomy* 173. The "things" referred to in the verse refer to the abhorrent practices of the nations who resided in the Holy Land before its conquest by the Children of Israel: burning one's child as a sacrifice, soothsaying, divination, sorcery, spellcasting, seeking to inquire of the dead.

41. *Sifre on Deuteronomy* 43.

42. *Avot de-Rabbi Natan* 36:1. The eschatological doctrines assumed here are that after the Messiah will come, the dead will come to life again. Then the Day of Judgment will arrive and those who will not be found guilty will then enjoy the world to come. It would appear that all the wicked as well as the righteous will be resurrected, with the sole exception being the very wicked who, as set forth here, will not be brought back to life. Therefore, they will not stand in judgment. For more information on this subject, see the chapters on the hereafter in Moore's *Judaism*, vol. 2, part 7, and Abraham Cohen's *Everyman's Talmud*, chap. 11. The source in the Talmud is *Sanhedrin* 107bff. Joshua, like Eliezer, is a *tanna* of the second generation while Nehemiah belongs to the fourth generation.

43. *Avot de-Rabbi Natan* 36:2–3. See also *Tosefta Sanhedrin* 13:9–10. *In re* the spies see Numbers, chaps. 13–14.

44. *Avot de-Rabbi Natan* 36:1. The passage deals with the young children of the wicked. The children died in infancy and did not sin. See also *Sanhedrin* 110b. Joshua's argument is that the text in Daniel speaks of the preservation of the stock of the tree, which symbolizes man's descendants. Therefore, the wicked will be utterly destroyed, but their young children will come to life in the world to come.

45. *Midrash on Psalms* 72:3. When justice is done on earth it is an extension of God's justice, and once punishment has been suffered on earth it suffices.

46. *Midrash on Psalms* 4:12. The fact that a king of Judah was dependent for his food upon the king of Babylon, a foreign ruler, was humiliating for the Jewish people. King Jehoiachin was forcibly taken to Babylonia and placed in prison in the land of his conquerors. When Evilmerodach came to the Babylonian throne he released the king of Judah from prison but kept him in house arrest and saw to it that Jehoiachin was fed daily.

47. *Kallah Rabbati* 2:11. The first question is phrased differently in *Kallah*, chap. 21: "What should a man do that his children prosper and flourish?" See *Kallah*, chaps. 21–23. On Rabbi Eliezer's counsel that a man speak seductively to his wife at time of intercourse, the *Gemara* on 52b explains that he should speak of his love and desire for her. Rabbi Judah bar Ilai was a fourth-generation *tanna*.

48. *Kallah* 1:20, *Kallah Rabbati* 2:10. See also *Shabbat* 32b, *Midrash on Ecclesiastes* 4:1. The text in *Shabbat* cites Jeremiah 2:30 as its proof-text. Rabbi Natan is a fifth-generation *tanna*, Rabbi Nehorai a fourth generation. The

passage in *Kallah Rabbati* omits the statement of Rabbi Natan and cites Rabbi Joshua instead of Rabbi Nehorai as the author of the last statement. Joshua was a contemporary of Eliezer. The verse quoted by Rabbi Eliezer from Ecclesiastes is preceded by the verse, *It is better not to vow than to vow and not fulfill* (Ecclesiastes 5:4).

49. *Yevamot* 63b–64a. Abba Hanan (or Hanin) was a contemporary of Rabbi Eliezer in the second generation of *tannaim*. Nadab and Abihu, the two sons of Aaron, suddenly died when they brought "strange fire" into the sanctuary (Leviticus, chap. 10).

50. *Berakhot* 13a. Bar Kappara was a *tanna* of the sixth generation. His name was linked here with that of Rabbi Eliezer, a second-generation *tanna*, by the redactors of the Talmud.

51. *Genesis Rabbah* 55:7. The point here is that God could have told Abraham at the outset to take his son Isaac to Mount Moriah but He keeps the righteous in doubt and suspense.

52. *Hullin* 92a. The chief cupbearer of Pharaoh tells his dream to Joseph in Genesis 40:9–11. All four rabbis mentioned in this passage are members of the second generation of *tannaim*. Rabbi Eleazar the Modaite came from Modiim.

53. *Exodus Rabbah* 2:5. The physical status of the Hebrew slaves was low, and they practiced the personal quality of modesty. Hence God Himself redeemed them from their lowly station.

54. *Song of Songs Rabbah* 2:2.

55. *Midrash on Psalms* 18:16 on the verse *He made darkness His hiding-place, His pavilion round about Him were dark waters, and thick clouds of the skies* (Psalms 18:12). Gehinnom, the valley of Hinnom, was a glen to the immediate south of Jerusalem where the god Molokh was worshiped by the heathen, the worship accompanied by the sacrifice of children, a fearful place—therefore a place for the punishment of the wicked in the hereafter, Gehenna, hell. The Great Sea refers to the Mediterranean. Rabbi Joshua stretched the meaning of his proof-text.

56. *Exodus Rabbah* 23:9. This passage is included in the traditional *haggadah*.

57. *Song of Songs Rabbah* 1:7. The Hebrew word *ekev* (*status constructus* form—*ikvei*) as a noun means "rear" or "consequence," associated with the word *akev* meaning "heel" or "back side," which as a verb means "to trace" or "to follow." As a conjunction, *ekev* means "in consequence of." Here the rabbis make use of a play on the word, *ikvei*, translated in the verse as "*in the tracks of.*" Each interpretation states a future occurrence *in consequence of* that which has already happened. Rabbi Eliezer gives an answer to Moses' doubts about providing for Israel in the future. God had caused a miracle for the word for "cakes" here is in the singular—one cake. Since it lasted so long, you may be assured that God will provide for all Israel's needs in the future. Rabbi Akiba speaks of God's protection for Israel—in the past, so in the future. The anonymous rabbis speak of food—just as God provided manna in the desert, so will He see to their food in abundance in the future.

58. *Numbers Rabbah* 23:2. An intellectual exercise in finding meaningful words for which *nahita*, "You led," could serve as an acronym. Notice that here, as in the passage just before, Rabbi Akiba's concern is for God's protection of His people, living as he did during a time of Roman persecution to which he fell a martyr.

59. *Leviticus Rabbah* 34:8. When Rabbi Simon is mentioned without a patronymic it is usually Rabbi Simon ben Johai, a fourth-generation *tanna*.

The "four lines of thought" are completely carried out save for the last. The verse in Leviticus occasioning the four lines of thought speaks of the need for kindness to a person in economic difficulty who is compelled to sell a part of his land. His closest relative able to redeem, to buy back, the land for him is called upon by the Torah to do so. The question about the angels eating arises from the fact that angels do not eat or drink. The question and answer are a later addition to the passage, for Rabbi Judan is a fourth-generation *amora*. The deduction, *a minori ad majus*, in Hebrew, *kal ve-homer*, is an inference that may be drawn from a minor premise to a major premise. It is the first of the thirteen principles whereby the Torah may be interpreted as given by Rabbi Ishmael in the first chapter of the Sifra. The manna is mentioned in chapter 16 of Exodus, the quail in the same chapter and in the eleventh chapter of Numbers, the clouds of glory and the pillars of fire in Exodus, chapter 13. Jethro was indebted to Moses because Moses rose to the defense of the daughters of Jethro, drew water for them and watered their flock (Exodus 2:16–19). The Kenites were supposed to be the descendants of Jethro. The Hebrew word *kali* is usually translated as "roasted grain." The last section of the passage must be another later addition for Rabbi Isaac is either a fifth-generation *tanna* or a second sage by that name, a third-generation *amora*. Feminine modesty dictated that Ruth sit *beside* the reapers and not among them.

60. *Numbers Rabbah* 20:18. The statement of Rabbi Joshua, a contemporary of Rabbi Eliezer, is added from *Midrash Tanhuma*.

61. *Numbers Rabbah* 9:10, *Sotah* 4a, *Yerushalmi Sotah* 1:2 (3c). The sages mentioned as giving the minima here, beginning with Rabbi Eliezer and continuing through Rabbi Judah ben Batyra, are all *tannaim* of the second generation with the exception of Rabbi Akiba of the third generation or, as some classify him, of the second half of the second generation. Rabbi Eleazar ben Phineas is a little-known *tanna*, found once in the Babylonian Talmud, once in the *Tosefta*, and once in the *Yerushalmi*. The passage in *Sotah* 4a changes his name to Rabbi Eleazar ben Jeremiah, whose name is found only here in the Babylonian Talmud. The name Penimon, like Eleazar ben Phineas, a little-known *tanna* of the *baraita*, is sometimes known as Abba Penimon or Penimin or as in *Yerushalmi Sotah* 1:2 (3c), Minimin. The practical application of the rabbis' selection of minima is to base the woman's subjection to the water ordeal upon the combined circumstances of the husband's jealousy and the wife's seclusion with another man. If either factor is missing, she cannot be subjected to the water ordeal and she remains permitted to her husband. The *sinnar* was a kind of petticoat or breech cloth. "Warmed up" as applied to Ben Azzai, a third-generation *tanna*, is a euphemism for his having sustained pollution. The quotation from Psalms is meant to imply that the matter was revealed to Ben Azzai through divine inspiration. Trial by ordeal was common in both ancient times and the Middle Ages among various peoples. The ordeal by water described in chapter 5 of the book of Numbers is the only example of it in Jewish law. It was abolished by Rabban Johanan ben Zakkai soon after the destruction of the Second Temple by the Romans in 70 c.e. Eliezer and Joshua were both his students, hence the discussion here is purely for academic purposes, not for practical use.

62. *Numbers Rabbah* 9:25. Three interpretations of a verse, Numbers 5:28. Eliezer and Joshua were contemporaries, Simon ben Johai, two generations later. Simon's opinion is that the woman found pure after the ordeal by water is still guilty of a wrong, having disregarded her husband's warning not to seclude herself with the other man.

63. *Numbers Rabbah* 13:15–16. Abba Hanan, sometimes Hanan, was, like Eliezer, a second-generation *tanna*. The force of the quotation linking the chiefs of the tribe of Issachar with Deborah was to state that they, like her, were prophets and judges.

64. *Berakhot* 61b, *Pesahim* 25a, *Sifre on Deuteronomy* 32. "Might" in this verse is understood by the rabbis to mean "possessions," "wealth," or "substance." See the comment of Akiba on the same verse, *Berakhot* 60b.

65. *Lamentations Rabbah, Proems* 27. The two rabbis reinterpret the Hebrew word, *"ad,"* usually meaning "until," "yet," "for." Rabbi Eliezer sees in it the word, *ed,* "witness," Rabbi Joshua, the word *od,* "more." In this connection it is well to remember that the words of the Torah as written by a scribe in a scroll do not have vowel marks, so the letter *ayin* and *daled* may be read as *ed, ad,* or *od* (defective, without the usual *vav* as the middle letter).

66. *Sotah* 13b. The word in the Talmud is *mils,* which equals 1, 226 yards. See earlier passage ending with note 12.

67. *Song of Songs Rabbah* 1:12. The point here is that God Himself need not be occupied in carrying out His wishes. His will is sufficient or one of His angels, like Michael, here called "the great prince," may be His messenger. For the story of Abraham in the fiery furnace see Louis Ginzberg, *The Legends of the Jews,* vol. 1 (Philadelphia, 1909–1946), pp. 198ff.

68. *Song of Songs Rabbah* 1:9. The verb *damah* or *demi* can mean "to be silent" or "to imagine," "compare," resemble," "be like." Hence the exposition by Rabbi Eliezer.

69. *Leviticus Rabbah* 19:1, *Song of Songs Rabbah* 5:11. The last half of the verse, *and black as a raven,* is interpreted in this way: *black, shahor,* is changed to red *shahar,* "dawn," and *raven, arev,* is read *erev,* "evening." The Hebrew words without vowel signs may be read either way. The statement by Rabbi Eliezer is from the Midrash on Proverbs, end of chap. 23.

70. *Ecclesiastes Rabbah* 11:2. Eliezer uses the verse from 1 Kings as a proof-text because there the previous verse mentioned that Elijah had sent his servant seven times so the text should have stated "at the last time." Therefore, "seventh" is interpreted to mean the Sabbath, and Elijah appealed to God to send rain through the merit of the Sabbath. Eliezer understands the act of Elijah putting his face between his knees as alluding to circumcision, and the prophet prayed that God should send rain through the merit of Israel's observance of circumcision. Joshua's inclusion of the principal holy days was to indicate that all of them are occasions when the blessing of *she-he-he-yanu* is pronounced: "Who has kept us in life, has preserved us, and enabled us to reach this season."

71. *Ecclesiastes Rabbah* 11:6, *Numbers Rabbah* 61:3. Eliezer interprets the text literally, whereas Joshua gives a metaphorical interpretation, the second coming from *Numbers Rabbah.*

72. *Ruth Rabbah* 7:7. The question raised here is, How did it happen that the closest relative of Ruth's late husband, who had the first right to marry her, happened to come along just as Boaz had gone to the gate of the town and sat down? It was too much to be a mere coincidence. Rabbi Eliezer's answer was that Boaz, Ruth, and Naomi each played a part in the unfolding drama. Whereupon God said, "I too have a part to play"—that is, to bring the kinsman along just as Boaz sat down, so that the closest relative would decline to exercise his prerogative to marry the widow Ruth and then Boaz could take her in marriage. The gate of the town was where most people would gather. The court sat there, the market would be there, people would

come and go. Rabbi Berekhiah, the second scholar by that name, was an *amora* of the fourth generation who is especially known for his activity in the field of *aggadah*. The term *Peloni Almoni* is used in rabbinic literature in the meaning of "So-and-so" or "Such a one."

73. *Leviticus Rabbah* 14:44. The verse speaks of God's works of creation, setting boundaries to the sea. The three sages are struck by the comparison of the sea to a woman.

74. *Tosefta Kelim Bava Kamma* 1:6. Rabbi Simon *ha-Tzanua*, which may be translated as "pious" or "modest" or "discreet" or "chaste" or "unassuming," was a *kohen*, a priest who served in the Temple before its destruction. This story is preceded by a difference of opinion between Rabbi Meir and the sages as to what the proper practice was in the Temple. Rabbi Meir held that priests whose hands and feet are not washed may enter the area between the hall leading to the interior of the Temple and the altar. The sages said that they may not, and Rabbi Eliezer agrees with them. See Louis Finkelstein, *The Pharisees*, vol. 1 (Philadelphia 1938; reprint, 1962), pp. CVIIff.

75. *Yerushalmi Hallah* 4:5 (60b). Rabbi Simon bar Kahana was a distinguished student of Rabbi Eliezer ben Hyrcanus and a teacher of Rabbi Simon ben Gamaliel II. In this passage the Leiden manuscript and *editio princeps* of the *Yerushalmi* reads Rabbi Eleazar, but Eliezer should be the preferred reading since it was he who was the teacher of Simon bar Kahana. Rabbi Eliezer here expresses his concern for the property of others, even to the extent of a sliver.

76. *Leviticus Rabbah* 34:10. Abbahu is an *amora* of the third generation. Of course, the implication here is that one should certainly give alms to every legitimate beggar and since it is virtually impossible to tell who is an imposter, it follows that one should respond charitably to every beggar.

77. *Leviticus Rabbah* 34:9. Vengeance or punishment comes to the Jews for not being responsive to the poor. The verses preceding our text in Deuteronomy speak of lending to the needy. Edom was an ancient neighbor of the Jewish kingdom but was often used by the rabbis as a code word for Rome. Could Rabbi Eliezer here be expressing the hope or the conviction that Rome would someday be punished by the Jews for its misdeeds?

78. *Seder Eliyahu Rabbah*, p. 151. This passage reads "the Emperor Hadrian," but the reference must correctly be to the emperor Trajan, who waged war in 115–117 C.E. against those who had rebelled against his rule. The Jewish community of Alexandria was destroyed, and the same can be said about the rest of Egyptian Jewry. This tells that the Jews were entrapped by guile, then destroyed by a sudden attack. The church historian, Eusebius, gives the same account, except that he tells that the attackers were the Greek civilians rather than the Roman military (Eusebius, *History of the Church* [New York, 1984], Book 4, p. 154). The passage in *Yerushalmi Sukkot* 5 (55b–c), which describes the Great Synagogue in Alexandria, ends with the words, "Who destroyed it? The wicked Trugeinos (Trajan)."

79. *Gittin* 57a. Most scholars ascribe this passage to the Bar Kokhba War, but Rabbi Eliezer was no longer alive at the time of this war (132–135 C.E.). The Valley of Yadayim has been identified as the Nile Delta. Like Jewish blood used as fertilizer, this writer in 1945 saw sacks of ash from the crematoria in the Dachau concentration camp stamped with the word "fertilizer" in German.

80. *Betzah* 15b. By "large barrels" Rabbi Eliezer meant the very rich, who count their wine by their large barrels. They left the study hall early because of the great amount of food and plentiful drink awaiting them on the

festival. They are simply gluttons. Then each successive group—the casks, pitchers, flasks, and beakers—is less rich then the group earlier but richer than the next following group and less in pursuit of material pleasure than the group before it but more so than that following it. When the sixth and last group walked out Rabbi Eliezer's anger was at its peak and he said, "These are the people of the curse." After the recounting of the story the *Gemara* asks, "But is not the celebration of a festival with good food and drink a religious obligation?" The answer is given that Rabbi Eliezer is consistent with his own view, for he said that such rejoicing on the festival is optional, that on a festival a person may either "eat and drink *or* sit and learn." Obviously, the preference of Rabbi Eliezer is for the latter, while Rabbi Joshua holds that one should do both.

81. *Sanhedrin* 92b. Rabbis Joshua and Judah ben Batyra are *tannaim* of the second generation, Eliezer ben Jose the Galilean a *tanna* of the fourth. Ezekiel lived in Babylonia, hence the revived dead had to go up to the Land of Israel. In rabbinic usage those who travel from any country to the land of Israel go up to that land.

82. *Sanhedrin* 95b. The rabbis believed that no natural cause could have destroyed overnight the powerful invading army of Sennacherib (2 Kings 18–19, Isaiah 36–37). Each explained the supernatural miracle that must have occurred. The angel Gabriel is charged with the responsibility for the ripening of fruit. The statement about evil spirits is from *Midrash Tanhuma, Ekev*, 4. Judah here should properly be Joshua, known as a transmitter of legends. A *bet rova* equals 104 1/8 square cubits, a cubit being 52 1/2 centimeters. A *kav* equals 220.39 centimeters. Sikhnin or Sukhnin was in Galilee.

83. *Leviticus Rabbah* 5:4, *Deuteronomy Rabbah* 4:8, *Yerushalmi Horayot* 3:4 (48a). The story varies a little among these sources; for example, the *Yerushalmi* says the name of the man was Abba Judah, not Judan—the origin of the latter is indeed the former. Further, it says he found a jewel, not a treasure. *Deuteronomy Rabbah* makes no mention of the use of a cow in plowing and that Abba Judan simply found a treasure in the field probably turned up by his plow. Antiokhia or Antioch was the capital of Syria and stood partly on a hill but also partly on a level surface. The valley of Antiokhia probably indicated an area in the latter. Our account is drawn from all three sources. Alon, *The Jews in Their Land in the Talmudic Age* 1:250, identified the location as either a place in northern Transjordan or near Antioch.

84. *Genesis Rabbah* 89:8. Rabbi Eliezer quotes the verse to show that the fulfillment of a dream actually follows its interpretation.

85. *Sanhedrin* 99a. Psalm 95:10's closing words are usually translated . . . *I was provoked by that generation*, but the word *akut*, "provoked," is connected with the root, "to hold," here in the sense "I shall rule over them." Rabbi Eleazer ben Azariah, a contemporary of Rabbi Eliezer, was a *tanna* of the second generation; Rabbi Dosa and Rabbi Judah ha-Nasi belonged to the fifth generation. The text here refers to the latter simply as "rabbi," commonly done throughout rabbinic literature, the rabbi *par excellence* and the redactor of the Mishnah. The interpretation of the proof-text of Rabbi Judah ha-Nasi, Isaiah 63:4, is *I had planned that My year of redemption*, that is, 365 days, of which each day shall be as long as a day of God's vengeance, which is a year, as in the case of the spies, on whose account the Israelites were condemned to wander forty years in the desert—one year for each day of their mission (*cf.* Numbers 14:34 and Rashi's commentary). *A generation and generations* (literal translation of *dor va-dor*) is minimally three generations.

86. *Sanhedrin* 71a. The explanation of "the condemned city" may be found in Deuteronomy 13:13-17. A *mezuzah* is an encased strip of parchment on which is written the first two sections of the *Shema*—Deuteronomy 6:4, 6:5-9, and 11:13-20. (The third section of the *Shema* is Numbers 15:37-41.) The case containing the parchment is affixed to the doorpost in accordance with Deuteronomy 6:9. Rabbi Jonathan is a *tanna* of the fourth generation.

87. *Deuteronomy Rabbah* 1:15, *Kiddushin* 31a-b, *Avodah Zarah* 23b-24a, *Yerushalmi Peah* 1:1, *Yerushalmi Kiddushin* 1:7. Our account includes elements from several sources. One variation tells that the father was asleep with the key to the jewel box under his pillow. Another was that Dama was paid the weight of the Red Heifer in gold pieces. The laws pertaining to the Red Heifer may be found in Numbers 19:1-10. Such an animal was uncommon, and therefore its price was always high. The stories about Dama must date before the destruction of the Temple in 70 c.e. Baron, *A Social and Religious History of the Jews* 2:239, describes Dama's behavior as "unreasonable extremes of religious piety."

88. *Kiddushin* 32a.

89. *Kiddushin* 31a. Rabbi Eliezer's answer reflects the sexist position of some of the ancient rabbis, but the status of the woman in rabbinic Judaism was higher than that in other contemporary cultures. Rabbi Joshua's answer makes it clear that although he could tell that the questioner was the son of a widow and not a divorcee and therefore this question was purely academic, nonetheless he would answer the question. From his eyelids it could be seen that he was a widow's son because they had been affected by weeping. Rabbi Joshua's last words are sarcastic.

90. *Yerushalmi Taanit* 2:12 (66b), *Yerushalmi Megillah* 1:4 (70d), *Tosefta Taaniyot* 2:5. Both Rabbi Eliezer and Rabbi Joshua held that it was forbidden to decree a fast to take place during Hanukkah. Hence Eliezer had his hair cut and Joshua bathed on the Hanukkah day that was supposed to be a fast day to show their opinion that the fast was null and void. Such is the law as stated in Mishnah *Taanit* 2:10. To be sure, Rabban Gamaliel there states that if the fast had already begun, it should be observed. But the *Tosefta* text cited above adds that as long as Gamaliel lived the law followed his opinion but not so after his death. Lod, of course, is Lydda.

91. *Taanit* 25b. In times of drought the practice was to pray and fast. Rabbi Akiba was younger than Rabbi Eliezer and his student.

92. *Sukkah* 27b. In biblical and rabbinic usage "the festival" always meant the festival of Sukkot. Rabbi Eliezer conducted his academy at Lod or Lydda for many years. See also a parallel story in *Tosefta Sukkah* 2:1, which is also quoted in *Yerushalmi Sukkah* 2:5 (53a). In this version Rabbi Eliezer asks Ilai, "Are you not among those who observe the festival? Have they not said that it is not praiseworthy for a person to leave his home on a festival?" The Babylonian Talmud concludes that although it is a *mitzvah* to visit one's teacher on a festival, that is so only if one may return to his home and dine with his family on the same day. See Lieberman, *Tosefta ki-fshutah* 4:849, and Alon, *The Jews in Their Land in the Talmudic Age* 2:471.

93. *Pesahim* 68b, *Betzah* 15b. The two rabbis were contemporaries.

94. *Sukkah* 27b and *Tosefta Sukkah* 1:9. Little is known about Rabbi Johanan ben Ilai. Caesarea was made an important city by Herod, who gave it its name in honor of Emperor Augustus Caesar. The Roman governors administered Judea from Caesarea, which had a garrison of Roman soldiers and a sizable non-Jewish population together with a rather large Jewish community. Rabbi Eliezer, conservative that he was, put off answering Rabbi

Johanan because he was not certain of the law and he would not make a legal decision without a precedent set by a predecessor. His teacher was Rabban Johanan ben Zakkai. The law pertaining to this subject was codified in the Mishnah, *Sukkah* 2:3, "If a person spread a sheet over the *sukkah* because of the sun . . . the *sukkah* is not valid. . . ." See Lieberman, *Tosefta ki-fshutah* 4:843–844.

95. *Sukkah* 28a. Rabbi Jose ben Rabbi Judah was the son of Rabbi Judah ben Ilai, a fourth-generation *tanna* (c. 140–c.165 c.e.). See *Baba Kamma* 85a and Mishnah *Nedarim* 8:6. This story and the one before it stress that Rabbi Eliezer relied upon precedent in making any legal decision, a common although not exclusive practice in jurisprudence today. Rabbi Eliezer's five-part statement shows that it was not for lack of knowledge that he hesitated to render a decision. He made use of all his time in the study hall from early morning to late at night, with no time wasted, to add to his learning. But his principle was to make no legal decision without knowledge of a precedent.

96. *Berakhot* 47b. In contemporary usage the expression *am ha-aretz* connotes an ignoramus. But clearly that was not the complete meaning of the term in rabbinic times or in biblical literature. It could imply ignorance of the law but more often in rabbinic literature it meant one who was indifferent to Jewish religious practice, negligent of the laws of ritual purity and impurity, of tithe-giving, and other religious rites. Therefore, George Foot Moore says "that such *ammei ha-aretz* should be regarded by the Pharisees as little better than the indigenous heathen who were properly designated by that opprobrious name" (Moore, *Judaism in the First Centuries of the Christian Era* 1:321). *Am ha-aretz* literally means "people of the land; plural, *amei ha-aretz*, "peoples of the land." See Genesis 23:7. It may mean the council of leaders of the people (see Mayer Sulzberger, *Am Ha-aretz, The Council of the People* [Philadelphia, 1909]). The *Shema* is the declaration of faith in the one God (Deuteronomy 6:4) and is recited in the daily morning and evening prayers, in the prayer before going to bed, the closing prayer on Yom Kippur, and in the last confessional before death. The *tefillin* are the phylacteries worn during the daily weekday prayers (Deuteronomy 6:8), and the *mezuzah* is the metal or wooden case containing Deuteronomy 6:4–9 and 11:13–21, placed on the doorpost of the Jewish home (Deuteronomy 6:9). *Tzitzit* are the fringes on the *talit*, the prayer-shawl, originally on the garment itself, the robe that was, in ancient times, the usual clothing worn by men. See Numbers 15:37–41. One theory has it that fringes were worn on the hem of the garments of nobility in antiquity and were to be worn by Jews, "a kingdom of priests and a holy nation."

97. *Pesahim* 49b. This is undoubtedly hyperbole but the exaggeration illustrates the hostility between the observant Jews who devoted themselves to learning and the untutored, somewhat nonpracticing Jews. See Rabban Gamaliel's aphorism. "No *am ha-aretz* can be pious (*Pirkei Avot* 2:5) or John 7:49, "But the people who do not know the law are cursed." See also the previous note.

98. *Sotah* 17a, *Berakhot* 6a, *Menahot* 35b. Rabbi Eliezer understands the verse literally, that the name of the Lord is proclaimed upon you refers to the phylactery that is placed by the worshiper on his head each morning save for the Sabbath and holidays. The new J.P.S. translation translates *alekha* as *over you*, not "upon you" and the note there explains, "i.e., the Lord recognizes you as His own; cf. Isaiah 4:1." The source in *Berakhot* 6a is prefaced by "How do we know that the *tefillin* are a source of strength to Israel? For it is written, "*And all the peoples of the earth shall see,*" etc.

99. *Pesikta Rabbati* 22:5, *Yerushalmi Berakhot* 2:3 (13b). Of course, the *tefillin* would not be worn after sunset, but Rabbi Eliezer would wear them all day until evening.

100. *Tefillin* (one of the minor treatises of the Talmud) 1:19–20 (63a). The interchange between Rabbi Eliezer and Rabbi Joshua is from the *Midrash on the Psalms* 1:17. Ubelin or Obelin was the name of a village near Jaffa and also of a village in Galilee near Sepphoris. A visit by Rabbi Eliezer to Obelin is mentioned in *Eruvin* 11b–12a. Rabbi Joshua interprets *yamim* in Exodus 13:10 in its original sense of "days" rather than in its derived sense of "year." For the importance of the *Shema* see note 96 *supra*.

101. *Pirkei de-Rabbi Eliezer*, chap. 3, beginning. The Talmud in *Megillah* 18a states that he who speaks God's praise to excess will be taken from the world, based on Job 37:20. The ministering angels are identified with "the sons of Elohim" of Job 1:6, and they are probably to be identified with "the angels of sanctification" mentioned in the Book of Jubilees 2, 2:18. *In re* "the heavenly host praising God" see Luke 2:13.

102. *Rosh Hashanah* 10b. See also *Genesis Rabbah* 22:4 and *Leviticus Rabbah* 29:1 where Rabbi Eliezer is quoted as saying that the world was created on the twenty-fifth day of *Elul* while man was created on Rosh Hashanah. *Nisan* is described as the seventh civil month in the Jewish calendar and the first ecclesiastical month.

103. *Ecclesiastes Rabbah* 3:20 and *Genesis Rabbah* 12:11. In Psalm 148 the angels, sun, moon, and all the heavenly bodies are described as being from heaven, while the sea monsters, ocean depths, and all the rest until man are described as being from the earth. See also *Yoma* 54b where a third opinion is stated, that of the sages who state that all that God created in heaven and earth were created out of Zion, the proof-text being Psalms 150:1–2.

104. *Yoma* 54b. The quotation of Psalms 50:1–2 is understood to mean that God *summoned the world from east to west* into being, that is, into creation.

105. *Bava Batra* 25a-b. An exedra in the ancient Greek world was an open room or area surrounded by a railing in front of a house where conversations or discussions were held. It was closed on three sides and open on the fourth. Rabbi Joshua's "tent" was completely closed by the firmament. The verse in Ecclesiastes speaks of the wind, but here it is taken to refer to the sun also. The last statement means that the sun traverses the eastern and western sides of the heaven in the summer when it is above the horizon, and goes around in winter when it is below the horizon. Of course, the ancients believed that the earth was the center of the universe, the sun revolving around it.

106. *Ecclesiastes Rabbah* 1:7, *Genesis Rabbah* 13:10, *Taanit* 9b. The latter adds "There is not even a hair's breadth between the drops of rainwater, which teaches you that a day of rain is as great as the day when heaven and earth were created." The flow that welled up from the ground (see Genesis 2:6 as quoted) was caused by the evaporation of the sea. Rabbi Joshua's question, "But are not the waters of the ocean salty?" implies the fact that rainwater is not salty. The Hebrew word here translated "sweetened" means both "pour down" and "be distilled," hence "sweetened."

107. *Pesahim* 117a.

108. *Berakhot* 34a; *Mekhilta, Vayassa*, chap. 1. The second part, telling of God's instruction to Moses, comes from *Exodus Rabbah* 21:8. The *Mekhilta* adds "the prayer of the righteous is short" and concludes with the statement, "For as Rabbi Eliezer used to say," etc.

109. *Pesikta Rabbati* 23:4. Aquila is identified as a translator of the

Scriptures from Hebrew into Greek. By birth he was a Gentile from Pontus. He joined the Christians but later left them to become a Jew. He finished his work of translation under the influence of Rabbi Akiba. His other teachers were Rabbi Eliezer and Rabbi Joshua ben Hananiah. See *The Jewish Encyclopedia* 2:34–38. Of course, during the procedure of conversion he had to undergo circumcision. Rabbi Eliezer's answer is that both the Sabbath, although included in the Ten Commandments, and circumcision were decreed before the revelation at Mount Sinai. Circumcision was ordained as a covenant between God and Abraham (Genesis 17:9–14).

110. *Mekhilta, Vayassa,* chap. 5. Gog and Magog are savage, barbarian peoples (or one people) who, in apocalyptic prediction, will attack Israel in the last of battles and will be defeated (see Ezekiel 38–39) prior to the Day of Judgment and the advent of the Messiah. See *The Jewish Encyclopedia* 6:19–20. The Great Day of Judgment or The Day of the Lord is a factor in Jewish eschatology, called also "that day" or simply "the day." It would come at the end of time, a day of punishment of the wicked or, sometimes, a day of punishment for the wicked and blessing for the righteous. Before the coming of the Messiah there would be great suffering.

111. *Berakhot* 3a. God roars like a lion over the loss of His temple but can do nothing until His people repent. But in time they will repent and Israel reborn will last forever. Commentators interpret "the night" in this passage as referring to the exile of the Jewish people. So the different watches and their respective signs refer to various dark periods in the history of the long Jewish exile. The Holy One suffers with His people's suffering. See Baron, *A Social and Religious History of the Jews* 2:114.

112. *Avot de-Rabbi Natan* 16:2 (24b), *Yerushalmi Yevamot* 13:2 (13c). His niece was Rabbi Eliezer's second wife. He was also married to Imma Shalom. This story illustrates the tenderness underlying Rabbi Eliezer's frequent bluntness of expression. The previous passage in *Avot de-Rabbi Natan* tells the story of how Rabbi Akiba resisted temptation when in Rome two beautiful women thrust themselves at him. The passage in *Yerushalmi* reads, "I am your maid to wash the feet of my master's slaves." By her question Rabbi Eliezer's niece was telling him that she desired to marry him. See 1 Samuel 26:41 where Abigail's message to David was *Your handmaid is ready to be your maidservant, to wash the feet of my lord's servants.* Baron points out (*A Social and Religious History of the Jews* 2:227) that out of several hundred talmudic sages, only two or three actually lived with two wives and in each case "some exceptional circumstance accounted for the deviation," as here.

113. Mishnah *Sotah* 3:4 and *Yerushalmi Sotah* 3:4 (18d). See Mishnah *Nedarim* 4:3, "though he may teach Scripture to his sons and his daughters." Ben Azzai here explains that if the daughters must drink the bitter water of the woman suspected of adultery (Numbers 5:11ff.), "she may know that the merit [that she has acquired through study] will hold her punishment in suspense." Rabbi Eliezer ben Hyrcanus in his attitude to women was conservative as he was generally in the development of the *halakhah*. The mainstream in the Talmud favors teaching the Torah to sons and daughters. About the place of women in the talmudic world, see Baron, *A Social and Religious History of the Jews* 2:235.

114. *Numbers Rabbah* 9:48, *Yerushalmi Sotah* 3:4 (19d). This story is a further illustration of Rabbi Eliezer's conservative position, as in the previous passage. The three kinds of death were by the sword, the water ordeal, and the plague (see *Numbers Rabbah* 9:47). As in the passage before, Rabbi Eliezer is consistent in this view that women are not to be taught the Torah, a view

not universally accepted. Hyrcanus in this story is identified by Hyman as Rabbi Eliezer's son in *Toldot Tannaim ve-Amoraim* 1:361. Hyrcanus was also the name of his father. A *kor* is equal to thirty seah or 364.4 liters. An interesting question is raised by this story: Was the giving of tithes still in practice after the destruction of the Temple? Rabbi Eliezer was a Levite but he was active in the years following the end of the Temple service. No definitive answer can be given to the question but this story would indicate that the first tithe was given. This is supported by Mishnah *Ma'aser Sheni* 5:9. As to the second tithe, the Mishnah (*Ma'aser Sheni* 1:5) states that such part of the crop that would have been redeemed for use in the pilgrimage festivals in Jerusalem should now—after the destruction of the Temple—be permitted to rot on the ground. In any case visits by Jews to Jerusalem were prohibited by the Romans.

115. *Kohelet Rabbah* 1:8 and *Bava Metzia* 59b. Rabbi Joshua's view was that by her repentance she had died to her past life and would never live in it again. See also *Avodah Zarah* 17a and Herford, *Christianity in Talmud and Midrash*, pp. 188–189. Herford assumes that the woman wanted to reject *Minut*—"in this instance Christian heresy"—for conversion to Judaism. Rabbi Eliezer, like Shammai, opposed converts, teaching that "it is because there is a bad streak in the stranger (*ger*, also meaning proselyte), that Scripture warns about him in so many passages" (Baron, *A Social and Religious History of the Jews* 2:148).

116. *Kohelet Rabbah* 1:7, *Genesis Rabbah* 13:9. The Great Sea is the Mediterranean, the largest ocean with which the ancients were familiar until the Romans invaded what is now England. The ship entered waters that seemed to be stationary and Rabbi Eliezer asserted that it must be a part of God's plan, that they use that water for a later test that would prove the verse, Ecclesiastes 1:7. Since the ocean water absorbed the other water and the flask did not overflow, that proved that no matter how many rivers flow into the ocean, it does not become full.

117. *Kohelet Rabbah* 11:1. Ship passengers would bring their own food, including live animals, and drink sufficient to last them for the voyage. Rabbi Eliezer and Rabbi Joshua accompanied Rabban Gamaliel II on a mission to Rome. See *Deuteronomy Rabbah* 2:24 and *Yerushalmi Sanhedrin* 7 (25d). For voyages to Rome by the rabbis see Alon, *The Jews in Their Land in the Talmudic Age* 1:124–131.

118. *Bava Batra* 74b. The leviathan is a mythical sea animal described in Job, chap. 40. Its flesh will be served at a feast for the righteous at the coming of the Messiah (*Bava Batra* 74a). It lives in the Mediterranean (*Bava Batra* 74a and *Bekhorot* 55b). The body of the leviathan, especially its eyes, possesses great illuminating power, as this story tells.

119. *Bava Metzia* 59a–b, *Yerushalmi Mo'ed Katan* 3:1 (81c-d). See Mishnah *Kelim* 5:10. Judah Goldin says of this story, "This is perhaps the most emphatic defense of intellectual 'freedom' (better, independence), preserved by the Talmud and is rightly cherished by students of Jewish literature and thought." ("On the Account of the Banning of R. Eliezer ben Hyrcanus," *The Journal of the Ancient Near East Society* 16–17 (1984–1985). Rabbi Eliezer argued that since the oven was made of separate parts with a layer of sand in between, it is not susceptible to ritual uncleanness. For each part cannot be regarded as a utensil and since sand separates the parts, they do not constitute a whole unit that can become unclean. The sages, however, argued that the outer coating of mortar or cement unites all the parts and makes it susceptible to uncleanness. Akhnai is probably the name of a respected

person. Although the story is told in legendary form it is a remarkable statement, for it asserts that the development of Jewish law depends on human reason. Human beings, by majority vote, exercise the final decision.

It was the traditional belief that Elijah never died and he appears from time to time. He is present at every *brit milah* and he will be the forerunner of the Messiah, heralding his coming.

Rabbi Akiba was concerned that if the wrong person told Rabbi Eliezer of his having been excommunicated, it might be told him in a tactless and cruel way. Rabbi Eliezer rent his garments and took off his shoes as a sign of mourning incumbent upon a person who had been placed under the ban. In ancient times mourners sat on the ground.

Rabban Gamaliel as *Nasi* and head of the Sanhedrin was in charge of the excommunication proceedings. The *tahnun* is a series of prayers in the weekday morning service that follows the *Amidah* or the Eighteen Benedictions. Originally it was a short interval for the offering of personal prayers and entreaties. They were called supplications and the supplicant fell on his face. Today the person bows his head on his arm as he sits to recite these prayers, now fixed, consisting of Psalm 6 or 130 followed by brief prayers. The *tahnun* is not recited on the Sabbath, holidays or their eve, or on *Rosh Hodesh*, the beginning of a new month in the Jewish calendar. Jewish months are either 29 days (defective) or 30 days (full). Imma Shalom was concerned that her husband, Eliezer, would pour out his story of humiliation and feelings of hurt before God, who would listen to him and punish her brother, Gamaliel. Thinking that the previous month consisted of 29 days and the next day would be *Rosh Hodesh* when *tahnun* prayers would not be recited, she relaxed her watch over her husband. But the day was actually the thirtieth day of the previous month and in those times the *tahnun* prayers were recited on the thirtieth day of a month. When she realized her mistake, she was sure that Eliezer had included in his *tahnun* prayers his grievance against her brother. The *Yerushalmi* source changes the order of the several elements in the story.

The stubbornness on both sides here and the extreme punishment of excommunication make it not unreasonable to suggest that a fundamental issue is involved: the tradition as received by an individual as opposed to the opinion of the majority, who also respect the tradition but believe it is open to interpretation.

The story of the resolution of the debate between Rabbi Eliezer and his colleagues casts light on the contemporary American debate over the original intent of the framers of the Constitution. By invoking heavenly intervention in his controversy with the other sages, Rabbi Eliezer asserted his belief in original intent: that it is God who exercises final authority on Jewish law. The sages, conversely, believed that the final authority rests with those who interpret the law and that Eliezer's approach is heresy. Therefore, they felt compelled to excommunicate him, for his conservatism would prevent the proper development of the oral law.

120. *Yerushalmi Moed Katan* 3:1 (81c-d). A sample of Rabbi Eliezer's sense of humor.

121. *Avodah Zarah* 16b–17a, *Tosefta Hullin* 2:24, *Ecclesiastes Rabbah* 1:8, Yalkut Shimoni on Micah 1 and Proverbs 5:8. The word translated here as "heresy" is *minut*, used generally in rabbinic literature for the beliefs and practices of sectarians or dissenters and, most often, of the early (Jewish) Christians. From the context it is clear that here *minut* means the Christian heresy. Herford, in *Christianity in Talmud and Midrash*, pp. 141–142, writes

that there was a general search for Christians in Palestine by the Romans in the year 109 C.E. during the reign of Trajan. Eusebius, in *The History of the Church from Christ to Constantine* 3:32-33, 142-144, speaks of this hunting down of Christians and says that Trajan called a halt to the search for Christians, "but if met were to be punished." The date of this exchange of letters between Trajan and the governor, Plinius Secundus, is 112 C.E. Herford concludes, "It appears to me probable that the arrest and trial of R. Eliezer took place during this official search after Christians, and is therefore to be dated A.D. 109 or thereabouts." See also Alon, *The Jews in Their Land in the Talmudic Age* 1:292 n. 24. Herford thinks that the trial took place in Caesarea "where Eliezer seems to have gone after his excommunication by the Rabbis of Jabneh." The Talmud in *Sanhedrin* 68a says that he died in Caesarea and his body was brought home to Lod. Jacob could not have learned his interpretation of the verse in Deuteronomy from his master, Jesus, says Herford, because "he belonged to the second or, perhaps, the third generation of disciples." Solomon Zeitlin, in "Jesus in the Early Tannaitic Literature" (Vienna, 1933), unlike Herford, does not believe this text to be authentic. Instead he says that this passage is of a later period and was "brought into the Tannaitic literature under the influence of the Gospels." On the other hand, Joseph Klausner, in *Yeshu ha-Notzri* (New York, 1925), pp. 29-37, is convinced of the authenticity of this passage. But he places the arrest of Rabbi Eliezer in the year 95 C.E. during the reign of Domitian. Unlike Herford, who writes that Rabbi Eliezer met Jacob a short time before the trial, Klausner thinks that the meeting took place many years earlier and that Jacob was an actual disciple of Jesus and an old man when he spoke with Rabbi Eliezer in about the year 60 C.E. Klausner even suggests that the Jacob in this story was Jesus' brother, known as James, who headed the disciples after the crucifixion. See Galatians 1:19. Our text of the Babylonian Talmud for this passage in *Avodah Zarah* 16b-17a does not identify Jacob. The *Tosefta* does identify him as quoting in the name of Jesus son of Pantiri (elsewhere Pandera or Pantira). The patronymic Pantiri, etc., is from the Greek and difficult to explain, says Herford, except that it may represent the point of view that Jesus was born of the union between his mother, Miriam or Mary, and a man not his legitimate father. Marcus Jastrow, in *A Dictionary of the Targumim, the Talmud Babli and Yerushalmi, and the Midrashic Literature* (New York, 1926), p. 1186, explains Pandera as "the surname of Joseph the father of Jesus of Nazareth."

The Munich manuscript of the Talmud in our passage identifies Jacob as "of the disciples of Jesus the Nazarene." Again, near the end of the passage the manuscript reads, "This is what Jesus the Nazarene taught me." In the same place in the story the Tosefta reads, "This is what Jesus ben Pantiri taught me." For the words added in the Munich manuscript see Raphael Nathan Rabinowitz, *Dikdukei sofrim* (Munich, 1867-1897), to *Avodah Zarah*.

Sekhaniah has been identified with Sukhnin or Sikhnin in Galilee. The high priest spent the entire night preceding the Day of Atonement in the precincts of the Temple and provision had to be made for his comfort. Compare the last statement of keeping away from the ruling power with *Avot* 1:10, "Seek no intimacy with the ruling power," and 2:3, "Be guarded in your relations with the ruling power." Alon, *The Jews in Their Land in the Talmudic Age* 1:293, writes of "the fairly familiar relations that occasionally existed between some of the early *tannaim* and some of the Jewish followers of Jesus—but, at the same time, the growing alienation between the two camps, approaching the proportions of a halakah forbidding discourse with *Minim* in matters of Torah."

Saul Lieberman has said that this *baraita* telling the story of how Rabbi Eliezer was accused of being a new Christian is of importance for knowledge of Roman trial procedure. He also called it the first authentic text of persecution of the Christians. This writer sat in Doctor Lieberman's class during the summer of 1958, in the Herbert Lehman Institute of Ethics. The subject of study was the talmudic text of *Avodah Zarah*. Professor Lieberman also wrote an article on Roman legal institutions in which he discusses this *baraita* (*Jewish Quarterly Review* 35 [July 1944]). He dates the trial, as does Herford, about 108–109 c.e. The source of this *baraita* is the passage in *Tosefta Hullin* 2. The final completion of the *Tosefta* took place at the beginning of the third century, and most of its material refers to the middle of the second century. The *Tosefta* therefore is a source almost contemporaneous with the events described and often eyewitnesses were still alive. Many attended the Roman trials, especially those referring to religious matters. Another reason for the reliability of this source is that the rabbis tell this story *en passant* without very much detail.

The Hebrew word *gardom*, translated here as "a raised platform," comes from the Latin, *gradus*, "a step." In a Roman court it was a moveable platform with a back. The accused stepped up on the platform, his back to its back as he faced the judge, with the arms of the accused bound under his armpits against the sides of the platform, unless the accused confessed at once. The trial was conducted in Greek with only the sentence pronounced in Latin. Here no accuser is mentioned. Evidently, there was none; Rabbi Eliezer was probably called to trial on the basis of an anonymous accusation. The question asked by the judge was a catch-question, a common Roman judicial procedure. Here the assumption underlying the judge's question is, Of course you are guilty of being a Christian, but how is that possible? Rabbi Eliezer gave an evasive answer because he did not want to reveal that he had been excommunicated by the rabbis, a story we have told earlier. That very fact could have caused the Roman judge to suspect that the Jews themselves were aware that Rabbi Eliezer had joined the new Christian group. The judge could hardly have been expected to believe that the ban was the result of a halakhic dispute.

A pagan accused by a Roman court of having become a Christian could escape punishment by obeying the order of the court to pour a libation before an idol. Jews could escape punishment by carrying out the Roman court's order to curse Jesus.

122. *Sanhedrin* 38b and *Nedarim* 32a. Compare with *Avot* 2:19, "Know how to answer a heretic." One must learn the Torah in order to answer a heretic because he tries to find support from the Torah for his beliefs. The Hebrew word here translated as "heretic" is *apikores*, which is related to the name of the Greek philospher Epicurus and is used in the Talmud in a play upon the word *pakor*, meaning to be free from restraint. Hence the *apikores* is one who denies God and His commandments.

123. *Berakhot* 28b, *Avot de-Rabbi Natan* 19:4, *Ecclesiastes Rabbah* 6:1. Perhaps Rabbi Eliezer was reminding his disciples that in their agreeing with his excommunication they had not been concerned about his honor. Jastrow, in his *Dictionary*, p. 331, explains the third piece of advice to the disciples, "restrain your children from recitation (parading a superficial knowledge of the Bible by verbal memorizing)." In their master's last hours his disciples ask him for a summing up of his wisdom and experience.

124. *Sanhedrin* 101a. Rabbah bar Bar Hana was a Babylonian *amora* of

the third generation. Rashi explains Rabbi Eliezer's opening words to his disciples as referring to himself. God must be very angry with him to have caused him such pain. But Graetz, in *Geschichte* 4:47, thinks that the reference is to Trajan's forthcoming attack on the Jews of various countries in 116–117 C.E. Rabbi Akiba's statement was that since his master was so wealthy, an owner of landed property, and prosperous in so many areas, his reward was already given him in this world with none for him in the world to come. But since he saw his pain he was comforted that his master's reward was awaiting him in the next world. Whereupon Rabbi Eliezer asked him what sins he could have committed to be expiated by the pain he was now suffering. To which Rabbi Akiba answered that you yourself have taught us the verse from Ecclesiastes, that there is no righteous person on earth who does only good and never sins.

125. *Sanhedrin* 101a–b, *Sifre on Deuteronomy* 32. Rabbis Joshua and Eleazar ben Azariah were contemporaries of Rabbi Eliezer, while Rabbis Tarfon and Akiba were younger and properly belong to the next generation. Rabbi Akiba makes the point that suffering not only leads a person to God but also makes atonement for the sufferer. The fact that "the men of Hezekiah" copied the proverbs of Solomon implies that they did so for the instruction of the people generally. Therefore, Manasseh, son of Hezekiah, certainly must have received instruction. Rabbi Akiba alone gives meaning to Rabbi Eliezer's suffering for, unlike his colleagues, he does not praise his master but instead makes clear the benefits of suffering that can bring results that even learning cannot produce.

126. *Sanhedrin* 68a, *Yerushalmi Shabbat* 2:7 (5b), *Ecclesiastes Rabbah* 6:1f., *Avot de-Rabbi Natan* 25:3 (27a). The story as told here largely follows the account in *Sanhedrin* with elements added from the other sources. It is only in *Sanhedrin* that Rabbi Akiba replied to Hyrcanus, son of Rabbi Eliezer, who is upset that his father's mind has become deranged. In all the other sources it is Rabbi Eliezer who replied to his son to tell him, in anger, that it is he, Hyrcanus, whose mind is deranged. Hyrcanus tried to remove his father's *tefillin* since the Sabbath was fast approaching and phylacteries are not worn on the Sabbath. But his father was more concerned that the Sabbath lights had not yet been kindled, nor had the Sabbath meal been put away to keep it hot. To do these things after the Sabbath had begun would be a violation of Scriptural law and even punishable by death at the hands of Heaven, while the wearing of *tefillin* on the Sabbath would be a violation only of a rabbinic prohibition.

The sages sat at a distance of four cubits from Rabbi Eliezer—a cubit is 49.5 to 52.5 cm.—because Rabbi Eliezer had been excommunicated. The question asked by Rabbi Eliezer, "And why have you not visited me more often?" is based on the text in *Avot de-Rabbi Natan*. Rabbi Eliezer was complaining about his long isolation after his excommunication. The sages endeavored to mollify him with their answer. Rabbi Eliezer predicts their unnatural death, with Rabbi Akiba's the worst. This was realized under Hadrian with the failure of the Bar Kokhba rebellion against Rome. All this would happen because of their disrespect to their teacher and their failure to visit him frequently when he could have taught them more of the Torah. His reference to the two scrolls of the Torah that are wrapped up means to say that such scrolls cannot be read or studied; so too his learning, for none of his disciples had come to study with him since he had been under the ban.

With regard to the "deep bright spot," a sign of leprosy, see Leviticus, chap. 13. The final question posed by the sages to Rabbi Eliezer concerned items made of leather, stuffed with hair or cotton. A leather utensil cannot become unclean unless it has a hollow in which something can be placed. The sages argued that since the hollow in these items is made in order to be filled, the items are not receptacles and therefore cannot become unclean. But Rabbi Eliezer maintained that since they do contain a hollow, although it be filled up, they can become unclean. See *Kelim*, chap. 23. In addition, when these items are placed in a ritual bath, the sages' opinion was that the stuffing is foreign matter and must be removed before the immersion. But Rabbi Eliezer felt that the stuffing is an integral part of the item—not foreign matter—and does not invalidate the immersion. That is why he answers "they are restored to their cleanness just as they are," that is, with the stuffing still inside; it does not have to be removed for immersion. Now that he was dying, they wanted to know if he still maintained his opinion. His answer affirmed that the filling is not to be regarded as foreign matter, which must be removed. Thus his answer was that he continued to maintain his views. The amulet served as a charm to ward off illness or evil and was worn about the neck. It contained mystic verses. The leather bag contained false or imitation pearls and was placed on cattle for the same purpose. Small weights were enclosed in leather to preserve them. The sages and Rabbi Eliezer differed about the status of a finished shoe still on the last where it was made. The sages argued that since it was a finished product it was susceptible to uncleanness. Rabbi Eliezer held that until it was removed from the last it was not a finished product and therefore not susceptible to uncleanness.

Rabbi Joshua declared the ban on Rabbi Eliezer lifted, and therefore a stone was not placed upon his coffin as would have been done were the excommunication still in effect (See *Eduyyot* 5:6).

The opening words of Rabbi Akiba's funeral address are a quotation from 2 Kings 2:12, the exclamation of Elisha when he saw his master, the prophet Elijah, being carried off to heaven. When Rabbi Akiba spoke of having many coins but no money changer to take them, he meant that he had many questions regarding Jewish law but now, with Rabbi Eliezer's death, he had no one to answer them.

The last question of the sages to Rabbi Eliezer about the leather items is found also in *Derekh Eretz Rabbah* 3:5 (56b).

127. *Song of Songs Rabbah* 1:3.

128. *Yerushalmi Avodah Zarah* 3:1 (42c) and *Yerushalmi Sotah* 9:16 (24c). The death of a person in a home causes the ritual uncleanness of articles in the home that are susceptible to uncleanness. The text here states that when Rabban Johanan ben Zakkai lay dying he uttered the same words except that he called for a throne to be prepared "for Hezekiah, king of Judah." Hezekiah in rabbinic literature is considered to be a man of unusual piety and even, by some, as the Messiah (see *Sanhedrin* 99a) or he was destined to be the Messiah but was thwarted (*Sanhedrin* 94a).

129. The first statement is found in *Yerushalmi Sotah* 9:16 (24c) and *Tosefta Sotah* 15:3. The same statement is made about the death of Rabban Gamaliel the Elder and Rabbi Akiba (Mishnah *Sotah* 9:15), the former because he loved those who studied Torah, the latter because he delved into every aspect of Torah learning. (I am indebted to Rabbi David Weiss-Halivni for this explanation.) The statement is made about Rabbi Eliezer as a tribute to his great learning. That is also true of the second statement whose source is *Sotah* 49b.

130. *Ecclesiastes Rabbah* 12:11. Our passage is a reconstruction of what is evidently a corrupt text, for most frequently the law followed the opinions of Rabbi Joshua.

Chapter 3

1. *Avot de-Rabbi Natan*, chap. 4. See also the same text, version B, in Solomon Schechter, *Aboth de Rabbi Nathan* (New York, 1967), p. 22. Our text may be found in Judah Goldin, *The Fathers According to Rabbi Nathan* (New Haven, 1955), p. 34. Joshua was a student of Rabban Johanan, one of his five eminent disciples (*Pirkei Avot* 2:10). See my *Legends of the Rabbis* 1:267f. When Rabban Johanan asked his disciples which is "the good way to which a man should cleave?" Rabbi Joshua's answer was to be a good friend (*Pirkei Avot* 2:13). He and Rabbi Eliezer, another disciple, carried Rabban Johanan out of Jerusalem in 70 c.e. during the Roman attack on the city so that their master could intercede with Vespasian for permission to establish an academy of learning at Jabneh (*Legends of the Rabbis* 1:273). Of Rabbi Joshua, Rabban Johanan said, "Happy is she who gave him birth" (*Pirkei Avot* 2:11). He survived both Gamaliel II and Eliezer ben Hyrcanus. He was a singer in the Temple before its destruction by the Romans in 70 c.e., and he was alive in 130 c.e. for he spoke with Emperor Hadrian in that year. He is not mentioned in connection with the Bar Kokhba rebellion (132–135 c.e.), so he must have died before its outbreak.

2. *Derekh Eretz Rabbah* 6:1 (56b–57a), *Kallah Rabbati* 9:1 (54b–55a). The story illustrates the importance placed by the rabbis upon the sanctity of a vow, especially when sworn on the Scriptures. The answer given by Rabbi Joshua to Rabbi Simon is hyperbole and is not to be taken literally. Nothing is known about Rabbi Simon ben Antipatros. There was a town north-north-west of Jerusalem that was founded by Herod the Great and named Antipatris after his father (*Gittin* 76a) – the second "t" is occasionally dropped. The town was on the border between Judea and Galilee. The opening statement in the story may be found in *Pesahim* 86b. Rabbi Joshua was concerned that Rabbi Simon might smite him upon his thighs because his reply to the question about going to the bathhouse was not strongly affirmative and Simon's reputation had alerted him. An entire tractate in the Talmud is devoted to the laws pertaining to vows.

3. *Yerushalmi Hagigah* 2:1 (77b). Rabbi Judah ben Pazzi's full name is Rabbi Judah ben Rabbi Simon ben Pazzi, as is found in the Babylonian Talmud wherever the name is mentioned. He was an early *amora* and here he quotes Rabbi Jose ben Judah, a fifth-generation *tanna*, his father being Rabbi Judah ben Ilai. The "Work of Creation" is a subject of ancient Jewish mysticism. At an early date this mysticism began to be viewed with suspicion. More will be said when we deal with Rabbi Eleazar ben Arakh, Ben Zoma, and Rabbi Akiba. See "The Origin of Jewish Mysticism," pp. 93–105 in Leo Baeck, *The Pharisees and Other Essays* (New York, 1947).

4. *Sukkah* 53a, *Tosefta Sukkah* 4:5, the latter quoted also in *Yerushalmi Sukkah* 5:2 (55b). Rabbi Joshua was a Levite and when he was very young he served in the Temple among the singers (see *Arakhin* 11b). Here he describes how busy was the day in the Temple, especially during *Simhat Bet ha-Shoevah* during the Sukkot festival when there took place a joyous procession to and from the well from which the water was drawn for libation on the festival. The procession was accompanied by music. The Talmud reports (*Sukkah* 51a) that he who has not witnessed this celebration has never seen real rejoicing.

5. *Pesahim* 49a. A sample of Rabbi Joshua's humor. The *kohen*, the priest or descendant of the priests who served in the Temple, stood on the top rung of the societal ladder, the levite, as was Rabbi Joshua, on the next

rung. The priests had a reputation for *hauteur* (see *Eduyyot* 8:7 or *Bekhorot* 30b).

6. *Bava Batra* 60b, *Midrash Tehillim* 137:6 and *Tosefta Sotah* 15:11–14. The latter differs somewhat in that specific fruits are mentioned—figs and grapes, and the reason for not eating bread is because two loaves of bread used to be brought as an offering and on the Sabbath the showbread was brought. The verse from Malachi is understood to mean that the Jewish people laid upon itself the vow to bring the tithe. It would not have been effective unless the entire people had done so. Therefore a hardship is not placed upon a people unless it be certain that the majority at least can tolerate it. The passage in *Bava Batra* continues, showing how one should mourn for the loss of the Temple; when a person stuccos his house he should leave a small part unstuccoed; a full-course meal should omit something; a woman may adorn herself with much jewelry but not with all of it; ashes should be placed upon the head of a bridegroom.

Rabbi Joshua's final declaration may be regarded as the authoritative view of the rabbis with regard to the destruction of the Temple and the loss of Jerusalem (see Baron, *A Social and Religious History of the Jews* 2:112). Rabbi Ishmael, who belonged to the generation after Rabbi Joshua, echoed his words in *Tosefta Sotah* 15:10 as well as in *Bava Batra* 60b.

7. Mishnah *Sotah* 3:4. A pious fool out of false modesty and ill-considered piety would not rescue a naked woman from drowning. A clever knave by shrewd logical arguments can attempt to confuse and mislead a judge. Rabbi Joshua objects here to the wife whose "piety expressed itself in a reluctance to normal marital life as degrading or impure" (Finkelstein, *The Pharisees* 2:837 n. 52).

8. Mishnah *Sotah* 9:12 and *Midrash Tanhuma, Tetzaveh* 13. Even though Rabbi Joshua warned against mourning excessively for the loss of the Temple, in this passage we see how deep was his grief. The very course of nature has been altered by the great tragedy. See Baron, *A Social and Religious History of the Jews* 2:111–112. The passage in *Tanhuma* includes a proof-text, *God pronounces doom each day* (Psalms 7:12). Rabbi Simon ben Gamaliel who quoted Rabbi Joshua in Mishnah *Sotah* was the second by that name and was active two generations after Rabbi Joshua.

9. *Eruvin* 41a. Rabbi Joshua was opposed to the Shammaitic tendencies of both the patriarch, Rabban Gamaliel II, and of his contemporary, Rabbi Eliezer ben Hyrcanus. For example, Rabbi Joshua was more considerate of proselytes and the poor. As Baron writes, "An artisan of limited means, he dealt with the patriarch on equal terms and boldly led his school of thought against that headed by R. Eliezer ben Hyrcanus, one of the country's richest landowners" (see Baron, *A Social and Religious History of the Jews* 2:276).

10. *Sanhedrin* 32b. Rabbi Joshua left the academy at Jabneh to establish his own school at Pekiin, a town between Jabneh and Lod (Lydda). Teaching was his principal occupation there but he earned his livelihood as a needlemaker (*Yerushalmi Berakhot* 4:1 [7d]) or/and a blacksmith (*Berakhot* 27b–28a). The interpretation of the verse implies that in order to pursue justice one must first learn the laws at an academy. The full text includes other academies as well.

11. *Derekh Eretz Rabbah* 5:3 (56b), *Kallah Rabbati* 9:1 (54b–55a). The point made here is that one should be on guard with all strangers but yet show them the highest respect. The *Gemara* in the latter text asks, "But it is not so! For we have learned, 'Do not judge your fellow human being until

you be in his position' (*Pirkei Avot* 2:5)." The answer is given that there is no contradiction. The statement in *Avot* refers to a person whom you know, while our passage concerns a person whom you do not know.

12. *Pesikta de-Rav Kahana,* supplement 5:2. The Fathers, of course, are Abraham, Isaac, and Jacob; the mothers, Sarah, Rebecca, Leah, and Rachel. Those Jews in ancient times who wished to disappear as Jews and to become Greek or Roman restored their foreskins, thus erasing the sign of the covenant with God begun by Abraham (Genesis 17:10). The Fathers and Mothers, except for Rachel, were buried in the Cave of Makhpelah in Hebron (see Genesis chap. 23). *In re* Jonadab ben Rechab, see Louis Ginzberg's *Legends of the Jews* 3:380.

13. *Sanhedrin* 97b–98a. Rabbi Eliezer argues that only when the Jewish people repent of their wrongdoing will God redeem them and restore them to their land. Rabbi Joshua, in the second-quoted source, maintains that the Messiah will come to redeem the Jewish people when their position in the world will have fallen to its lowest point, whether they will have repented or not. Rabbi Joshua's position was that of those Jews in the Middle Ages who followed the false Messiahs such as Shabbetai Zevi. The last quotation from Daniel was a clincher in that it simply predicts the redemption at the end of a certain period of time with no mention of repentance.

14. *Pirkei de Rabbi Eliezer,* chap. 43 (60a). In the previous passage Rabbi Joshua affirms that at a certain time the Messiah will come—when Jewish suffering will be at its worst—whether or not the Jews will all repent. However, that does not in the least minimize his appreciation of the importance of repentance, as this passage indicates. See also *Sanhedrin* 10:2, 101b and 103a, and *Yerushalmi Sanhedrin* 10:2 (28c). The first editions read "the leaders of the troops of the king of Assyria," which is supported by 2 Chronicles 33:11. That verse, however, does say that Manasseh was carried off to Babylon, then a province of the world empire of Assyria. Later Babylonia succeeded Assyria as the ruling power of the Middle East. Manasseh's father, King Hezekiah, prayed to God when Assyria's armies stood at the walls of Jerusalem and the Assyrian troops did not take the city (Isaiah 37). He prayed again when he fell dangerously ill and he recovered (Isaiah 38). See the Prayer of Manasseh in *The Jewish Encyclopedia* 8: 281. The Prayer of Manasseh, a Greek poetic composition, though found in Latin translation in some Vulgate manuscripts, was never recognized as canonical by the Church, but was accepted by Luther and is included in the authorized English version of the Apocrypha. Dove or pigeon flyers, like dice players, are not permitted to serve as witnesses or judges (Mishnah *Sanhedrin* 3:3).

15. *Midrash on Psalms* 9:15, *Tosefta Sanhedrin* 13:2. The word *Sheol* means the netherworld, the realm of the dead, Hades, hell. The position of Rabbi Joshua, in contradistinction to that of Rabbi Eliezer, is that only the wicked of the nations of the world—like the wicked among the Jews—will descend after death to *Sheol.*

16. *Tosefta Sanhedrin* 13:1. Rabbi Joshua believed that the righteous of all peoples have a share in the world to come. Of course, Rabban Gamaliel here is Rabban Gamaliel II of Jabneh.

17. *Ecclesiastes Rabbah* 1:6 and *Leviticus Rabbah* 15:1. The proof-text from Isaiah is difficult in the Hebrew. The 1978 Jewish Publication Society translation states "the meaning of the Hebrew is uncertain" and renders the verse as *Nay, I who make spirits flag,/Also create the breath of life.* The 1917 J.P.S. translation has it as *For the spirit that enwrappeth itself is from Me,/And the souls which I have made.* In our midrashic passage the word *ya'atof* is translated

"becomes faint" based on the same verb in the reflexive mode found in Jonah 2:8, *hitatef*, which the earlier J.P.S. version translates as "fainted"—*When my soul fainted within me*. The point of the quotation of the verse from Isaiah in our text is that since God made the souls of human beings, He protects them from the violence of nature's forces.

18. *Pirkei Avot* 2:16. "The evil eye" has been explained by commentators in various ways: an envious disposition, stinginess, a begrudging person, one dissatisfied with his lot, a passion for wealth. "The inclination to do evil" is the impulse within each individual to do wrong, side by side with the impulse to do good. Both are natural instincts within the human being and the person is to so train himself as to follow his good impulse and not his evil inclination. Hatred of one's fellow human beings is the very opposite of what Jews have been taught, *Love your neighbor as yourself* (Leviticus 19:18). "Drive a person out of the world" means either shorten a person's life or cut that person off from human society, driving him out of the world of human relationships.

19. Mishnah *Sotah* 3:4. A *kab* is a dry measure equaling four *logs* and one *log* equals the contents of six eggs, about 33.4 cubic inches.

20. *Yevamot* 62b and *Avot de-Rabbi Natan* 3:6–7 (19b). Rabbi Joshua was not advocating polygamy here for although there was no legal prohibition against it in talmudic times, the rabbis had a strong aversion to it. Of all the rabbis mentioned in the Talmud there is not one who is described as having more than one wife. It was not until the time of Rabbi Gershom, "the Light of the Exile," 960–1028, that polygamy was expressly forbidden, although his decree was accepted only by Ashkenazic Jews. Rabbi Joshua was urging men to remarry after a first marriage was terminated by death or divorce. He explained that perhaps the children of one's later years may be better than those of the earlier years. The actual words of Ecclesiastes 11:6 are *if both are equally good*. Similarly, do not hesitate to perform a *mitzvah* again during the course of a day because one never knows which *mitzvah* will stand him in good stead in the future. A *perutah* was the lowest copper coin available.

21. *Ecclesiastes Rabbah* 5:5. The thought expressed here is that one should be very careful with his speech. One should not speak needlessly or without thought. Like jewels, speech should be guarded. There were groups of Jews in Lithuania in the *musar* movement of the nineteenth century who took it upon themselves not to speak at all for days. Professor Louis Ginzberg once did not speak for forty days. This teaching of Rabbi Joshua may be based on Ecclesiastes 5:5. It is reminiscent of the Yiddish expression, *A rendel a vort* and the proverb, "Silence is golden." A *sela* was equal to two *shekels* or four *dinars* or 768 *perutahs*.

22. *Tosefta Ahilot* 16:6, *Tosefta Parah* 4:7, *Sanhedrin* 99a–b. Studies were transmitted orally and therefore when one learned something it had to be repeated again and again and perhaps organized with other teachings on the same or a similar subject in order to be safely committed to memory. This held until the end of the second century of the Common Era when Rabbi Judah ha-Nasi collected the oral law and redacted the vast body of tradition into the Mishnah. The prior collections of Rabbi Akiba and Rabbi Meir were available to him. The second statement is from the Midrash on Proverbs, chap. 1, near the beginning. It is not certain that this reading is correct or whether the reverse is the correct text. The text is a comment on Job 28:12.

23. *Mekhilta Vayassa*, chap. 3. The rabbis were aware that not every farmer or artisan could spend all day in study as they did. But they were anxious that they devote at least a little time in study before and after the

working day. One is reminded of the *shtiblakh,* the small chapels of the various tradesmen and craftsmen in Vilna and other Lithuanian cities to which the workers would repair at the end of the day to enjoy an hour or two in study of the Talmud. See also Alon, *The Jews in Their Land in the Talmudic Age* 2:530.

24. *Genesis Rabbah* 17:8. Rabbi Joshua's answers are hardly scientific! It is not news to say that women were considered inferior to men in ancient cultures. If anything, the status of women in ancient Judaism was higher than that of women in other contemporary cultures. The questions reveal some interesting practices of Rabbi Joshua's time: Jewish men would go out bareheaded! For women walking in front of a corpse in a funeral procession, see *Sanhedrin* 20a. The assumption is that Adam and Eve would have lived forever but Eve persuaded Adam to eat of the fruit of the tree of knowledge and the punishment was that death came into the world. See Genesis 2:17 and 3:19. In the verse from Job the words, *innumerable are those who precede him,* are taken to refer to women and not in a temporal sense. For the separation of dough when baking bread, see Numbers 15:18–21. Jewish women sanctify the bread eaten by the family and spread the cheer of the Sabbath as symbolized by the light they kindle at its onset.

25. *Yerushalmi Sotah* 9:15 (24c), *Yerushalmi Peah* 1:1 (16b), *Tosefta Avodah Zarah* 1:20, *Midrash on Psalms* 1:17. The second paragraph in our text comes from the last-cited source. The sources vary as to the initial question asked of Rabbi Joshua. The two *Yerushalmi* sources say the question is as we have phrased it—about teaching one's son the Greek language. The *Tosefta* states the question as, "What is the law as to a man teaching his son a book in Greek?" The *Midrash on Psalms* puts it this way, "At what time may a father teach his son the wisdom of the Greeks?" The answer is at no time since one is to be occupied both day and night with the study of the Torah. The study of the Torah is to be without limit and it should take all one's time. The text in both *Yerushalmi Peah* and *Sotah* following our passage speaks of Jewish informers who would spy on their own people for the Romans and therefore it would appear that the subject of our passage should properly be a prohibition against teaching one's son the Greek language rather than a Greek book or Greek wisdom. Familiarity with the Greek language might enable someone to pass treasonous information to the Roman authorities occupying the land of Israel. Rabbi Joshua's stricture against Greek runs counter to what is known about the realities among Jews in the first centuries of the Common Era. See Saul Lieberman, *Greek in Jewish Palestine.* In the introduction he writes, "The Greek language was known to the Jewish masses; certain formulas of oriental Graeco-Roman law were popular among them in the original language; the current motifs of Hellenistic literature may have infiltrated into them, but real Greek culture was probably scarce in Jewish Palestine" (p. 2). Lieberman also writes, "The Jewish leaders felt that not only is 'Greek Wisdom' indispensable for proper relations with the Roman government but that Greek philosophy is a useful instrument in religious discussions, especially with the Gentile Christians who became more and more influential" (p. 1). See also Alon, *The Jews in Their Land in the Talmudic Age* 1:138, 2:714; G. F. Moore, *Judaism in the First Centuries of the Christian Era* 1:48; and Baron, *A Social and Religious History of the Jews* 2:141f. Rabban Gamaliel II, at the end of the first century C.E., maintained at his patriarchal court a school for a thousand children, of whom "five hundred studied the Torah and the other five hundred were trained in Greek wisdom (*Sotah* 49b)." Rabbi Judah ha-Nasi at the end of the second century agreed

that Jews may teach their sons Greek (*Yerushalmi Avodah Zarah* 2:2 [40d]). *Tosefta Avodah Zarah* 3:5 replaces the name of Rabbi Judah ha-Nasi with that of Rabban Gamaliel. But Rabbi Ishmael of the first half of the second century agreed with Rabbi Joshua that it is prohibited to teach Greek wisdom to one's son and quoted the same proof-text used by Rabbi Joshua (*Menahot* 99b). However, a daughter may be taught Greek because "it is a jewel for her" (*Yerushalmi Peah* 1:1). See "Greek Language and the Jews" in *The Jewish Encyclopedia* 6:85ff.

Rabbi Joshua's statement that a father should not even take time away from Torah study with his son to teach him a craft is contradicted by the majority opinion of the rabbis. They say that a father is obliged to teach his son a handicraft by which he could earn his living; Rabbi Akiba adds even to teach him to swim (*Kiddushin* 29a-b and 30a; *Tosefta Kiddushin* 1:11; *Yerushalmi Kiddushin* 1:7 [61a]; *Midrash Tanhuma, Shelah* 26). The occupations of many rabbis are mentioned in the Talmud; see *The Jewish Encyclopedia* 10:294f.

26. *Exodus Rabbah* 21:2 and 28:8 on *Exodus* 14:15.

27. *Exodus Rabbah* 23:9. In the *haggadah* of Passover this statement is attributed to Rabbi Jose the Galilean, a contemporary of Rabbi Joshua.

28. *Ecclesiastes Rabbah* 4:3. What we have here is an ingenious word play in which common words like wrath, destruction, annihilation, anger, and fury are personified and given their Hebrew names. It should be noted that elsewhere *Hemah* is an allegorical name of an angel of justice. Abraham's question, after God tells him that his descendants will inherit the Promised Land, shows a lack of faith in God. What this *midrash* teaches is that it took both God's compassion and Moses' efforts to rescue the people of Israel and save them from disaster.

29. *Zevahim* 116a–b. Modiim was the native town of the Hasmoneans, some fifteen miles northwest of Jerusalem. Rabbi Eleazar of Modiim was a contemporary of Rabbi Joshua. The pagan kings were moved to sing a song of reverence to God. The new J.P.S. translation replaces "palace" with "temple" in Psalms 29:9. In Genesis 9:11 God swears that He will not again destroy all flesh by the waters of a flood. For more information about *mabbul shel aish*, "a flood of fire," see Louis Ginzberg's article, "*Mabbul shel aish*," in his *Al halakhah ve-aggadah* (Tel Aviv, 1960), edited by this writer, pp. 205–214. The Torah is the treasure that God has given Israel and it is Israel's strength. The Midrash says it existed before Creation and God consulted in His work of creating the world. See *Genesis Rabbah* 1:1, *Song of Songs Rabbah* 5:11. Rabbi Eleazar ben Azariah was another contemporary of Rabbi Joshua. Since "heard" in his proof-text refers to the drying up of waters, it has a similar connotation with reference to Jethro.

30. *Exodus Rabbah* 2:4. Rabbi Joshua details the various gifts given to the Children of Israel in the wilderness of Sinai. For the well see Numbers 21:16–17. The *Shekhinah*, God's presence, was close to them in the desert. *In re* the manna and quail see Exodus 16. God called Israel *a kingdom of priests and a holy nation* (Exodus 19:6). The construction of the Tabernacle is described in Exodus 25–27, 35–38. See Exodus 13:21f. for the divine cloud.

31. *Midrash Tanhuma* on Genesis 10:16. See also *Genesis Rabbah* 92:1 and *Berakhot* 5a. If God disciplines a person but he is still able to study Torah, then the discipline has been blended with mercy and the person is blessed. But if the person be unable to study Torah, then divine mercy has been withdrawn and the discipline is that of punishment.

32. *Genesis Rabbah* 57:4. A rather farfetched conjecture.

33. *Mekhilta, Vayassa*, chap. 2. The agricultural output of the land of

Israel suffered under the unfavorable political conditions of Roman occupation. The armies of Vespasian and Hadrian inflicted deep wounds upon the country. Inflation was rampant. Recurrent famines were caused by difficulties of transportation more than by failures of crops. See Baron, *A Social and Religious History of the Jews* 2:245.

34. *Genesis Rabbah* 82:8. Alon, in *The Jews in Their Land in the Talmudic Age* 2:648f., quotes this source and dates this text in the time following the defeat of Bar Kokhba and his forces (135 C.E.). He writes, "the harsh suffering that followed created a mood of despair among many of the survivors. There must have been many who abandoned their Jewish identity . . . for not everyone had the fortitude to resist the prolonged religious persecution." Alon points to the apostate soldier in our text, a member of the occupying forces, "apparently himself a former student of Rabbi Joshua ben Hananiah." The Hebrew of "sons of the Torah" really means those who have amassed much learning in Jewish studies and who constantly devote themselves to it. The apostate soldier taunts the students of Rabbi Joshua and challenges them to show the courage that he himself did not possess.

35. *Song of Songs Rabbah* 6:10. Rabbi Joshua is evidently commenting on the fear felt by the Jews during his time because of the commanding officers of the Roman occupying forces.

36. *Eduyyot* 8:7. Simon ben Johai is of the fourth generation of *tannaim*. Elijah is to be the forerunner of the Messiah.

37. *Perek Hashalom* 59a-b. The literal translation of the close of the Exodus verse is "we will do and obey." The word "strength" in the verse from Psalms is taken to mean a synonym for Torah. Much has been written about the contrasting roles of the priest and the prophet. For example, see the striking essay by Ahad Ha'am, *Kohen ve-navi*, "Priest and Prophet," in his *Al perashat ha-derakhim*, vol. 1 (Berlin, 1921), or in Leon Simon, editor, *Selected Essays* (Philadelphia, 1936), pp. 125–138. Here Rabbi Joshua states that despite their differences, both priest and prophet are messengers of the Lord.

38. *Ecclesiastes Rabbah* 7:8. Aquila, according to *The Jewish Encyclopedia* 2:34ff., "was by birth a Gentile from Pontus, and is said by Epiphanius to have been a connection by marriage of the emperor Hadrian and to have been appointed by him about the year 128 C.E. to an office concerned with the rebuilding of Jerusalem as 'Aelia Capitolina.' " He was at first converted by the Christians but left them to become a proselyte to Judaism. His teachers, according to the Talmud, were Rabbi Eliezer, Rabbi Joshua, and Rabbi Akiba. His translation of the Hebrew Scriptures into Greek was widely used in the ancient world. Eusebius, in *The History of the Church*, refers to it on pp. 212 and 256. "For the sake of heaven" is an idiomatic phrase meaning for pure unadulterated motive. Leviticus 24:5ff. tells of the showbread. His students thought that Rabbi Joshua's first answer to Aquila was too fanciful.

39. *Midrash on Psalms* 104:4. The effort is made here to explain why the author of the Psalms had to use the comparative form of the adjective, "very great," instead of using the simple adjective, "great." God cannot be compared to any other being. Rabbi Berekhiah, an *amora*, quotes both Rabbi Eleazar ben Azariah and Rabbi Joshua ben Hananiah, *tannaim* of the second generation.

40. *Genesis Rabbah* 13:6. "Gentile" here probably means a heathen, not a member of the new Christians. The fact that the meadows were covered by flocks of sheep means that rain had fallen, resulting in much fresh green grass upon which the sheep were feeding.

41. *Numbers Rabbah* 14:4. Rabbi Johanan ben Beroka was, like Rabbi Joshua, a second-generation *tanna*. He took literally the verse from Leviticus

that on Sukkot the obligation to use the citron (*etrog*), the palm branch (*lulav*), myrtle twigs (*hadas*), and the willow branches (*aravot*) during services fell only on the first day of the festival, and rabbinic injunction extended it through the remaining days of the holiday. Rabbi Simon ben Halafta was a *tanna* of the sixth generation. The verse from Ecclesiastes is taken to mean that both the Scriptures and rabbinic law have been given by God, for the latter ultimately has its roots in the former.

42. *Leviticus Rabbah* 28:5. The Israelites were told to bring the first sheaf of the spring harvest to the priest. Rabbi Hama ben Ukba was an *amora* of the third generation, the student of Rabbi Jose ben Hanina. The ceremony of the sheaf waving together with the burnt offering, the meal offering, and the libation (Leviticus 23:13) were to take place in gratitude on the first day of Passover. Seven weeks later the Feast of Weeks would be celebrated—on the fiftieth day.

43. *Yerushalmi Nedarim* 8:1 (40d). Although Hanukkah is a minor festival, one is not to fast during the holiday. The fast here may have been proclaimed in prayer for rain or in repentance for wrongdoing. Rabbi Joshua told the people in Lod (Lydda) that they had done wrong in having fasted on Hanukkah, and he ordered that they fast after the festival as punishment.

44. *Exodus Rabbah* 30:20. This text is somewhat reminiscent of the teaching of Rabbi Hananiah ben Akashyah, a fourth-generation *tanna*, found in Mishnah *Makkot* 3:16, which is repeated at the end of each chapter of *Pirkei Avot*. The scriptural portion referred to here is *Mishpatim*, Exodus 21:1-24:18, a portion that includes various kinds of laws: civil, criminal, torts, etc. The story of Balaam is told in Numbers 22-25, of Doeg in 1 Samuel 21- 22, of Ahithophel in 2 Samuel 15-17, of Gehazi in 2 Kings 4-5 and 8. These four individuals are cited in *Sanhedrin* 90a as having no share in the world-to-come.

45. *Yerushalmi Yevamot* 1:6 (3a). Rabbi Dosa Ben Harkinas (sometimes Hyrcanus and in the *Yerushalmi* usually Arkinas) was, of course, older than Rabbi Joshua and his name is even linked with that of Rabban Johanan ben Zakkai, as in *Ketubbot* 13:1. This passage is the reason for the statement in *Pirkei Avot* 2:11, "Rabbi Joshua ben Hananiah—blessed be she who bore him."

46. *Song of Songs Rabbah* 1:1 on verse 1:3. At first glance this statement and an almost identical one preceding it in the Midrash by Rabbi Eliezer seem highly immodest. But the thrust here is not to tell of the great learning of these sages but of the infinite content of the Torah. No matter how extraordinary be the learning of anyone, there is so much more to be studied. Even the greatest scholar has taken from the potential knowledge of the Torah only the amount equal to what a pencil can take from the ocean when dipped into it. Rabbi Akiba, in the same passage, says that he cannot match his teachers, for they did take something from the Torah while he has taken no more than one takes from a citron when smelling it.

47. *Gittin* 48a, *Lamentations Rabbah* 4:2, *Yerushalmi Horayot* 3:4 (48b), *Tosefta Horayot* 2:5-6. The last two sources end with "And concerning him Scripture has said, *The precious children of Zion;/Once valued as gold—/Alas, they are accounted as earthen pots,/Work of a potter's hands* (Lamentations 4:2)! When it became urgent to plead at Rome the case of the Jews of the Land of Israel, Rabban Gamaliel of Jabneh and Rabbi Eleazar ben Azariah, the two heads of the Academy, led the delegation that included Rabbi Joshua ben Hananiah and Rabbi Akiba, the youngest of them all. A second purpose for visiting Rome was to strengthen relationships with the Jewish community there,

occupying so important a geographical place at the seat of the Roman Empire. There must have been a series of visits to Rome by the sages of that generation; on the earlier ones Rabban Gamaliel, the Patriarch, was accompanied by Rabbi Eliezer and Rabbi Joshua, while on the later journeys Rabbi Eleazar ben Azariah and Rabbi Akiba also went. The several journeys are mentioned in *Deuteronomy Rabbah* 2:24, *Yerushalmi Sanhedrin* 7 (25d); *Maaser Sheni* 5:9, *Tosefta Betzah* 2:3, Sifre on Deuteronomy 43 and parallel passages. See Lieberman, *Tosefta Kifshuto* 5:955 and Alon, *The Jews in Their Land in the Talmudic Age* 1:124–131. The latter points out that it is impossible to fix exact dates for the several missions to Rome except to say they took place after the time of the Flavian emperors (96 C.E.) and before the outbreak of the Bar Kokhba revolt against Rome in c. 132 C.E. Finkelstein, in *The Pharisees* 1: cxxxi, writes, "These scholars . . . wished to impress on the Imperial government the distinction between the Pharisaic practice of their faith and the warlike nationalism that had led to the rebellion against Rome."

48. *Yerushalmi Sanhedrin* 7:13 (25d). This is an unusual story, telling, as it does, of the practice of magic by a renowned rabbi. Official Judaism had long denounced belief in magic or sorcery, the Pentateuch even ordering capital punishment for its practitioners (Exodus 22:17 and Deuteronomy 18:10–11). But foreign influences, the Chaldean astral religion, and Egyptian practices of magic and sorcery had their effect upon Jews. See Baron, *A Social and Religious History of the Jews* 2:15–23. Lieberman, in *Greek in Jewish Palestine*, pp. 97–114, shows how the sages reinterpreted a number of practices of magical and superstitious origin. The Rabbi Judah ben Batyra mentioned at the end of this story is the second by that name. He was a *tanna* of the third generation and in Mishnah *Ohalot* 11:7 he differs with Rabbi Eleazar ben Shammua, while in *Bekhorot* 55a he differs with Rabbi Simon ben Johai. The first Rabbi Judah ben Batyra was a contemporary of Rabbi Joshua, Rabbi Eliezer, and Rabban Gamaliel of Jabneh.

49. *Sanhedrin* 90b. This page in the Talmud and page 90a contain an anonymous answer to the question asking for scriptural proof for the resurrection of the dead, as well as answers by (*seriatim*) Rabbi Simai, Rabban Gamaliel II, Rabbi Joshua ben Hananiah, Rabbi Eliezer ben Rabbi Jose, and others. The books of the Bible vary in their views as to what happens after the death of a human being. One can find the opinion that the dead go down into a netherworld (*Sheol*) where they live a colorless existence. Only an occasional person might escape and be taken to heaven where God dwelled. In the book of Job there is expressed a longing for resurrection (14:13–15). The Psalmist believed that the wicked went to *Sheol* and the souls of the righteous went directly to God. The hope for a Messiah encouraged the belief in resurrection so that more would share in the Messianic kingdom (Isaiah 26:19, Daniel 12:1–4). In the Apocryphal books of Pharisaic origin one finds a belief in resurrection. Rabbinic arguments for resurrection are found in *Sanhedrin* 90b–92b, and both the Pharisees and the Essenes believed in it. The Sadducees rejected belief in resurrection (*Sanhedrin* 90b, *Avot de-Rabbi Natan* 5, Josephus, *Antiquities* 18:1:4, and *Wars of the Jews* 2:8:14, Acts 23:8 ["For the Sadducees say that there is no resurrection, neither angel, nor spirit . . ."]). The Pharisees emphasized their belief in resurrection as a fundamental conviction (*Sanhedrin* 10:1, see also *Pirkei Avot* 4:22 and *Sotah* 9:15) and placed it in the *Shemoneh Esreh*, "The Prayer," as the second blessing. The Hebrew of the verse quoted by Rabbi Joshua would indicate that the question of the Romans is in order. The cantillation of the verse also supports their question. But Rabbi Joshua is joined by Rabbi Simon and

Rabban Gamaliel II in the use of this proof-text, while other rabbis chose different proof-texts.

50. *Genesis Rabbah* 28:3, *Leviticus Rabbah* 18:1, and *Ecclesiastes Rabbah* 12:5. The question is, From what part of the body will the dead grow into a living being at the time of the resurrection? The answer is, From the coccyx, the small triangular bone at the lowest part of the spinal column. Even if the rest of the body disintegrates in the earth this will remain intact and will be the starting point for the body's restructuring of itself at the resurrection. The passage in *Ecclesiastes Rabbah* feels it is not enough to say of Hadrian, "May his bones rot!" and therefore adds "And may his name be obliterated!" Hadrian, the ward of Trajan, was ruler of the Roman Empire from 117 to 138 C.E. and during his latter years the Jews revolted against him under the leadership of Bar Kokhba and Rabbi Akiba. His response was a massive slaughter of the Jewish rebels and the tortured death of the rabbis.

51. *Shabbat* 119a. The emperor is Hadrian.

52. *Genesis Rabbah* 10:3. Rabbi Joshua's answer is that the universe spread inwards from the six balls that were set on its outer limits. Hadrian wondered at the reply, doubting whether God could really place the balls at such widely separated points. Rabbi Joshua explained to him that just as he, the emperor, could easily touch the walls of the small room, so God could encompass the four corners of the earth as well as above and below.

53. *Hullin* 59b–60a. In all the stories telling of conversations between Rabbi Joshua and the emperor, the latter is Hadrian.

54. *Hullin* 59b. Amos uses the metaphor of a lion roaring and the consequent fear simply to show cause and effect. Hence, if God speaks to the prophet, he must prophesy. He was not comparing God to a lion. Rashi explains the word, "Be-Ilai," as a forest by this name, but according to Jastrow it refers to the mountains of interior Asia (p. 520, top of first column). A parasang is an ancient Persian measure of length equal to about three and a half miles, in Persian, *farsang*.

55. *Hullin* 60a. Rebita, some say, is the name of a river, but others suggest that it is an area on the shore of the Mediterranean.

56. *Taanit* 7a-b and *Nedarim* 50b. In the latter source the emperor is not mentioned. His daughter carries on the dialogue with Rabbi Joshua after the royal wine was spoiled. Evidently Rabbi Joshua was not handsome.

57. *Hullin* 60a. Lepers were given skeins of wool and spools on which to wind the wool so that they would have something to do while sitting in the open square of Rome, the object of the glances of all passersby.

58. *Genesis Rabbah* 78:1 and *Lamentations Rabbah* 3:23. As we have observed earlier, the imprecation frequently follows Hadrian's name because of the great sufferings of the Jews during his reign, especially during and after the Bar Kokhba War. The "river of fire" is mentioned in Daniel 7:10. The *Hayyot*, literally, "the living creatures," are the celestial beings described in the first chapter of Ezekiel. Bet Peor was the site of an idolatrous shrine, a town on one of the hills overlooking the lower valley of the Jordan. See Deuteronomy 3:29.

59. *Hagigah* 5b. The word *min* used in the text is usually applied to a Judaeo-Christian, a Jew who has joined the new Christians. Christian censors often had the word replaced in the text by "Sadducee" or *"Kuti."*

60. *Esther Rabbah* 10:11. Of course, the sheep is the Jewish people, the seventy wolves are the nations of the world, and the shepherd is God. Hadrian desires to praise the Jews for having survived the attacks upon them by so many peoples of ancient times but Rabbi Joshua retorts that the praise is due God for having preserved them.

61. *Ecclesiastes Rabbah* 2:8. See earlier note for the reason for calling Hadrian "accursed." Nizhana is mentioned nowhere else. It may be a corrupted form of Nazareth. Sidon was a Phoenician town, Akhbrin, a town in upper Galilee, and Gush *Halav* or Giscala in Galilee. "Others say from Akhbrin" because that town was in the Land of Israel described in the proof-text, while Sidon was not.

62. *Ecclesiastes Rabbah* 9:4 and *Ruth Rabbah* 3:2. The story has Hadrian quoting Scripture! Of course, Jewish law permits—even mandates—the violation of the Sabbath for the purpose of saving a life.

63. *Pesikta Rabbati* 21:3. See also *Arakhin* 13b and *Midrash on Psalms* 81:13. This passage is linked with Psalm 92:4, *with an instrument of ten strings, with the psaltery,* but the Hebrew is translated instead, "For me the ten (commandments), for me the obloquy." In addition to having journeyed to Rome (note 47) with other scholars, Rabbi Joshua witnessed Hadrian's visit to the Land of Israel, and he followed him to Alexandria in 130 c.e. The conversations between Rabbi Joshua ben Hananiah and the Roman emperor as preserved in Talmud and midrash have been modified greatly and are characterized by much exaggeration, but Bacher, in *The Jewish Encyclopedia* 7:291, concludes, "But they nevertheless present in general a just picture of the intercourse between the witty Jewish scholar and the active, inquisitive emperor, the *curiositatum omnium explorator,* as Tertullian calls him." Hadrian is correct in this story in that the first five commandments include God's name, the latter five do not. Hence Hadrian concluded that the first five were given to the Jewish people, the second five to all peoples. Lot's two daughters gave birth to Moab and Ben-ammi, the father of the Ammonites (Genesis 19:37–38). Rabbi Joshua's answer to the question put to him is that the Ten Commandments in their entirety and the Torah itself were indeed offered by God first to non-Jewish nations. It was only after they refused the offer that all the Ten Commandments and the entire Torah were offered to the Jews who accepted them. There is no division between the first five and the last five of the Ten Commandments.

64. Dr. Aharon Jellinek, compiler and editor, *Bet ha-midrash*, vol. 5 (Jerusalem, 1938), pp. 132–133. The vague description of the "king of one of the nations of the world" must refer to the Roman emperor Hadrian, the only king familiar to Rabbi Joshua ben Hananiah, Trajan having died in 117 c.e.

65. *Genesis Rabbah* 64:10. For the historicity of this story see Alon, *The Jews in Their Land in the Talmudic Age* 2:430ff. His conclusion is, "The most that we can derive from the midrash is this: at one point the Roman government promised to rebuild the Temple but then reversed itself. The Jews were very upset by this, and there were signs of revolt in some quarters, but the would-be rebels were cooled down by Rabbi Joshua ben Hananiah and his colleagues. All the rest of the details are either legend, or at best dubious." There seem to have been two strands to the story, one a promise about the city of Jerusalem, the other about the Temple. The Church Father, Epiphanius, who lived in the fourth century, wrote of Hadrian's decision to restore the city but not the Temple (Alon, 2:441–443). A Syriac chronicle of the eighth or ninth century tells that in the year 129 the Jews were about to rebuild both Jerusalem and the Temple, while another Christian chronicler, Alexander the Monk, writing in the ninth century, says that Hadrian ordered that the city be rebuilt but not the Temple (Alon, 2:444–446). *Genesis Rabbah* was probably composed in the fifth century, some three hundred years after the events in our text. The story in its details has a distinctly legendary ring.

The tradition that two important men, Pappus and Lulianus (perhaps Julianus) were put to death by Trajan, Hadrian's predecessor, is found in a number of sources: *Sifra* 5:2, 9:5; *Yerushalmi Taanit* 2:12 (66a), *Megillah* 1:4 (70c); *Taanit* 18b; *Semahot* 8:15; *Ecclesiastes Rabbah* 3:17. Tannaitic sources affirm that the two men were seized and killed during the rule of Trajan, in variance with our story. The *Yerushalmi* sources say that they were killed on the twelfth day of Adar; the midrash in *Ecclesiastes Rabbah* gives the place of their execution as Laodicea. *Pesahim* 50a says they were brothers and calls them "the martyrs of Lydda."

However, Graetz accepts the historic value of our story (*History of the Jews* 2:403–404). He identifies Pappus and Julianus (*sic*) as two courageous men from Alexandria who led the rebellion in Judea against Trajan (116–117). According to Graetz, they were caught but escaped or were released and so lived to welcome the Jews coming from Babylonian exile in our story and, as Alon explains, to help them by exchanging money for them or to give them loans. Graetz dates Hadrian's promise to have the Temple rebuilt as early in his reign and to meet the demand of the Jewish rebels before they would lay down their arms. He writes that the Jews recognized Hadrian's new conditions, that the Temple must be built in a new place or on a smaller scale, as temporizing, and they were not willing to permit themselves to be played with. Therefore, Graetz continues, many Jews armed themselves and assembled in the valley of Rimmon on the plain of Jezreel. A new rebellion seemed imminent but the lovers of peace sent for their leader, Rabbi Joshua, who calmed the crowd. But the idea of rebellion did not die and burst out less than two decades later under Bar Kokhba.

66. *Genesis Rabbah* 10:9. See also *Megillah* 9a and *Yerushalmi Megillah* 1:9 (71d). Despite the fact that Rabbi Joshua's name is not mentioned here, we have included it here because he was one of the elders who visited Rome more than once. The name of King Ptolemy is probably a copyist's mistake. Read instead—"a certain philosopher." The Ptolemaic kings ruled in Egypt after the death of Alexander the Great. The text of the passage is generally in poor condition and the translation is an attempt to make sense of it.

67. *Midrash on Psalms* 117:1. It must be remembered that in the Middle East rain falls only in its season, and often it is late in coming and so threatens the food crop for the next harvest. See the similar story earlier, ending with note 40.

68. *Genesis Rabbah* 20:4. Rabban Gamaliel's face turned pale from embarrassment that he could not answer the question. The dog was called "a wild beast" because in ancient times dogs were semi-wild and not fully domesticated. Two different dogs are mentioned in rabbinic literature—the ordinary dog, described by Rabbi Meir as a domestic animal, and the Cyprian dog, resembling a fox, called a wild animal. See *The Jewish Encyclopedia* 4:630–632. According to Rabbi Joshua's answer, the cattle bear at seven times fifty days or 350 days, approximately a year (the Jewish year, a lunar year, is 354 days and a fraction) and the serpent seven times that or seven years. He interprets the verse this way: you, the serpent, are more cursed than the cattle to the same extent that cattle are more cursed than beasts. The expression, "offered to me on the end of a cane," is an idiom for something that is done with complete ease. See *Bekhorot* 8b.

69. *Bekhorot* 8b–9a. A fanciful and lengthy tale demonstrating the superiority of the Jewish sages to the wise men of Athens. The wit of Athens is defeated by the cleverness of the sages. See also *Lamentations Rabbah* 1:1. There is a historical basis for this account in that Joshua had an association with the emperor Hadrian. He visited Rome and Athens where he engaged in discussions with Athenian scholars and philosophers. Louis Ginzberg

wrote about this story, "In later times when it was thought impossible that a sacred book like the Talmud should contain anything amusing, much ingenuity was displayed in order to read into these jests a deep and secret significance" (*The Jewish Encyclopedia* 2:266, s.v. "Athenians in Talmud and Midrash").

Instead of "cushions" Rashi has here "chairs." Bran dust or flour was scattered in front of the entrance to the school of the Athenian wise men so that the footsteps of those entering or leaving could be detected. Only those were punished who entered without prior permission. Rabbi Joshua's scheme resulted in his entering the school without concern. The question about the lender assumed that if he encountered difficulty recovering his money from the first borrower, he would not lend again. The answer about the woodsman says that although he had problems with his first borrower, the next one might be easier. A *zuz* was half a *shekel*. That Rabbi Joshua made use of the Divine Name and was able to hang in midair serves as an illustration of the belief that certain individuals have the mystical ability to use the permutations of the Hebrew names of God to effect miracles and healings. The founder of Hasidism, Israel ben Eliezer, was better known as the Baal Shem Tov, the Master of the Divine Name, and he was, according to the stories about him, a faith healer and miracle worker. Rashi explains the "straits" as referring to the Mediterranean Sea about which there was the belief that it absorbs all the waters of the world that flow into it.

This somewhat cryptic account of an intellectual contest between the sixty wise men of Athens and Rabbi Joshua ben Hananiah in which the Jewish scholar showed his superior cleverness is the only real piece of *aggadah* of any length in the tractate of *Bekhorot*.

70. *Niddah* 69b–71a. The text calls him Rabbi Joshua ben Hinnena, this patronymic being incorrect. Saul Lieberman wrote about the puzzling questions posed by the people of Alexandria: "All those riddles were in the typical spirit of the Alexandrian schools of that time. . . . The contact of Rabbi Joshua with this particular branch of Alexandrian 'exercises' is thus well established; it can be therefore safely assumed that he was acquainted with the methods and practices prevalent in the rhetoric schools of Alexandria at that time." (From "The Publication of the Mishnah" in *Hellenism in Jewish Palestine* [New York, 1950].) The three questions having to do with *Halakhah*, Jewish law, are the following: (1) How long do the corpses of those who died while having a flux or a woman in her menstrual period or a leper impart ritual impurity to those who carry them?; (2) Is the daughter of a woman who was divorced and remarried by her first husband permitted to marry a priest?; (3) If the sacrifices of two lepers were mixed up and after the sacrifice of one of them was offered, one of them died, what is to be done about the survivor? This last question pleased Rabbi Joshua and he called it "a wise inquiry" (see end of *Tosefta Negaim*). The third series of questions in the text treats of *divrei borot*, explained by Rashi, the noted medieval commentator, as "silly questions" or "nonsense." But Professor Lieberman prefers the meaning of "hypothetical questions" or questions divorced from any real existing situation.

The story of Lot's wife who turned into a pillar of salt may be found in Genesis, chap. 19, and the story about Elisha and the Shunamite woman in 2 Kings, chap. 4.

For more information about the Jewish community of Alexandria and the twelve questions put to Rabbi Joshua see "Response to the Introduction by Professor Alexander Marx" by Saul Lieberman in Judah Goldin, *The Jewish*

Expression (New York, 1970), pp. 119–133, and *The Jewish Encyclopedia* 1:361–366. Rabbinic sources tell us little about the Jews of Alexandria, but see Mishnah *Hallah* 4:10, *Yerushalmi Eruvin* 3, end, *Yerushalmi Kiddushin* 3:14.

71. *Bet ha-midrash*, vol. 5, *Maasiyot* 3, pp. 135–136. This must be a late story, perhaps originating during the Middle Ages. The language shows unusual syntax and grammatical forms. The tunic or flowing robe was the standard garment worn by both sexes during the rabbinic period. It was loose, permitting the circulation of air, and so was comfortable in hot weather. The white tunic was worn on the Sabbath and festivals. When Jews moved to European countries they kept what had been a kind of national Jewish dress, the white tunic, for use on Yom Kippur, during the *seder* on Passover evening, and were clothed in it for burial.

72. *Midrash on Proverbs*, chap. 2. Rabbi Joshua's calling Rabbi Eliezer "my son" raises a question since both were contemporaries and the language would normally be used by a teacher speaking to a student. One is reminded of Burton L. Visotzky's statement that "one finds dialogues between Rabbi Eliezer and Rabbi Joshua recorded only in Midrash on Proverbs, for the simple reason that they took place only in the imagination of Midrash on Proverbs' redactor." See Visotzky's introduction to his translation of the *Midrash on Proverbs*.

73. *Midrash on Proverbs*, beginning of chap. 5. See Proverbs 7:5–10 where the forbidden woman and the promiscuous woman are identified as meaning the same. In this story not only does Rabbi Joshua call Rabbi Eliezer "My son," but Rabbi Eliezer addresses him as "Master," this despite the fact that both were contemporaries. See previous note.

74. *Midrash on Proverbs*, chap. 6. Yet rabbinic teaching advises that one must give charity even to the person you suspect may not really need it.

75. *Midrash on Proverbs*, chap. 6. During the second century there were problems with those who informed on the Jews to the Roman authorities. Most often these informers were to be found among the new Christians. See Baron, *A Social and Religious History of the Jews* 2:142 and 385 n. 18.

76. *Midrash on Proverbs*, chap. 6. On the two rabbis who were contemporaries and not student and teacher see note 72. The text here reads Rabbi Eleazar but should correctly be Rabbi Eliezer. Proverbs 6:6 reads, *Lazybones, go to the ant;/Study its ways and learn.*

77. *Midrash on Proverbs*, chap. 10. About the relationship between the two rabbis in this dialogue see note 72. For centuries it has been deemed desirable by Jews to die in the Land of Israel or, at least, to be buried there. The power of the Land of Israel to effect atonement is found also in *Midrash on Proverbs* 17:1. See also *Sifre on Deuteronomy* 333. The meaning of the verse from Deuteronomy is uncertain. The hermeneutical principle, an inference from the minor to the major, *kal va-homer*, is the first of the thirteen principles of logic set forth by Rabbi Ishmael (*Sifra*, chap. 1). Rabbi Joshua's statement that the righteous depart from this world free of sin is part of a theodicy that explains why the righteous suffer in this world. They depart for their reward in the world to come.

78. *Midrash on Proverbs*, chap. 11. Rabbi Joshua's opening statement about the two hands is derived from the Hebrew of "assuredly," which in the Hebrew is literally "hand upon hand," a gesture attesting to a sworn oath. The comparison of the verse from Proverbs with the verse from Exodus in order to learn the meaning of the former from the meaning of the latter is a hermeneutic principle called *gezeirah shavah*, an inference from similarity of phrases in texts. It is the second in the thirteen principles of logic set forth by

Rabbi Ishmael (*Sifra*, chap. 1). See Lieberman, *Hellenism in Jewish Palestine*, p. 61, for more about this principle. The wicked person swears to pay the prostitute her full fee and then pays her less afterward.

79. *Midrash on Proverbs*, chap. 17, end. As to the relationship between the two rabbis, who were not master and disciple, see note 72.

80. *Midrash on Proverbs*, chap. 22, near beginning.

81. *Midrash on Proverbs*, chap. 23, near beginning. For the relationship between these two sages, see note 72. For the counting of the days, see Ginzberg, *The Legends of the Jews* 6:58 n. 300; 59 n. 303. The *omer* was a measure of roasted barley offered daily in the Temple between Passover and the Feast of Weeks (see Leviticus 23:10–21). The *omer* offering came to an end when the Temple was destroyed by the Romans in 70 C.E., as did the other Temple practices mentioned here. For the showbread, see Leviticus 24:5–9; for the garments of the high priest, see Exodus, chap. 28; for the *shekel* payments see Exodus 30:11–16. Libations of wine accompanied the sacrifices, and water libations occurred during the Feast of Tabernacles. The answer of Rabbi Joshua reflected the difficult economic conditions in the Land of Israel during the second century of the Common Era under Roman rule.

82. *Hagigah* 3a–b; *Mekhilta* 131:3, chap. 16 (*Pisha*), Lautenberg pp. 131–133; *Tosefta Sotah* 7:9–12; *Yerushalmi Hagigah* 1:1 (75d); *Yerushalmi Sotah* 3:14 (18d–19a); *Soferim* 18:6 (42b); *Numbers Rabbah* 14:4; *Avot de-Rabbi Natan* 18:2 (25b). The latter begins the story with "When Rabbi Joshua was an old man. . . ." Rabbi Johanan ben Beroka and Eleazar Hisma were younger members of the second generation of *tannaim*. Pekiin is sometimes spelled Pekiim or Bekiim. It was located in southern Palestine between Jabneh and Lydda. The younger scholars' courteous response was meant to say, "We accept only your authority" or "We cannot tell you anything you do not already know." But Rabbi Joshua deprecated the thought that there were no other great teachers from whom he could learn. Rabban Gamaliel II, the patriarch and president of the academy, had been deposed from the latter post because of his humiliation of Rabbi Joshua and other scholars. Rabbi Eleazar ben Azariah was elected to take his place. When Rabban Gamaliel was later reinstated, the new arrangement was that he would give during each month discourses on three Sabbaths and Rabbi Eleazar ben Azariah on one Sabbath (*Berakhot* 27b–28a). For more details see my earlier section on Rabban Gamaliel II. To state that the women came only to listen implies feminine ignorance. But not necessarily so. *Lishmoa*, "to listen," in Hebrew has the implication of understanding, comprehension. *Hakhel* refers to the practice enjoined upon the ancient Jewish kings to assemble the people every seventh year during the festival of Sukkot for the purpose of reading the Torah to them (Deuteronomy 31:10–13). The verse in Ecclesiastes is of uncertain meaning, hence its translation varies. The words in 2 Samuel 7:23 are also found in 1 Chronicles 17:21. A nail contracts because of corrosion. The words of the Torah could contract because of forgetfulness. Of course, the leader referred to is Moses. A generation may be called orphaned if it lacks a spiritual leader. Several sources mention that the younger scholars came from Jabneh to Lod to Pekiin.

83. *Eruvin* 53b, *Lamentations Rabbah* 1:1, *Derekh Eretz Rabbah* 6:3 (57a) with some variations among them. *Pe'ah* referred originally to the corners of the field whose harvest the farmer was not to reap but to leave for the poor and the stranger (Leviticus 19:9–10). Here the derived meaning is that while the waitress should not leave anything in the pot for herself, the person being served should leave some food in the plate for her in the nature of a tip. In

connection with Rabbi Joshua saying that he had already had a meal earlier in the day, it might be noted that Professor Louis Ginzberg in a class lecture on Jewish practices with regard to the Sabbath stated that Jews in ancient times ate two meals a day on a weekday and three meals on the Sabbath. The woman gently rebuked Rabbi Joshua for not having left some food for her on the first two days. The little girl chided Rabbi Joshua for using a path across a field that was private property and not a public thoroughfare. The long way but the short way took longer to the city but it was a clear road unencumbered by obstacles.

84. *Lamentations Rabbah* 1:1. Garlic and onions would sweeten the water when its taste is not the best. Eliezer, Abraham's servant, rewarded Rebekah with gifts (Genesis, chap. 24). Evidently, several more children got the better of Rabbi Joshua.

85. *Shabbat* 152b. As indicated earlier, the word "emperor" may mean the representative of the emperor, the Roman governor of Judea.

86. *Hagigah* 5b. Rabbi Joshua defended Judaism against attacks upon it by pagans. The verse from Jeremiah in the text is not a statement but a question and the word translated here as "children" is often understood to mean "prudent." Rabbi Joshua interpreted "children" as "children of Israel" or the Jews. The verse from Genesis he interpreted to mean that Esau, a name used for non-Jews, will keep up with Jacob or Israel but will not get ahead of him. Gentiles will not best the Jews in theological argumentation.

87. *Mishnah Sotah* 9:15, *Yerushalmi Sotah* 9:16 (24c), *Tosefta Sotah* 15:3. With Rabbi Joshua's death men of counsel and reflection were said to be no more because he often defended Judaism against heathen attacks. These statements form a tribute to Rabbi Joshua ben Hananiah and speak of the admiration for him by his contemporaries and by those of later generations.

Chapter 4

1. *Berakhot* 27b. This was the reason given for his being chosen to replace Rabban Gamaliel II as *Nasi* (patriarch) and head of the academy at Jabneh (*Berakhot* 28a). Louis Ginzberg maintained that he replaced Gamaliel only as head of the academy and not as *Nasi*, but Gedaliah Alon rejects Ginzberg's reasoning (Alon, *The Jews in Their Land in the Talmudic Age* 1:320). See the story of the revolt against Rabban Gamaliel in my chapter about him (chap. 1). Other sources tell of the wealth of Rabbi Eleazar ben Azariah: *Shabbat* 54b, *Betzah* 23a and cf. *Kiddushin* 49b. Despite the reappropriation and redistribution of the land by the Roman authorities, Rabbi Eleazar ben Azariah managed to retain his large landed properties. See Baron, *A Social and Religious History of the Jews* 2:104–105. Rabbi Eleazar ben Azariah was born about 70 c.e. and died before 135 c.e. He had property in Sepphoris and may have died there.

2. *Yevamot* 86b. This story is based on a controversy between Rabbi Eleazar ben Azariah and Rabbi Akiba, his junior, found in *Yevamot* 86a and b. Rabbi Akiba held that the heave-offering belonged to the priest and the first tithe to the Levite, as Scripture requires. But Rabbi Eleazar said that the first tithe belonged to the priest. The question was asked, "To the priest, but not to the Levite?" Scripture assigns it to the Levite! To which the answer was given, "Read 'to the priest also,' " in addition to the Levite. In this story Rabbi Eleazar, a priest, would collect the first tithe from this garden but Rabbi Akiba

made that impossible by changing the position of the gate so that it opened on a cemetery, on whose soil a priest is not permitted. *In re* the position taken by Rabbi Eleazar ben Azariah see also *Bava Batra* 81b, *Ketubbot* 26a, and *Hullin* 131b. He was said to be the twenty-sixth in descent from Aaron, the first priest. When the Temple was destroyed in 70 C.E. by the Romans, the priests and Levites no longer had any sacerdotal functions to perform and, therefore, the offerings to them should have ceased. But the rabbis insisted that such gifts should continue even though that was resisted by the people. Times were hard and the people, in addition, felt that since the priests and Levites could not work in the Temple, they should no longer be given the traditional offerings. (See Alon, *The Jews in Their Land in the Talmudic Age* 1:254–258 and the next note.)

Rabbi Akiba in his early life was a shepherd (cf. *Ketubbot* 62b), and Meiri explains that Eleazar ben Azariah was saying that in time of economic distress, Rabbi Akiba could return to taking up again his shepherd's wallet, but he, Rabbi Eleazar, could manage to live without his tithe.

3. *Betzah* 23a. A proof of Rabbi Eleazar ben Azariah's wealth. Several sages were rich men: Rabbi Eliezer ben Hyrcanus, Rabbi Eleazar ben Azariah, Rabbi Tarfon, and Rabbi Ishmael. "The continued enjoyment of wealth by any Jewish family [during the instability of conditions in the Roman Empire] for more than a generation or two," writes Salo Baron, "must have been quite rare in Palestine and even rarer in other parts of the empire" (*A Social and Religious History of the Jews* 2:420 n. 46). Rav was a first-generation *amora*, early third century, while Rabbi Judah lived a generation later. Tosafot *ad locum* asks, "How was it that Rabbi Eleazar ben Azariah gave the annual tithe since he was active after the destruction of the Temple and in *Bekhorot* 53a it is stated that after the Temple's destruction all tithes of animals came to an end?" Several answers are given: (1) Tithes of animals came to an end slowly, not at once; (2) the word "tithe" here means not the tithe offering to the Levite, but Rabbi Eleazar ben Azariah gave one tenth of his yield each year to the Roman government. In any case the number of calves mentioned in this text may well be somewhat of an exaggeration.

4. Mishnah *Shabbat* 5:4, Mishnah *Betzah* 2:7 and 23a. Rashi explains that it was because Rabbi Eleazar regarded the strap as an ornament, but the sages thought it to be not an ornament but a burden. The Gemara, since the language speaks of "Rabbi Eleazar ben Azariah's cow," asks, "Did he then have only one cow? He gave ten thousand calves annually as tithe from his herd!" The answer is given that the cow spoken of was not his cow but that of a neighboring woman, but since he did not restrain her, it is referred to as his.

5. *Yerushalmi Sukkah* 2:4 (52d), *Yerushalmi Eruvin* 1:7 (19b). Rabbi Eleazar argued that a moving ship is not an appropriate place for a *sukkah*. His junior by a generation, Rabbi Akiba, maintained that it was.

6. Mishnah *Yoma* 8:9, *Yerushalmi Yoma* 8:7 (45b). Since the verse mentions *before the Lord*, Rabbi Eleazar takes the verse to mean the wrong-doings a person commits against God are at once atoned for on Yom Kippur.

7. *Yoma* 86a. See also *Yerushalmi Shevuot* 1:6 (33b). In the order of sins the worst is profanation of the Divine Name, committing an act that desecrates the name of God. Such an act is performed in defiance of religious and ethical principles and reflects badly on all Jews (see Leviticus 22:32).

8. *Ecclesiastes Rabbah* 2:8. *Ketubbot* 49a, *Yerushalmi Berakhot* 4:1 (7d). The academy to which the scholars repaired after the destruction of Jerusalem and the Temple was at Jabneh. See my chapter on Rabbi Johanan ben Zakkai,

who had the foresight to create such a school of learning, in my *Legends of the Rabbis*, vol. 1. This seat of the sages came to be known as *kerem be-Yavneh*, "the vineyard at Jabneh," and Rabbi Eleazar ben Azariah gives the reason for it. The Sanhedrin and the seat of the patriarch were also in Jabneh, a small town to the northwest of Jerusalem.

9. *Genesis Rabbah* 22:2. This fanciful statement stems from the fact that Scripture does not here speak periodically of the passing of time as it does in the opening chapter.

10. *Genesis Rabbah* 32:3. The Hebrew proverb has it: "A part of a man's praise in his presence; all of it in his absence." See *Eruvin* 18b.

11. *Genesis Rabbah* 65:10. An explanation of why so righteous a man as Isaac was smitten with impaired vision.

12. *Sifre on Deuteronomy*, 50.

13. *Berakhot* 9a. Rabbi Abba was an *amora* and Rabbi Akiba was of the third generation of *tannaim*, the younger colleague of Rabbi Eleazar ben Azariah.

14. *Numbers Rabbah* 3:6. Rabbi Eleazar is playing with words here. In *ba-kosharot* he sees the words, *bakho*, "to weep," and *sharu*, "they sang." The word is translated in the 1982 translation of the Jewish Publication Society as "safe and sound."

15. *Avot de-Rabbi Natan* 2:3 (18b). Rabbi Eleazar could not abide the thought that Moses had dared on his own to break the tablets of the Ten Commandments given him by God (Exodus 32:19). He therefore quoted the final words of the Pentateuch as the summing up of all the actions of Moses, which were undoubtedly performed only at God's command, including the breaking of the tablets.

16. *Pesikta Rabbati* 52:4. The verse from 1 Kings refers to the story of Elijah telling the boy to go up seven times and to look out to the sea for a sign of rain. The last time he did so the verse could well have read, "and the last time." Therefore, Rabbi Eleazar takes the reading *and the seventh time* to refer to the Sabbath, the merit of which was invoked by Elijah in his prayer for rain. In addition, the expression that *Elijah . . . put his face between his knees*, implying that he was looking in the direction of his circumcision, meant that he was invoking the merit of that *mitzvah* in his appeal for rain. The eight generations from Abraham to Joshua were the following: Abraham, Isaac, Jacob, Levi, Kohat, Amram, Moses, and Joshua. Rabbi Joshua's closing argument is that the verse could have read simply *and*, but since it reads *and also*, the word *also* serves to include the other holidays that he enumerates.

17. *Pirkei Avot* 3:21–22 and *Avot de-Rabbi Natan* 22:1 (26a). The latter's version is with some variants and in reverse order. The Hebrew translated here as "right conduct" is more popularly translated as "good manners." But the meaning here is much wider, referring to the way a person relates to other human beings. If he has not studied Torah he will not know how to relate ethically and morally to others; even, for example, not to embarrass another in public. And he who knows how to conduct himself toward others can climb even higher on the ladder of right living by studying more Torah for its own sake. So too one cannot attain true reverence for God without studying Torah, just as one cannot truly engage in the study of Torah without some measure of reverence. *The beginning of wisdom is the fear of the Lord* (Psalms 111:10). Similarly, without the ability to analyze and to synthesize, one cannot develop knowledge, while conversely, if one does not have the knowledge to aim at a goal, there cannot be necessary understanding. If a person lacks sufficient food, his mind cannot devote itself fully to study. Rabbi Eleazar concludes that if a person forsakes the study of Torah in order

to amass wealth, in the end he will lose his riches or his enjoyment of his wealth. He then follows his statement with an illustration, the roots of a tree serving as a symbol for the person's good deeds.

18. Midrash *Tanhuma, Aharei* 11. The first pot mentioned is for boiling, the second for stewing. Rabbi Eleazar ben Shammua was a *tanna* of the fourth generation. Here the advice is not to overeat or drink too much and not to spend one's money needlessly.

19. *Genesis Rabbah* 84:8. Wise counsel about the unhappy results of favoritism among children by a parent. Resh Lakish or Rabbi Simon ben Lakish was an *amora* of the second generation. The subject of the biblical verse is Joseph's brothers.

20. *Genesis Rabbah* 93:11.

21. *Exodus Rabbah* 30:19. The Ten Commandments, the essence of the entire Torah, are followed by the laws that flow from them and that govern the relationships among human beings. Justice refers not only to the courtroom and the decisions issuing from it. Justice is far more comprehensive. It directs proper behavior to the poor and the powerless, indeed, to all human beings.

22. *Genesis Rabbah* 34:14, *Yevamot* 63b, *Tosefta Yevamot* 8:7. The logic is if the last commandment here be violated, then the two former ones are transgressed. The text in *Yevamot* quotes Rabbi Eliezer as having said, " . . . is as though he had shed blood," and Rabbi Eleazar ben Azariah as having said, " . . . diminished the divine image."

23. *Nedarim* 31b and *Yerushalmi Nedarim* 3:9 (38a). The proof-text refers to *Egypt, Judah, Edom, the Ammonites, Moab and all the desert dwellers who have the hair of their temples clipped.* Not a convincing proof-text, for it includes Judah. And should one argue that what is meant are the wicked in Judah, what does one do with the end of the verse, . . . *but all the House of Israel are uncircumcised of heart?* The latter means that their minds are blocked to God's commandments.

24. *Pesahim* 118a. The meaning of the first verse quoted is uncertain. The second verse is taken to be an allusion to the happening at the Red Sea when the walls of water closed again. Rabbi Shizvi, a Babylonian *amora* of the third or fourth generation, studied in the land of Israel with Rabbi Johanan for a short time and there he learned the traditions of Rabbi Eleazar ben Azariah.

25. *Pesahim* 118a. See previous note with reference to the two quoted verses.

26. *Pesahim* 118a and *Makkot* 23a. Rabbi Sheshet was a Babylonian *amora* of the third generation. This teaching is another example of the hermeneutical principle of *semukhin*, deducing a lesson from the fact that biblical verses are in close proximity to one another.

27. *Pesahim* 118a. See previous note for the hermeneutical principle involved. Rashi explains "despises the festivals" as meaning doing unnecessary work on the intermediate days of the festival.

28. *Eruvin* 64b–65a. Having been described as "drunk" prior to the destruction of the Temple, Israel, still bearing the stigma, could not be held responsible for its actions. For Rabbi Sheshet, see note before the last.

29. *Avodah Zarah* 19a. The commentators understand this statement to refer not to a lazy hunter of game but to a negligent or lazy student who studies superficially and who does not review what he has learned. The exposition is based on a play on words: *yah'rokh*, "to hunt" or "to have game" and *yihyeh*, "to live," together with *yaarikh* (*yamim*), "enjoy length (of days)." *In re* Rabbi Shizvi, see note *supra*.

30. *Midrash on Proverbs*, chap. 5.

31. *Yerushalmi Yevamot* 1:6 (3a-b). The elders or sages came to Rabbi Dosa ben Harkinas, a contemporary of Eleazar, to ask about the question of whether co-wives may enter into levirate marriage, which was approved by the school of Shammai. In the group of sages were Rabbi Joshua ben Hananiah, Rabbi Eleazar ben Azariah, and Rabbi Akiba. Another opinion says that Rabbi Tarfon was also with them. Rabbi Dosa here speaks of Rabbi Eleazar's wealth and eminent priestly ancestry.

32. *Yerushalmi Sanhedrin* 7:13 (25d). The hot baths of Tiberias, a natural hot spring, were famous in ancient times and continue to exist today. No patronymic is given in the text for Rabbi Eleazar. In most such instances, where the story is about *tannaim*, Rabbi Eleazar ben Shammua is meant. But he is a *tanna* of the fourth generation and it would be questionable to have him here with Rabbi Joshua ben Hananiah—in the *Yerushalmi* often Hanina—of the second generation and Rabbi Akiba, of the third. Besides, Eleazar here speaks to Rabbi Joshua as an older colleague, not as one much younger. "Sectarian" in the original text is a *min*, a heretic, an infidel, often referring to a Jew who had joined the new Christian sect. As for the practice of magic on both sides, Baron writes, "Use of magic aids cuts across national and religious lines." See *A Social and Religious History of the Jews* 2:15–23. This despite the fact that the Pentateuch decreed the penalty of capital punishment for the practice of magic and sorcery. See Deuteronomy 18:10, Exodus 22:17.

33. *Yerushalmi Berakhot* 1:3 (3b), quoting the Mishnah. The *mishnah* of the Babylonian Talmud, *Berakhot* 1:3, sets forth the difference between the schools of Shammai and Hillel with regard to a person's position while reciting the *Shema*. However, our story is not found there. The *Shema* is the basic creed of Judaism, *Hear, O Israel! The Lord is our God, the Lord alone* (Others: . . . *the Lord is one*) (Deuteronomy 6:4). It is recited during the daily morning and evening prayers and before going to sleep. The school of Shammai held that one should recline while reciting the evening *Shema* but in the morning the person should stand when reciting it. Their proof-text was . . . *when you lie down and when you get up* (Deuteronomy 6:7). The school of Hillel argued that a person may recite the *Shema* each in his own way and their proof-text was . . . *and when you are away* (Deuteronomy 6:7). With only very few exceptions the law generally follows the school of Hillel. Rabbi Ishmael was a third-generation *tanna*, a younger colleague of Rabbi Eleazar.

34. *Pesikta de-Rab Kahana* 20:7. Messianic times are meant, when the peoples of the world will flock to Jerusalem.

35. *Derekh Eretz Rabbah* 3:4 (56b). Cf. *Berakhot* 28b and *Pirkei Avot* 4:15. By "stand up to pray" the *Amidah* is meant. The advice to be concerned about the honor of one's friends is similar to *Ethics of the Fathers* 2:13, "Let the honor of your friend be as precious to you as your own."

36. Mishnah *Sotah* 9:15 and *Yerushalmi Sotah* 9:16 (24c). The second quotation is from *Sotah* 49b, *Yerushalmi Sotah* 9:16 (24c), and *Tosefta Sotah* 15:3. Few of the sages had wealth, but the second quotation is an attempt to explain Proverbs 9:15, that the only wealth—but it is the true wealth—of the sages was their wisdom.

Chapter 5

1. *Ethics of the Fathers* 2:13–14, The *Fathers According to Rabbi Nathan*, chap. 14. These were not his only disciples. Another group is mentioned in

Bava Batra 10b, among whom are Rabban Gamaliel II, Rabbi Eleazar of Modiim, and Rabbi Nehuniah ben ha-Kanah. The expression, "Go and see" in the Hebrew is equivalent to "Consider" or "Think about this." The first question asked by Rabban Johanan ben Zakkai of his five outstanding students was "How may one live the good life?" "A liberal eye" has the connotation of recognizing the good in other people, being free of envy and ill will, generous in all respects, the opposite of "a grudging eye." The answer "A good friend" means to be a good friend to all. So, too, to be "a good neighbor," for to be a good neighbor is the first step to extending love and assistance to all human beings. The expression, "foreseeing the future" has the implication of understanding the link between cause and effect, of seeing where any action will lead and thus having the ability to choose only those actions that will effect good. Rabban Johanan ben Zakkai chose the answer of "a good heart" above the rest because a good heart, which the ancient rabbis saw as the source of both emotion and understanding, will be kind and generous, will see good in others, will inspire its possessor to be a good friend and neighbor, will understand the effect of any action, and will motivate one to do good. "A good heart" includes all the qualities suggested by the other disciples as to the secret of the good life. *Avot de-Rabbi Natan*, chap. 14, enlarges the last answer to "a good heart toward Heaven and toward humanity." It would seem that Rabbi Eleazar ben Arakh was the favorite student of Rabban Johanan ben Zakkai. But of the five, Rabbi Eliezer ben Hyrcanus and Rabbi Joshua ben Hananiah became the more famous.

2. *Pirkei Avot* 2:19, *Avot de-Rabbi Natan*, chap. 17. Without conscientiousness, enthusiasm, diligence, and eagerness—all of which may be understood in the Hebrew word, *shakud*—the student will not attain excellence in his studies. That is also needed to reply to the mocking questions of the unbeliever. See *Sanhedrin* 38b as to questions from a Gentile unbeliever and from a Jewish unbeliever. Finally, be aware always that you work in the presence of God who will see to it that you be rewarded justly. See Psalms 62:12. The Hebrew word for "unbeliever" is *apikoros*, the Hebraized form of Epicurus, the Greek who denied the reality of God. The sages applied this word to one who rejects the teachings of Judaism or who treats the teachings of Scripture and the tradition skeptically and frivolously.

3. *Avot de-Rabbi Natan* 14:6 (24a). Rabban Johanan knew intuitively that Rabbi Eleazar ben Arakh would succeed in comforting him, hence he told his servant to make the preparations for going to the bathhouse, a practice not engaged in by a mourner. David, too, ended his mourning for his son by bathing and putting on fresh clothes (see 2 Samuel 12:20). With regard to the soul as a trust, see Louis Ginzberg's *Legends of the Jews* 5:255 n. 259. Rabbi Eleazar's comforting of Rabban Johanan ben Zakkai is reminiscent of Beruriah's comforting of her husband, Rabbi Meir, upon the death of their sons (*Midrash on Proverbs*, chap. 31).

4. *Hagigah* 14b, *Yerushalmi Hagigah* 2:1 (77a), *Tosefta Hagigah* 2:1, with minor differences among them. For example, the Babylonian Talmud indicates that the tradition of not teaching the Work of the Chariot to an individual unless he be a sage who understands it on his own is the teaching of Rabban Johanan ben Zakkai. Similarly with the Tosefta. But the Palestinian Talmud quotes it in the name of the sages. It is found in the Mishnah, *Hagigah* 2:1. The Work of the Chariot refers to mystic speculations on the divine chariot in the vision of Ezekiel, chap. 1:4ff. Such esoterics may involve speculation as to the very nature of God and the heavenly beings that surround Him. Hence the sages restricted such speculation to only those few

who could be taught it without it affecting them adversely. Here we see at least two of Rabban Johanan ben Zakkai's most distinguished disciples indulging in such esoteric speculations. The ancient rabbis looked with suspicion upon men whose minds were deeply involved in such abstract meditations. The summer solstice, literally, "the cycle of *Tammuz*," is mentioned because in the land of Israel the sky is sunny and cloudless normally during the summer months, yet the day became overcast with a rainbow appearing in a cloud. Dining couches and not chairs were used for formal meals in antiquity. Each person leaned on a couch, in front of which was a small table upon which the food was placed. When the dinner was finished, the small tables were removed. Seven classes of persons are admitted after death into God's presence according to the *Midrash on Psalms* 11:7, the third class being designated for the righteous.

5. *Midrash on Psalms* 1:19. When the counsel given by Rabbi Eleazar to people resulted in a felicitous future, they would call him a prophet, an appellation he rejected as untrue.

6. *Midrash on Ecclesiastes* 7:7. Cf. *The Fathers According to Rabbi Nathan*, end of chap. 14. Jabneh was the academy founded by Rabbi Johanan ben Zakkai when Jerusalem fell to the Romans in 70 C.E. See my *Legends of the Rabbis* 1:275. Emmaus, a town on the road between Jerusalem and Jaffa, was known for its springs and the luxurious life there. Rabbi Eleazar had not studied with his colleagues for some time and he forgot his learning. The rabbis taught that one should always study together with a comrade. See *Ethics of the Fathers* 1:6, 4:12. One explanation of the question asked of Rabbi Eleazar by his colleagues maintains that they asked a question of law, not simply one of mere taste. A parenthetical statement in the text adds that Rabbi Eliezer and Rabbi Jose say that "relish" here means two articles of food combined.

Chapter 6

1. *Yevamot* 16a, *Yerushalmi Yevamot* 1:6 (3a–b). A co-wife of a daughter is explained in this fashion: a man married his brother's daughter, his own niece, and, in addition, married another woman. Should he die childless, his brother, in fulfillment of the levirate obligation, could not marry his own daughter, now his brother's widow, but the question is, Is he permitted to marry his deceased brother's other wife, the co-wife of his daughter? Mishnah *Yevamot* 1:4 tells that the school of Shammai permits such a levirate marriage, while the school of Hillel forbids it. *In re* levirate marriage see Deuteronomy 25:5–10. On the prevalence of the custom of levirate marriage (*levir*, from the Latin for "brother-in-law"), see *Bekhorot* 1:7. The rabbis made it obsolete during the second century, although rare cases continued to occur later. Rabbi David Hoffman permitted a levirate marriage to take place in Berlin during the latter part of the nineteenth century.

Cardinians came from a region east of the Tigris and south of Armenia. Palmyra was an oasis in the Syrian desert. The question here had to do with the blemished ancestry of these peoples.

Rabbi Dosa ben Harkinas—Dosa, an abbreviated form of the Greek name, Dosithai or Dositheos—lived a long life, perhaps c. 10 C.E. to c. 90 C.E. Harkinas is likely of Greek origin also. He was active during the time of Rabban Johanan ben Zakkai and also during the time of his disciples. In the

Palestinian Talmud his patronymic is Arkinas. He is mentioned as an organizer of the order of prayers (Mishnah *Arakhin* 3:9).

2. *Ethics of the Fathers* 3:14, *The Fathers According to Rabbi Nathan* 21:1 (26a). Morning sleep wastes valuable time that could be spent in study. See Proverbs 6:9–11. To sleep late is to oversleep the time for the recital of the *Shema* and the morning prayers. Wine certainly is not prohibited in Jewish religious practice but wine during the early afternoon makes study and work impossible. See Proverbs 23:29–33. Listening to childish prattle also is a waste of time that could be better used. So too with attending gathering places of the ignorant. *The Fathers According to Rabbi Nathan* explains "these are their theaters and circuses." Rabbi Dosa was a wealthy man and he knew the practices of wealthy men among his contemporaries. They would engage in lengthy meals with much drink and would attend the Roman theaters and circuses. See also Psalms 1:1.

Chapter 7

1. *Yerushalmi Sotah*, end, *Song of Songs Rabbah* 8:9, and *Tosefta Sotah* 13:3 with variations. Samuel the Small was held in high esteem by his colleagues. But there is a difference of opinion among the authorities as to when he was active. Zechariah Frankel in his *Darkei ha-Mishnah*, p. 73, states that there is no doubt that Samuel the Small was active during the time of Gamaliel II because it was Samuel who composed the prayer against the sectarians that is included in the *Shemoneh Esrei*, finalized by Gamaliel II [*Berakhot* 28b, *Yerushalmi Berakhot* 4:8 (a)]. Hanoch Albeck, the author of *Mavo ha-Mishnah* (Tel Aviv, 5719; reprint, 5727), p. 224, is of the same opinion, as is Herman Strack in his *Introduction to the Talmud and Midrash* (Philadelphia, 1931; reprint, 1945), p. 112. However, Aharon Hyman, in *Toldot tannaim ve-amoraim*, p. 1148, expresses surprise at such a view, since Samuel the Small in our text is linked with Hillel. He further argues that Samuel was a student of Hillel, who died about 10 C.E., and Samuel must have been then about twenty years of age. Hence, he must have been active during the time of Gamaliel I and the first generation of *tannaim*. But Baron, in *A Social and Religious History of the Jews* 2:220, says that Samuel "lived to a ripe old age of ninety." Thus he was active during the first generation of *tannaim* and the early years of the second. Herford in *Christianity in Talmud and Midrash*, pp. 132–134, also speaks of Samuel the Small dying a very old man.

There is a difference of opinion, too, as to the reason for the name, Samuel the Small. One view is that he was so called because he would never inflate his own importance; he was modest and unassuming (*Yerushalmi Sotah* 9:13). Others held that the reason was a physical one, that he was short in stature. Another theory is that he was given the name because he died young, but there is no support for this view in talmudic literature. It is most likely a conjecture based on his name.

See my *Legends of the Rabbis* 1:24 for a story about Gamaliel I and Samuel for an illustration of the latter's character and the former's high regard for him.

2. *Ethics of the Fathers* 4:19, in some editions 4:24. The words ascribed to Samuel the Small are a quotation of two verses from Proverbs 24:17–18. Evidently, he would quote these verses often. A parallel may be found in Job 31:29. God, Himself, does not rejoice when the wicked meet destruction as

may be seen in the rabbinic story in *Arakhin* 10a: The angels were singing when the Egyptians were drowning in the Red Sea, but God rebuked them with the words, "My creatures are drowning in the sea and you sing!"

3. *Derekh Eretz Zuta* 9:13 (59a).

4. *Midrash on Psalms* 94:4. The theodicy frequently espoused by the ancient rabbis was that the righteous may suffer in this world to atone for any of their wrongdoings. But in the next world they will enjoy their reward for their generally righteous life. On the other hand, the wicked may enjoy prosperity in this life but will suffer eternal punishment in the next life.

5. *Ecclesiastes Rabbah* 7:15. See previous note about rabbinic theodicy. God is anxious that the righteous person live his entire life in goodness. Therefore, if there be the possibility that he be tempted to change his ways in the future, his life comes to an end sooner. But since God is patient and long-suffering, He grants continued life for the wicked person, hoping that he will seize the opportunity and repent before his death. See Ephraim Urbach, *The Sages—Their Concepts and Beliefs*, vol. 1 (Jerusalem, 1975), pp. 491–492.

6. *Taanit* 25b. To fast was a common practice used to avert a calamity, and, of course, the fast was accompanied by prayers. Samuel the Small did not think that in either of the two instances cited the prayers were quickly answered because of the righteousness of the congregation. Had they been so deserving of praise, rains would have instantly come when the people recited the *Shemoneh Esrei*—which includes the words, "He causes the rain to fall," words added during the rainy season in the land of Israel; and, of course, the *Shemoneh Esrei* is recited thrice daily.

7. *Shabbat* 33a. He acknowledged that it was a sin of his that had brought on the illness, hence his quick recovery.

8. *Tosefta Sotah* 13:4, *Sotah* 48b, *Sanhedrin* 11a, *Semahot* 8:8, *Song of Songs Rabbah* 8:9. Who these martyrs Simon and Ishmael are is not clear. Rashi (*Sotah* 48b) says that they were Simon ben Gamaliel the Elder and Ishmael the High Priest, both of whom died during the Roman destruction of the Temple in 70 c.e. At first glance it might appear that the prophecy was about martyrs during the Bar Kokhba War (133–135 c.e.). But if so, why were not far more prominent martyrs such as Rabbi Akiba and Rabbi Haninah ben Teradyon mentioned? Alon, in *The Jews in Their Land in the Talmudic Age* 2:424–425, argues that the martyrs Simon and Ishmael (not the colleague of Akiba) were executed during the lesser-known war staged by the Roman emperor Trajan and his general, Quietus (115–117 c.e.). See Alon 2, chap. 3, "The War of Quietus."

9. *Semahot* 8:8 (Higger edition, p. 153), *Sanhedrin* 11a, *Song of Songs Rabbah* 8:9, *Sotah* 48b. See note 1 with regard to the age of Samuel the Small. In brief, if the phrase, "worthy disciple of Hillel," is not just a general compliment—"worthy enough to have been Hillel's disciple"—but literally true, then Samuel, who was an older contemporary of Gamaliel II and Eleazar ben Azariah, must have died at an advanced age, perhaps ninety, as Baron says (note 1).

Chapter 8

1. *Tosefta Megillah* 4:10. Hanina, the son of Gamaliel the patriarch, is mentioned only five times in the Mishnah. He died before his brother Simon

succeeded their father as patriarch (see *Sotah* 49b and *Bava Kamma* 83a). It was the practice to have a *meturgeman* at services who would translate into Aramaic the Torah reading of the day. In our text Rabbi Hanina tells the *meturgeman* not to translate for the public the first half of the verse that tells about Reuben taking his father's concubine, the mother of his half-brothers, to bed. It is too indelicate. The rabbis generally stress clean speech. Indeed, the Torah itself seems to find the subject distasteful. The verse breaks off in the middle and veers to the subject of the number of Jacob's sons. Kabul was a town or village southeast of Acre.

2. Mishnah *Sotah* 5:5. An example of the theological discussion of whether God should be served out of love or out of fear. There are sufficient texts in Scripture to support both points of view, although one of the best known is Deuteronomy 6:4. This *mishnah*, like *Sotah* 5:2, 5:3, and 5:4, begins with the words "That same day . . .," referring to the day when Rabban Gamaliel II was deposed. See my earlier section on Gamaliel II and *Berakhot* 27b *et seq*. The statement that "the matter is in doubt" refers to the fact that the Hebrew of the verse differs in the *keri* and *ketiv*, the traditionally articulated and the written forms of the word *lo*. The Hebrew homophone *lo* may mean "no," "not," "to him," or "for him." It was the wish of Rabbi Joshua ben Hananiah that Rabban Johanan ben Zakkai, the founder of the academy at Jabneh, come alive again to see how a later scholar dares to take issue with him.

3. *Kiddushin* 81a-b. Plemo's name occurs rarely in the Talmud: *Berakhot* 48b, *Pesahim* 8b, *Sotah* 4a, *Taanit* 25a, and *Menahot* 37a. Satan in Job and Chronicles is merely the Accuser, an instrument of God's will, but under Persian influence he began to assume a significance almost rivaling that of God (see Baron, *A Social and Religious History of the Jews* 2:43). He is the tempter, the personification of the impulse to do evil. On the eve of Yom Kippur, Jewish families are at home, eating the final meal before the fast.

4. *Sanhedrin* 94a. Rabbi Pappias' name is found half a dozen times in the Babylonian Talmud and once each in the *Mekhilta* and the *Avot de-Rabbi Natan*. In our text he criticizes the king Hezekiah for not offering a song of thanksgiving. Hezekiah indeed did so upon his recovery from his dangerous illness (see Isaiah, chap. 38). However, there is no record of his having done so after the destruction of the Assyrian army that was besieging Jerusalem (*Isaiah*, chap. 37). In addition, it was evidently not enough for Rabbi Pappias that Moses and the Israelites sang the great song of thanksgiving only after they had successfully passed through the Red Sea (Exodus, chap. 15).

5. *Avot de-Rabbi Natan* 27:2 (28a). The verse quoted is a weak support for Rabbi Pappias' statement and it has been suggested that Song of Songs 1:9 should be read here for it states the high regard for Pharaoh's horses since God compares His love for the Jewish people to a highly prized mare in Pharaoh's chariots. The text of this passage is evidently in disorder.

6. *Hagigah* 3b and *Midrash on Psalms* 25:13. See also *Yadayim* 4:3. The name, Dormaskit, is understood to mean, the Damascene, that is, the son of a woman from Damascus. See *Sifre*, beginning of Deuteronomy. That Damascus was called Darmesek, with the extra "r," may be seen in 1 Chronicles 18:5. Our story would indicate that he was a student of Rabbi Eliezer ben Hyrcanus. See also *Hagigah* 3b. The lands of Ammon and Moab in Transjordan, according to Rashi, refer only to that part of the two countries conquered by Sihon and Og and later taken from them by the Israelites. See Numbers 21:21–35 and *Hullin* 60b. But according to Rabbenu Tam in the *Tosafot*, the reference is to the rest of the two countries not captured by Sihon

and Og. During every seventh year Jewish farmers in the land of Israel would let their lands lie fallow (see Leviticus 25:2ff.). A tenth of the harvest in the third and sixth years was given to the poor. But Jewish farmers in Ammon and Moab were not subject to the laws of the seventh year. Therefore, they were here required to give a tenth of their crops to the poor, even though they had done so the year before. See Deuteronomy 14:28–29 and *Sifre ad loc.*

Rabbi Eliezer lost his temper because despite the fact that he was a leading authority of the times he had not been informed that such a decision was to be acted upon. The expression, "a law going back to Moses at Sinai," is idiomatic for a statute of immemorial practice.

7. *Sifre on Deuteronomy* 43 and *Numbers Rabbah* 9:24. A play on the word *ma'ayanot* ("fountains"), which is similar to the word *ayin* ("eye") to show that God's punishment is measure for measure.

8. *Midrash Tanhuma on Genesis* 4:30 and *Pesikta Rabbati* 38:1; our story is a blend of the two sources. There may be also implied here that if someone offends you and later comes to ask your forgiveness you should show compassion and forgive him. Even so will God forgive you when you seek His forgiveness for your wrongdoings. But if you do not show such mercy neither will He. In this connection, see Mark 11:25, Matthew 6:12, 14–15, Luke 11:4.

Chapter 9

1. *Ta'anit* 18b, *Ecclesiastes Rabbah* 3:17, *Sifra* 9:5, *Semahot* 8:15 (47b). The last-mentioned sources say that his eyes were gouged out as his punishment. The story of Hananiah, Mishael, and Azariah, who were thrown into a fiery furnace at the order of Nebuchadnezzar, is found in Daniel, chap. 3. The three young men, together with Daniel, were originally taken into the king's service and were given the names of Shadrach, Meshach, and Abednego (Daniel, chap. 1).

The villain of this story cannot be Trajan. The end of the story proves it, for if dispatches arrived from Rome ordering his execution, they must have come from the emperor. Besides, Trajan died a natural death. It has been suggested that the villain here was Trajan's general, Lusius Quietus, who indeed was executed by Trajan.

Trajan, during his last years—he was succeeded as emperor by Hadrian on August 8, 117—had the same ambition as his predecessors, especially Nero, to secure the eastern provinces of the empire by defeating Parthia. When Trajan, after winning victories elsewhere, planned his attack on Parthia, hoping that such a conquest would also protect the important trade routes to India and China, Jewish uprisings broke out in Egypt, Cyprus, and Cyrenaica. The participation of the Jews of Palestine was minimal. Eusebius claims that the Jews' primary target was not Rome but their local non-Jewish neighbors (see Eusebius, *The History of the Church*, Book 4, pp. 154–155). The revolt of the Jews threatened the communications and supply lines of the Roman armies in the east. Trajan ordered a violent repression of the revolt, and tens of thousands of Jews were killed. Lusius Quietus, a Roman general, subdued the Jews in Babylonia and was then appointed governor of Palestine, while Marcius Turbo commanded the Roman forces in the Mediterranean region. Pappus and Lulianus were the leaders of the minor Jewish insurrection in Palestine that was quickly repressed by Lusius Quietus who executed the two leaders—the basis for our story. Thereafter they were known as "the martyrs of Lod." *Pesahim* 3a states that "No one can stand in close proximity to martyrs slain by the government" because of their holiness. "And who are they? if you say Rabbi Akiba and his colleagues [executed under Hadrian] they were holy even during their lifetime. What it means are those killed at Lod."

Genesis Rabbah 64:8 says mistakenly that Pappus and Lulianus were active during the reign of Hadrian, confusing them with the later revolt against Rome led by Bar Kokhba. But *Sifra* 5:2 preserves the tradition that they were executed during the reign of Trajan.

Laodicea is also Lydda or, in Hebrew, Lod.

2. *Ecclesiastes Rabbah* 9:10. God has avenged Pappus and Lulianus by placing them in the highest position in paradise. There is a Rabbi Aha who was a *tanna* contemporary with Rabbi Judah ha-Nasi. But this Rabbi Aha of our text was a leading *amora* of the fourth generation and lived in Lod. Hence the information about Pappus and Lulianus, who were executed in Lod, was of special interest to him. Rabbi Alexandri was of the second or third generation of *amoraim*.

3. *Lamentations Rabbah* 1:16. See also 4:19. On the ninth day of *Av* annually the Jews fast and mourn for the destruction of the Temple in Jerusalem. On Hanukkah Jews rejoice because of the victory of the Jews under Judas Maccabeus over the Syrians and King Antiochus IV in 165 B.C.E., and they light candles on each of the eight evenings of the festival. This entire story is marked by hyperbole. It probably reflects the repression of the minor insurrection by the Jews of Judea against the Romans. See note 1.

4. *Lamentations Rabbah* 3:5 and 3:10. Vespasian was the Roman general who in 68 C.E. conquered Galilee, after the revolt of the Jews, as well as other regions to the north and south of Jerusalem. In 69 C.E. he became emperor of Rome, leaving the destruction of Jerusalem and the Temple to his son Titus. Trajan was emperor of Rome from 98 to 117 C.E. and in the latter years of his reign Jews rebelled in Egypt, Cyprus, and Cyrenaica and, to a lesser degree, in Judea. Trajan ordered the bloody suppression of the rebels. See note 1.

5. *Yerushalmi Sukkah* 5:1 (55a–b), *Sukkah* 51b, *Tosefta Sukkah* 4:6, also 4:17. A text that reveals the prosperity and the large population of the Jewish community in Alexandria in the latter years of the first century and the beginning of the second. The passage also sheds light upon the crafts practiced by Jews then. While the *Yerushalmi* states that there were seventy thrones in the great basilica, the *Tosefta* says there were seventy-one and is probably correct for the *gerusia* or council of elders that governed the large local Jewish community numbered seventy-one. The Alexandrian Jewish community dated back to the days of Alexander the Great and quickly grew in numbers so that Jews were a majority in two of the five districts of the city. They enjoyed self-government and both the Ptolemies—at least the early members of that dynasty—and the Roman emperors, with the exception of Caligula, treated them with consideration. But the revolt of the Jews in Egypt, Cyprus, and Cyrenaica (114–117) was put down, at Trajan's orders, with violence and enormous loss of life, and the Jews of Alexandria were massacred. See *The Jewish Encyclopedia* 1:361–366. With regard to the Jewish basilica, see Lieberman, *Tosefta ki-fshutah* 4:889–890.

Bibliography

Ancient Nonrabbinic Sources

Early Christian Writings: The Apostolic Fathers. Translated by Maxwell Staniforth. New York, 1968.

Eusebius. *The History of the Church from Christ to Constantine.* Translated by G. A. Williamson. New York, 1984.

Josephus, Flavius. *Works.* Translated by William Whiston. New York, 1872.

Plutarch. *Lives of Noble Grecians and Romans.* Translated by John Dryden, revised by Arthur Hugh Clough. New York, n.d.

Tacitus. *The Annals of Imperial Rome.* Translated by Michael Grant. New York, 1984.

Rabbinic Sources

Aboth: Sayings of the Fathers. Edited and translated by Joseph H. Hertz. London, 1943; New York, 1945.

Aboth de-Rabbi Natan. Edited by Solomon Schechter. Vienna, 1887; reprint, New York, 1967.

The Babylonian Talmud. Translated into English. Edited by Isidor Epstein. 34 vols. London, 1935–1948. 16 vols. London, 1961.

The Fathers According to Rabbi Nathan. Translated by Judah Goldin. Yale Judaica Series 10. New Haven, 1955.

Judah ben Kalonymos. *Yehusai tannaim ve-amoraim.* Edited by Yehuda Leib Fishman. Jerusalem, 1942.

Masekhet Avot im Talmud Bavli ve-Yerushalmi. Edited by Noah Chaim ben Moshe mi-Kobrin. New York, n.d.

Masekhet Derekh Eretz Zuta. Edited by Jacob Landau. Tel Aviv, 1970–1971. With commentary by Daniel Sperber. Jerusalem, 1979.

Masekhet Ketanot [The minor tractates of the Talmud]. Translated under the editorship of Abraham Cohen. London, 1965.

Mekilta de-Rabbi Ishmael. Edited and translated by Jacob Z. Lauterbach. 3 vols. Philadelphia, 1933–1935 and 1976.

Mekhilta de-Rabbi Shimon ben Johai. Edited by J. N. Epstein and E. Z. Melamed. Jerusalem, 1955.

Midrash Abba Gurion. Edited by Salamon Buber. Vienna, 1886.

Midrash ha-Gadol. Edited by S. Frisch. Jerusalem, 1975.

————. Genesis. Edited by Mordecai Margoliot. Jerusalem, 1947.

————. Exodus. Edited by Mordecai Margoliot. Jerusalem, 1956.

————. Leviticus. Edited by Adin Steinsaltz. Jerusalem, 1975.

————. Numbers. Edited by Zvi Meir Rabinowitz. Jerusalem, 1967.

————. Deuteronomy. Edited by Shlomo Fish. Jerusalem, 1972.

Midrash Lekah Tov. Edited by Salomon Buber. 2 vols. Vilna, 1884.

Midrash Mishlei. Edited by Salomon Buber. Lwow, 1893.

Midrash on Proverbs. Translated by Burton L. Visotzky. New Haven, 1992.

Midrash on Psalms. Translated by William G. Braude. 2 vols. New Haven and London, 1959.

Midrash Rabbah. 2 vols. Vilna, 1878.

Midrash Rabbah. Translated into English under the editorship of H. Freedman and Maurice Simon. 10 vols. New York and London, 1939. 3rd edition, 1983.

Midrash Tanhuma. New York–Berlin, 5684.

Midrash Tanhuma. Edited by Salomon Buber. Vilna, 1885.

Midrash Tanhuma. Genesis. Translated by John T. Townsend. Hoboken, 1989.

Midrash Tehillim. Edited by Salomon Buber. Vilna, 1891; reprint, New York, 1948.

Mishnah. Horeb edition. Berlin, 1914.

Mishnah. Edited by Chanoch Albeck. 6 vols. Jerusalem, 1952–1958.

The Mishnah. Translated by Herbert Danby. Oxford, 1933.

Mishnah, Shishah Sidrei. Edited and with commentary by Jakob Kornberg. Israel, 1967.

Mishnat Rabbi Eliezer. Edited by Hyman G. Enelow. New York, 1933.

Pesikta de-Rab Kahana. Edited by Salomon Buber. Vilna, 1925; New York, 1962.

Pesikta de-Rab Kahana. Edited by Bernard Mandelbaum. 2 vols. New York, 1962.

Pesikta de-Rab Kahana. Translated by William G. Braude and Israel J. Kapstein. Philadelphia, 1975.

Pesikta Rabbati. Edited by Meir Friedman. Vienna, 1880.

Pesikta Rabbati. Translated by William G. Braude. 2 vols. New Haven, 1968.

Pirke Abot: With Commentary. Edited by Eliezer Levi. Tel Aviv, 1951–1952.

Pirke Aboth. Edited and translated by R. Travers Herford. London, 1930.

Pirke Aboth: Sayings of the Fathers. Edited and Translated by Isaac Unterman. New York, 1964.

Pirkei de-Rabbi Eliezer. Edited by Samuel Luria. Warsaw, 1852; New York, 1946.

Pirkei de-Rabbi Eliezer. Translated by Gerald Friedlander. London, 1916; New York, 1981.

Seder Eliyahu Rabbah. Edited by Meir Friedman. Vienna, 1900.

Seder Olam Rabbah. Edited by Jeruchim Leiner. Warsaw, 1904; New York 1952.

Sifra on Leviticus. Edited by Louis Finkelstein. 4 vols. New York, 1983–1990.

Sifre: A Tannaitic Commentary on the Book of Deuteronomy. Translated by Reuven Hammer. New Haven and London, 1986.

Sifre on Numbers. Edited by Zvi H. Wolk. Jerusalem, 5714.

Sifre Zuta. Edited by Saul Lieberman. New York, 1968.

Siphre on Deuteronomy. Edited by Louis Finkelstein. New York, 1969.

Talmud Bavli [The Babylonian Talmud]. Zhitomir, 1863.

The Talmud, Minor Treatises of. Translated by A. Cohen. 2 vols. London, 1971.

The Talmud of the Land of Israel. Edited by Jacob Neusner and translated by Jacob Neusner and Roger Brooks, Edward A. Goldman, Martin S. Jaffee, Irving J. Mandelbaum, Alan J. Avery-Peck, Tzvee Zahavy. 32 vols. Chicago, 1982–1993.

Talmud Yerushalmi. 2 vols. Berlin, 5689.

Talmud Yerushalmi. 7 vols. Bnei Brak, 5740–5751.

Talmud Yerushalmi. Translated by Adin Steinsaltz. Jerusalem, 1981.

Talmud Yerushalmi (Ahavat Tzion). Berakhot and Pe'ah. Edited by Zechariah Frankel. Reprint. Jerusalem, 1971.

Tanna de-be Eliyyahu. Translated by William G. Braude and Israel J. Kapstein. Philadelphia, 1981.

Tanna de-ve-Eliyahu. Warsaw, 1881–1908. Jerusalem, 1965–1966.

The Tosefta. Edited by Moses Samuel Zuckermandel. Pasewalk, 1880; Jerusalem, 1937 and 1963.

The Tosefta. Translated by Jacob Neusner. 6 vols. Hoboken, 1977–1986.

The Tosefta According to Codex Vienna with variants from Codex Erfurt, Genizah MSS. and *editio princeps* (Venice, 1521). Edited and brief commentary by Saul Lieberman. New York, 1955.

The Tosefta According to Codex Vienna. Edited by Saul Lieberman. New York, 1962.

Yalkut Makiri on Psalms. Edited by Salomon Buber. Berditchev, 1899.

Yalkut Shimoni. Vilna, 1908–1909; New York and Berlin, 1926.

Postrabbinic Sources

Azulai, Haim Yosef David. *Yalkut Shemuel al massekhet Avot*. New York, n.d.

Culi, Yaakov. *Me'am loez (The Torah Anthology)*. Translated by Aryeh Kaplan. 6 vols. New York and Jerusalem, 1979.

Emden, Yaakov. *Etz Avot*. New York, 5710.

Ibn Habib, Yaakov. *Ein Ya'akov*. 4 vols. Vilna, 1922. Translated by S. H. Glick. 5 vols. New York, 1916–1922.

Ma'aseh Book. Translated by Moses Gaster. 2 vols. Philadelphia, 1934; reprint (1 vol.), Philadelphia, 1981.

Serilio, Solomon ben Joseph. *The Palestinian Talmud According to Solomon ben Joseph Serilio*. Edited by H. Y. Dinglas. Jerusalem, 1952.

Aggadot Talmud Yerushalmi. With commentaries of Moses Margalit and Elijah ben Solomon Abraham ha-Kohen. Jerusalem, 1964–1965.

Ahad Ha-am. *Al perashat ha-derakhim*. 4 vols. Berlin, 1921.

Albeck, Hanoch. *Mavo ha-Mishnah*. Tel Aviv, 5719; reprint, 5727.

Alon, Gedaliah. *Mehkarim be-toldot Yisrael*. 2 vols. Tel Aviv, 1957–1958.

———. *Toldot ha-Yehudim be-Eretz Yisrael bi-tekufat ha-Mishnah ve-ha-Talmud*. 2 vols. Tel Aviv, 1952–1955.

———. *The Jews in Their Land in the Talmudic Age*. 2 vols. Jerusalem, 1980.

———. *Jews, Judaism and the Classical World*. Jerusalem, 1977.

Ashkenazi, Shmuel Yafeh. *Yefei Mar'eh*. Warsaw, 1898.

Avi-Yonah, M. *The Jews under Roman and Byzantine Rule*. Jerusalem, 1984.

Bacher, Wilhelm. *Die Agada der Tannaiten und Amoraer*. 2 vols. Strassburg, 1902. Hebrew translation by A. Z. Rabinowitz. *Aggadot ha-tannaim*. Tel Aviv, 1928.

Baeck, Leo. *The Pharisees and Other Essays*. New York, 1947.

Baron Jubilee Volume. Edited by Saul Lieberman, Arthur Hyman, associate editor. New York, 1975.

Baron, Salo. *A Social and Religious History of the Jews*. 18 vols. New York, 1937–1983.

Baumgarten, A. J. "The Akiban Opposition." *Hebrew Union College Annual* 50 (1979): 179–187.

Bergman, Yehuda. "Perakim be-aggadah u-be-folklor." In *Kovetz madai le-zekher Moshe Shor*, edited by Louis Ginzberg and Avraham Weiss, 42–56. New York, 5705.

———. *ha-Folklor ha-Yehudi*. Jerusalem, 1953.

Bialostotzky, Binyamin Yaakov. *Fun unzer oytzer*. New York, 1939.

Bin Gorion [Berdyczewski], Michah Yosef. *Mimekor Yisrael*. Edited by Emanuel Bin Gorion, translated by I. M. Lask. 3 vols. Bloomington, IN, and London, 1976.

Damesek, Gershon Zeeb. *le-Or ha-aggadah*. New York, 1955.

Daube, David. *The New Testament and Rabbinic Judaism*. London, 1956.

Derenbourg, Joseph. *Mas'a Eretz Yisrael* [History of the Land of Israel from Cyrus to Hadrian]. Translated by Menahem M. Mibashan. 2 vols. in 1. Jerusalem, 1969–1970.

Dubnow, Simon. *Divrei am olam*. 11 vols. Tel Aviv, 1923–1940.

Eisenstein, Judah David. *Otzar midrashim*. New York, 1915.

Encyclopedia Judaica. 16 vols. Jerusalem, 1971–1972.

Entziklopediyah Talmudit. 16 vols. Jerusalem, 1969–1980.

Epstein, J. N. *Mavo'ot le-sifrut ha-tannaim*. Jerusalem, 1957.

Epstein-Halevi, Elimelech. *ha-Aggadah ha-historit-biografit*. Tel Aviv, 1975.

Essays and Studies in Memory of Linda R. Miller. Edited by Israel Davidson. New York, 1938.

Finkelstein, Louis. "Introductory Study to Pirke Abot." *Journal of Biblical Literature* 57 (1938): 13–50.

———. *Mavo le-masekhtot Avot ve-Avot de-rabbi Natan*. Texts and Studies of Jewish Theological Seminary 16. New York, 1950.

_____. "The Pharisees: Their Origin and Their Philosophy." *Harvard Theological Review* 22 (1929): 185–261.

_____. *The Pharisees: The Sociological Background of Their Faith*. 2 vols. Philadelphia, 1938; reprint, 1962.

_____. *New Light from the Prophets*. London, 1969.

_____. "Studies in Tannaitic Midrashim." *Proceedings of the American Academy for Jewish Research* 6 (1934–1935): 215.

_____. "Midras, Halakot we-Haggadot." In *Baer Jubilee Volume*, edited by Salo Baron, B. Dinur, S. Ettinger, and I. Halpern, 28ff. Jerusalem, 1961.

Fishman, Zekhariah. *Aggadot eretz ha-Kedoshah*. Tel Aviv, 1927.

Frankel, Zacharias. *Darkhei ha-Mishnah*. Warsaw, 1923.

Gibbon, Edward. *The Decline and Fall of the Roman Empire*. Vol 1. New York, n.d.

Ginzberg, Louis. *Al halakhah va-aggadah*. Edited by Judah Nadich. Tel Aviv, 1960.

_____. *The Legends of the Jews*. 7 vols. Philadelphia, 1909–1946.

_____. *The Legends of the Bible*. Philadelphia, 1956.

_____. *On Jewish Law and Lore*. Philadelphia, 1955.

_____. *Perushim ve-hiddushim bi-yerushalmi*. 4 vols. New York, 1941–1961.

Goldin, Judah. *The Jewish Expression*. New York, 1970.

_____. *The Living Talmud—The Wisdom of the Fathers*. New York, 1957.

_____. "On the Account of the Banning of R. Eliezer ben Hyrqanus: An Analysis and a Proposal." *The Journal of the Ancient Near East Society* 16–17 (1984–1985): 85–97. Reprinted in his *Studies in Midrash and Related Literature*. Philadelphia, 1988.

Graetz, Heinrich H. *Geschichte der Juden von den Altesten Zeitung bis auf die Gegenwart*. 11 vols. in 13. Leipzig, 1902–1909.

_____. *History of the Jews*. 6 vols. Philadelphia, 1891–1898.

Grant, Michael. *The Jews in the Roman World*. New York, 1984.

Grayzel, Solomon. *A History of the Jews*. Philadelphia, 1948.

Gross, Moses David. *Otzar ha-aggadah*. 3 vols. Jerusalem, 1953–1954.

Gutman, Mattathias Ezekiel. *Aggadot Talmud Yerushalmi*. Jaffa, 1953–1954.

Halevy, Isaac. *Dorot ha-rishonim*. 6 vols. Pressburg and Jerusalem 1897–1939; reprint, Jerusalem, 1966–1967.

Halperin, Jehiel. *Seder ha-dorot*. Warsaw, 1897.

Herford, R. Travers. *Christianity in Talmud and Midrash*. London, 1903; reprint, Clifton, NJ, 1966.

_____. *Pharisaism: Its Aims and Its Method*. London, 1912.

_____. *The Pharisees*. New York, 1924.

Heschel, Abraham Joshua. *Torah min ha-shamaim be-aspeklariah shel ha-dorot*. Added title page, *Theology of Ancient Judaism*. 2 vols. London and New York, 1962–1965.

Hesronot ha-Shas. Cracow, 1895.

Higger, Michael. *Aggadot ha-Mishnah*. New York, 1937.

_____. *Aggadot ha-tannaim*. New York, 1929.

————. *Halakhot ve-aggadot*. New York, 1933.

————. *Otzar ha-braitot*, New York, 1938.

————. *Mesikhtot Derekh Eretz*. New York, 1935.

————. *Mesikhtot Kallah*. New York, 1936.

————. *Seven Minor Treatises*. New York, 1930.

Hyman, Aaron. *Toldot tannaim ve-amoraim*. 3 vols. London, 1910.

Jastrow, Marcus. *A Dictionary of the Targumim, the Talmud Babli and Yerushalmi, and the Midrashic Literature*. New York, 1926.

Jellinek, Aharon, compiler and editor. *Bet ha-midrash*. 6 vols. Jerusalem, 1938.

Jewish Encyclopedia. 12 vols. New York, 1901–1906.

Juster, Jean. *Les Juifs dans l'Empire Romain*. Paris, 1914.

Kadushin, Max. *A Conceptual Approach to the Mekilta*. New York, 1969.

————. *Organic Thinking: A Study in Rabbinic Thought*. New York, 1938.

————. *The Rabbinic Mind*. New York, 1952.

————. *The Theology of Seder Eliahu*. New York, 1932.

Kahn, Israel Meir. *Hafez Haim al aggadot ha-Shas*. Edited by Samuel Charlap. Jerusalem, 1964.

Kanter, Shamai. *Rabban Gamaliel II: The Legal Traditions*. Ann Arbor, 1980.

Kasowski, Chaim Joshua. *Otzar leshon ha-Talmud*. Jerusalem, 1953–1954.

Katz, Ben-Zion. *Perushim, Tzedukim, Kanaim, Notzrim*. Tel Aviv, 1947.

Kaufman, Yehezkel. *Toledot ha-emunah ha-yisraelit*. 8 vols. in 4. Tel Aviv and Jerusalem, 1955–1960.

Klausner, Joseph. *Yehudah ve-Romi*. Tel Aviv, 1946.

————. *Yeshu ha-Notzri*. 2 vols. Jerusalem, 1922. Translated by Herbert Danby (*Jesus of Nazareth*). New York, 1925.

————. *ha-Ra'ayon ha-meshihi be-Yisrael* (The Messianic Idea in Israel). Tel Aviv, 1949–1950; reprint, 1956. Translated by William F. Stinespring. New York, 1955.

Klein, Isaac. *A Guide to Jewish Religious Practice*. New York, 1979.

Lazarus, Moritz. *The Ethics of Judaism*. Translated by Henrietta Szold. 2 vols. Philadelphia, 1900–1901.

Levner, J. B. *Kol aggadot Yisrael*. Jerusalem, 1943–1944.

Lewin, B. M. *Otzar ha-geonim*. 13 vols. Vol. 1, Haifa, 1928. Vols. 2–12, Jerusalem, 1930–1943. Vol. 13, n.d.

Lieberman, Saul. *Greek in Jewish Palestine*. New York, 1942.

————. *Hellenism in Jewish Palestine*. New York, 1950.

————. *Tosefta ki-fshutah*. 8 vols. New York, 1955–1973.

————. *Tosefta rishonim*. Jerusalem, 1938.

————. *ha-Yerushalmi ki-fshuto*. Jerusalem, 1969.

————. *Texts and Studies*. New York, 1974.

————. "Roman Legal Institutions in Early Rabbinics and in the *Acta Martyrum*." *Jewish Quarterly Review* n.s. 35 (July 1944): 1–57.

————. "Achievements and Aspirations in Modern Jewish Scholarship." In *American Academy for Jewish Research Jubilee Volume*, pp. 375–376 and p. 373 n. 14. Jerusalem, 1980.

Marcus, Ralph. "A Selected Bibliography of the Jews in the Hellenistic-Roman Period." *Proceedings of the American Academy for Jewish Research* 16 (1946–1947): 97–183.

Margolioth, Moses. *Pene Moshe*. Amsterdam and Leghorn, 1754 and subsequent editions and reprints.

Margolis, Max, and Marx, Alexander. *A History of the Jewish People*. Philadelphia, 1945.

Markus, Mordecai Zvi. *Mafteah ha-aggadot mi-kol ha-Shas*. Vilna, 1870.

Meilin, Yehudah Yitzhak. *Shir ha-shirim im targum ha-targum ha-arami l'ivrit*. Haifa, n.d.

Melamed, Ezra Zion. *Midrashei halakhah shel ha-tannaim be-Talmud Bavli*. Jerusalem, 1943.

_____ . *Parashiyot mei-aggadot ha-tannaim*. Jerusalem, 1962.

Mishkin, Mordecai. *Agodes fun Talmud un Midrash*. New York, 1932.

Moore, George Foot. *Judaism in the First Centuries of the Christian Era: The Age of the Tannaim*. 3 vols. Cambridge, MA, 1927. Sixth edition, Cambridge, 1950.

Nadich, Judah. *The Legends of the Rabbis*. Vol. 1. Northvale, NJ, 1994.

Neusner, Jacob. *Eliezer ben Hyrcanus*. 2 vols. Leiden, 1973.

_____ . *From Politics to Piety: The Emergence of Pharisaic Judaism*. Englewood Cliffs, NJ, 1973.

Pin, Benjamin. *Jerusalem contre Rome*. Paris, 1938.

Piron, Mordecai. *bi-Netivei aggadot Hazal*. Tel Aviv, 1970.

Rabinovitz, Z. W. *Sha'are Torath Eretz Yisrael*. Jerusalem, 1940.

Rabinowitz, Raphael Nathan. *Dikdukei soferim*. 15 vols. Munich, 1867–1897.

Radin, Max. *The Jews among the Greeks and Romans*. Philadelphia, 1915.

Rapoport, Solomon Judah. *Sefer erekh millin*. Warsaw, 1914; Jerusalem, 1969–1970.

Rappoport, Angelo. *The Folklore of The Jews*. London, 1937.

Ravnitzki, Yehoshua H., and Bialik, Hayyim Nahman. *Sefer ha-aggadah*. 6 vols. in 3. Vol. 1, Cracow, 1905. Vols. 2–3, Odessa, 1910; reprint (1 vol.), Tel Aviv, 1952.

Raz, Simhah. *Aggadot ha-Talmud*. 3 vols. Jerusalem, 1991.

Rokeah, David. *Jews, Pagans and Christians in Conflict*. Jerusalem and Leiden, 1982.

Rosenstein, Abraham Moses, and Karlin, Arye. *ha-Tannaim u-mishnatam*. Tel Aviv, 1952–1953.

Roth, Cecil. *History of the Jews*. New York, 1964.

Sachar, Abram Leon. *A History of the Jews*. New York, 1965.

Schechter, Solomon. *Some Aspects of Jewish Theology*. New York, 1909.

Scripta Hierosolymitana 22 (1971).

Segal, Alan F. *Rebecca's Children: Judaism and Christianity in the Roman World*. Cambridge, MA, 1986.

Simon, Leon, editor. *Selected Essays* by Ahad Ha-am. Philadelphia, 1936.

Solomon, Nissim N. *Entziklopediah le-aggadot ha-Talmud*. New York, 1951.

Strack, Herman L. *Introduction to the Talmud and Midrash*. Philadelphia, 1931; reprint, 1945.

Sulzberger, Mayer. *Am Ha-aretz, the Council of the People*. Philadelphia, 1909.

Urbach, Ephraim E. *The Sages—Their Concepts and Beliefs*. 2 vols. Jerusalem, 1975.

Waxman, Samuel. *Yalkut Shemuel al masekhet Avot.* Jerusalem, 1937–1938.

Webster, Graham. *The Roman Imperial Army.* Totowa, 1985.

Weiss, Isaac Hirsh. *Dor dor ve-doreshav.* 5 vols. Berlin and New York, 1924.

Weiss-Halivni, David. *Mekorot u-mesorot (Sources and Traditions).* 2 vols. Tel Aviv and Jerusalem, 1968.

Wertheimer, Solomon Aaron. *Batei midrashot.* 2 vols. Jerusalem, 1951–1953.

————. *Midrashim kitvei yad.* Jerusalem, 1923.

————. *Otzar midrashim.* Jerusalem, 1913–1914.

Wilken, Robert L. *The Christians as the Romans Saw Them.* New Haven and London, 1984.

Wohlman, M. *Misterei ha-aggadah.* Tel Aviv, 1929–1930.

Wolfson, Harry Austryn. *The Philosophy of the Church Fathers.* Cambridge, MA, 1956; 2nd rev. ed., 1964.

Yoreh Deah. Vilna, 1900.

Zahavy, Tzvee. *The Traditions of Eleazar ben Azariah.* Missoula, 1977.

Zeitlin, Solomon. "Jesus in the Early Tannaitic Literature." Reprint from *Abhandlung Zur Erinnerung an Hirsch Perez Chajes.* Vienna, 1933.

Name and Place Index

Athens, 93, 94, 178–179 n. 69
Augustus Caesar (e. of Rome), 157 n. 94
Azariah, 129, 192 n. 1
Azzai, 43, 153 n. 61

Baal Shem Tov (Israel ben Eliezer), 179 n. 69
Babylonia, xi, 8, 29, 30, 38, 73–74, 127, 147 n. 14, 147–148 n. 16, 150 n. 32, 151 n. 46, 156 n. 81, 169 n. 14, 185 n. 24, 185 n. 26, 192 n. 1
Bacher, W., 136 n. 26, 177 n. 63
Baeck, Leo, 167 n. 3
Bar Kappara, 39, 152 n. 50
Bar Kokhba, 146 n. 5, 173 n. 34, 178 n. 65. See also Subject Index: Bar Kokhba rebellion
Baron, Salo, x, 133 n. 9, 134 n. 12, 135 n. 20, 137 n. 26, 137 n. 27, 150 n. 31, 157 n. 87, 160 n. 111, 160 n. 112, 160 n. 113, 161 n. 115, 168 n. 6, 168 n. 8, 168 n. 9, 171 n. 25, 173 n. 33, 175 n. 48, 180 n. 75, 182 n. 1, 183 n. 3, 186 n. 32, 189 n. 1, 191 n. 3
Baumgarten, A. J., 134 n. 12
Ben Azzai, 29, 43, 59, 144 n. 68, 153 n. 61, 160 n. 113
Ben Kalba Savua, 27, 146 n. 3
Ben Zaza, 18
Ben Zizit Ha-Kaset, 27, 146 n. 3
Ben Zoma, 167 n. 3
Berekhiah, 47, 82, 155 n. 72, 173 n. 39
Beruriah, 187 n. 3
Betar, 28, 146 n. 5
Bet Peor, 88
Bet Shearim, 144 n. 71
Bialik, xi
Boaz, 47
Boethus ben Zeno (Zunin), 15, 140 n. 51
Braude, William G., 149 n. 25
Brindisi, 12

Caesarea, x, 54, 66, 163 n. 121
Caligula (e. of Rome), 193 n. 5
Cardinia, 120, 188 n. 1
Cave of Makhpelah, 72, 169 n. 12
China, 192 n. 1
Cohen, Abraham, 151 n. 42
Ctesiphon, xi
Cyprus, xi, 130, 192 n. 1, 193 n. 4, 193 n. 5
Cyrenaica, xi, 192 n. 1, 193 n. 4, 193 n. 5

Dama ben Natina, 52
Damascus, 191 n. 6
Danby, Herbert, 134 n. 13
Daniel, 192 n. 1
Domitian (e. of Rome), x, 132 n. 8, 135 n. 20, 136 n. 26, 163 n. 121
Domitilla, 137 n. 30
Dosa ben Harkinas, 19, 51, 83, 113, 119–120, 143 n. 66, 156 n. 85, 174 n. 45, 186 n. 31, 188 n. 1–189 n. 2

Earth. See Subject Index: Earth
Edom, 48, 155 n. 77, 185 n. 23
Egypt, 48, 130, 185 n. 23, 192 n. 1, 193 n. 4, 193 n. 5. See also Subject Index: Egypt
Eleazar ben Arakh, 25, 115–118, 145 n. 1, 167 n. 3, 186 n. 1–188 n. 6
Eleazar ben Azariah, x, 8, 9, 10, 11, 12, 21, 22, 31, 51, 64–65, 82, 103, 104, 107–114, 119, 122, 136–137 n. 26, 137 n. 28, 140 n. 51, 144 n. 68, 148 n. 22, 156 n. 85, 165 n. 125, 172 n. 29, 173 n. 39, 174 n. 47, 175 n. 47, 181 n. 82, 182 n. 1–186 n. 36, 190 n. 9
Eleazar ben Jeremiah, 153 n. 61
Eleazar ben Phineas, 43, 153 n. 61
Eleazar ben Shammua, 111, 113, 175 n. 48, 185 n. 18, 186 n. 32

Lud. *See* Lod
Lulianus, 92, 129, 177–178 n. 65, 192–193 n. 1, 193 n. 2
Lusius Quietus. *See* Quietus
Luther, Martin, 169 n. 14
Lydda, 178 n. 65

Mabgai, 13, 139 n. 40
Manasseh, 65, 73–74, 165 n. 125, 169 n. 14
Marcius Turbo, 192 n. 1
Marx, Alexander, 179–180 n. 70
Mattiah ben Heresh, 107
Me'arat ha-Makhpelah, 144 n. 71
Mediterranean Sea, 40, 152 n. 55
Meir, 17, 29, 142 n. 57, 155 n. 74, 170 n. 22, 178 n. 68, 187 n. 3
Meshach, 192 n. 1
Mishael, 129, 192 n. 1
Moab, 127, 185 n. 23, 191 n. 6
Modiim, 78, 172 n. 29
Moore, George Foot, 131 n. 1, 151 n. 42, 158 n. 96, 171 n. 25
Moses, 89, 97, 109, 184 n. 15
Mount Sinai, 45

Nakdimon ben Guryon, 27, 146 n. 3
Natan, 38, 62, 151–152 n. 48
Nazareth, 177 n. 61
Nebuchadnezzar, 29, 129, 147 n. 14
Nehemiah, 36
Nehorai, 38, 151–152 n. 48
Nehuniah ben ha-Kanah, 187 n. 1
Nero, 192 n. 1
Nerva (e. of Rome), x
Nile River Delta, 155 n. 79
Nizhana, 88, 177 n. 61
Noah, 108

Obelin. *See* Ubelin
Og, 191–192 n. 6

Palestine, x, 134 n. 12, 139 n. 40, 163 n. 121, 181 n. 82, 192–193 n. 1
Palmyra, 120, 188 n. 1

Pappias, 126, 191 n. 4, 191 n. 5
Pappus, 92, 129, 177–178 n. 65, 192–193 n. 1, 193 n. 2
Parthia, 192 n. 1
Pekiin academy, 71, 103, 168 n. 9, 181 n. 82
Penimon, 43, 153 n. 61
Persia, 8, 191 n. 3
Phrygia Major, 192 n. 1
Plemo, 125–126, 191 n. 3
Plinius Secundus, 163 n. 121
Pontus, 160 n. 109, 173 n. 38
Proklos ben Philosophos, 4
Ptolemy (k. of Egypt), 92–93. *See also* Subject Index: Ptolemic Egypt

Quietus (Roman general), 190 n. 8, 192–193 n. 1

Rabbah bar Bar Hana, 64, 164–165 n. 124
Rabinowitz, Raphael Nathan, 163 n. 121
Rashi, 135 n. 20, 141 n. 55, 147 n. 11, 156 n. 85, 165 n. 124, 176 n. 54, 179 n. 69, 179 n. 70, 183 n. 4, 190 n. 8, 191 n. 6
Rav, 28, 107, 146 n. 5, 183 n. 3
Red Sea, 40, 46, 79, 112, 126, 185 n. 24, 191 n. 4
Rehoboam, 137 n. 27
Rimmon, valley of, 178 n. 65
River of Fire, 88, 176 n. 58
Rome, x, 9, 10, 135 n. 20, 150 n. 32, 161 n. 117. *See also* Subject Index: Roman Empire

Samaritans, 92
Samuel, 34, 149 n. 29
Samuel the Small, 28, 121–123, 132 n. 6, 146 n. 4, 189 n. 1–190 n. 9
Schechter, Solomon, 148 n. 22, 149 n. 29, 167 n. 1
Sekhaniah (Jacob of Kfar), 63, 163 n. 121
Sennacherib, 49, 156 n. 82

Subject Index

Bar Kokhba rebellion, 134 n. 12,
149 n. 30, 155 n. 79, 165 n.
126, 167 n. 1, 173 n. 34, 175
n. 47, 176 n. 50, 176 n. 58,
178 n. 65, 190 n. 8, 193 n. 1
Barrenness, water ordeal after
adultery, 44
Bastardy, 31
Bathhouses, 4, 18, 113, 134 n. 13,
142 n. 62, 186 n. 32
Bathing, 55
Hanukkah and, 53, 157 n. 90
mourning and, 23, 116, 187 n. 3
purification and, 34, 149–150 n.
31
Beggars, imposters as, 48, 155 n.
76
Bible, language of, 136 n. 25, 150
n. 36. *See also* Language
Bitter herbs, 141 n. 51
Blindness, 147 n. 10
Borrowing. *See also* Debt
Borrowing, good conduct and,
115
Bribery, 3
Bridegrooms, 2
Brief prayer, dangerous places
and, 35, 150 n. 35
Burial, 149 n. 27
death and, 23–24, 144 n. 70,
144 n. 71
in Israel, 101, 180 n. 77
Burnt offering, Passover and, 174
n. 42. *See also* Offerings
Business, law and, 97

Calamity, fasting and, 122, 190 n.
6
Calendar, 62–63
altar wood and, 32, 148 n. 23
circumcision and, 46, 154 n. 70
creation and, 56, 159 n. 102
law and, 19–20, 143 n. 66
numerology and, 109–110, 184
n. 16
Passover and, 174 n. 42
summer solstice and, 117–118,
188 n. 4

Ten Commandments and,
102–103, 181 n. 81
Chaldean astral religion, 175 n. 48
Charity, 47, 140 n. 48, 146 n. 6
childbearing and, 38, 151 n. 47
imposters and, 48, 155 n. 76
pe'ah, 104–105, 126–127, 181–182
n. 83, 191–192 n. 6
poverty and, 17, 141–142 n. 56
repentance and, 100–101, 180 n.
74
Chastisement, Torah study and,
79, 172 n. 31
Chastity, righteousness and,
98–100, 180 n. 71
Childbirth, 80
charity and, 38, 151 n. 47
dream interpretation, 51, 156 n.
84
water ordeal after adultery, 44
women and, 47
Child rearing
favoritism of children and, 111,
185 n. 19
Torah study and, 102
Children, 13, 31, 138–139 n. 39
death of, 38
generational worth, 29–30, 113
remarriage and, 75, 170 n. 20
requirement for bearing, 39,
97–98, 112, 158 n. 22
restraint of, 64, 164 n. 123
sacrifice of, 151 n. 40, 152 n. 55
of wicked, 37, 74, 151 n. 44,
169 n. 16
wisdom of, 105
Christianity, 2, 132 n. 6, 133 n. 9,
133 n. 12, 136 n. 24, 137 n.
29, 137–138 n. 32. *See also*
Heathens; Heretics and heresy; Pagans and paganism
answering to, 115, 187 n. 2
conversion to Judaism by
women, 60, 161 n. 115
Greek language and, 171–172
n. 25
heresy, 63–64, 162–164 n. 121
informers and, 101, 180 n. 75

magic and, 113, 186 n. 32
persecution and, 164 n. 121
sign language and, 88, 176 n. 59
Circumcision, 10, 110, 184 n. 15
calendar and, 46, 154 n. 70
covenant and, 59, 159–160 n. 109
wickedness and, 112, 185 n. 23
Cities, condemned, 52
Cleanliness, ritual cleanliness, 61–63
Clothing
of dead, 33, 149 n. 27
righteousness and, 98–100, 180 n. 71
Coccyx bone, resurrection, 85, 176 n. 50
Collegiality, conduct and, 114
Commandments, 16. See also Ten Commandments
Community, 58
Compassion, God and, 127, 192 n. 8
Condemned city, 52
Condolences, on death of slave, 35, 150 n. 34. See also Mourning
Conduct. See also Righteousness
collegiality and, 114
law and, 97–98
rules of, 120, 189 n. 2
Torah and, 110, 111, 184–185 n. 17, 185 n. 18
Conversion, 78, 172 n. 29
circumcision and, 160 n. 109
God's relation to converts, 81–82, 173 n. 38
to Judaism, 18, 22, 142 n. 62, 144 n. 68
pagan to Christian, 164 n. 121
by women to Judaism, 60, 161 n. 115
Corruption, 2, 132 n. 8
Cosmology. See Creation
Counsel, prophets and, 118, 188 n. 5

Courage, persecution and, 79–80, 173 n. 34
Courts. See also Law
judgment and, 38
justice and, 28
Covenant, circumcision and, 59
Co-wives. See also Marriage; Wives
levirate marriage and, 113, 186 n. 31
marriage to daughter's, 119–120, 188–189 n. 1
Crafts. See also Labor; Occupation
of Jews, 130, 193 n. 5
Torah study and, 76, 171–172 n. 25
Creation, 5–6, 7, 136 n. 23
calendar and, 56, 159 n. 102
heaven and earth, 56–57, 159 n. 103
mechanism of, 86, 176 n. 52
rain and, 57–58, 159 n. 106
sex differences and, 75–76, 171 n. 24
teachings on, 70, 167 n. 3
time and, 92–93, 108, 178 n. 66, 184 n. 9

Dangerous places, prayer and, 35, 150 n. 35
Daughters, Greek language study and, 172 n. 25
Death
of children, 38
of Eleazar ben Azariah, 114
of Eliezer ben Hyrcanus, 66–67, 166 n. 126
evil and, 33–34
funerals and, 23–24, 144 n. 70, 144 n. 71
of Johanan ben Zakkai, 118
of Joshua ben Hananiah, 105–106
law and, 96–97, 179 n. 70
mourning and, 12, 23, 122–123, 144 n. 71, 190 n. 9
repentance and, 28, 146 n. 6

Sabbath and, 109–110, 184 n. 16
Rationality, ritual cleanliness,
    61–63, 161–162 n. 119
Rebuke
    fearsomeness of, 111
    of Satan, 125–126, 191 n. 3
Reclining, 15, 16, 140 n. 51, 141
    n. 53
Redemption, repentance and, 73,
    122, 169 n. 13
Red Heifer, 32, 52, 97, 148–149 n.
    25, 157 n. 87
Relatives
    kindness to, 41–43, 153 n. 59
    marriage to, 59, 160 n. 112
Remarriage, 75, 170 n. 20, 179 n.
    70
Repentance. See also Atonement
    atonement and, 107–108, 183 n.
    7
    charity and, 100–101, 180 n. 74
    death and, 28, 146 n. 6
    law and, 96–97
    messianism and, 73, 169 n. 14
    power of, 73, 169 n. 14
    redemption and, 73, 122, 169 n.
    13
Respect, teacher/student relation-
    ships, 28–29, 64, 146–147 n.
    10, 164 n. 123
Restraint, of children, 64, 164 n.
    123
Resurrection, 11–12, 33, 36, 37,
    49, 138 n. 32, 149 n. 27, 151
    n. 42, 151 n. 44
    body part from which grows,
      85, 176 n. 50
    burial in Israel, 101, 180 n. 77
    scriptural proof of, 85, 175–176
    n. 49
Right conduct. See Conduct
Righteousness, 36, 151 n. 42. See
    also Conduct
    affliction despite, 108–109, 184
    n. 11
    animals and, 109
    children and, 113
    classes of, 118, 188 n. 4

death and, 121–122
doubt and, 39
God and, 91–92
good deeds and, 102
law and, 83
love and, 33, 34–35, 150 n. 32
repentance and, 100–101, 180 n.
    74
resurrection and, 85, 175–176 n.
    49
reward for, 121, 190 n. 4
safety and, 102, 181 n. 78
sin and, 101, 180 n. 77
wealth and, 98–100, 180 n. 71
Ritual, Temple and, 47, 155 n. 74
Ritual cleanliness, 61–63
Ritual impurity, law and, 97, 179
    n. 70
Rivers, oceans and, 60, 161 n. 116
Robbery. See Theft
Robe, righteousness and, 98–100,
    180 n. 71
Roman baths, 4, 134 n. 13
Roman Empire, 150 n. 32
    agriculture and, 79, 172–173 n.
    33
    Alexandria destroyed by, 48,
    155 n. 78
    Bar Kokhba rebellion, 134 n.
    12, 176 n. 50, 176 n. 58
    Caesarea and, 54, 157–158 n. 94
    Christian heresy, 63–64,
    162–164 n. 121
    Christian informers and, 101,
    180 n. 75
    fear of, 80, 173 n. 35
    Greek studies and, 76, 145 n.
    73, 171–172 n. 25
    Hadrianic persecution, 143 n. 68
    Hyrcanus and, 145–146 n. 3
    Jerusalem attacked by, 167 n. 1,
    188 n. 6
    Jewish populations in Rome,
    84, 174–175 n. 47
    Jewish revolts against, xi,
    129–130, 136–137 n. 26, 192
    n. 1, 193 n. 3, 193 n. 4, 193
    n. 5

Roman Empire (*continued*)
land redistributions of, 182 n. 1
law, 164 n. 121
poverty and, 102–103, 137 n.
27, 141 n. 55, 181 n. 81,
183 n. 3
poverty as punishment against
Israel and, 48, 155 n. 77
rebuilding of Temple and, 92,
177–178 n. 65
sages' visits to, 84, 174–175 n. 47
taxation and, ix, 133 n. 10
Temple destroyed by, 69, 70–71,
129–130, 167 n. 1, 168 n. 6,
168 n. 8, 181 n. 81, 183 n.
2, 190 n. 8, 193 n. 3
Torah study and, 3, 133–134 n.
12
Root, 38
Rosh Hashanah, calendar and,
46, 154 n. 70
Rosh Hodesh, 18, 142 n. 64

Sabbath, 9–10, 12, 18, 137 n. 29,
142 n. 61
foods and, 85–86
keeping of, rewards for, 59
law of observance, 65, 165 n.
126
mourning and, 144 n. 71
rain and, 109–110, 184 n. 16
violations of, to save life, 89,
177 n. 62
witnesses and, 18–19, 142–143
n. 65
women and, 76, 171 n. 24
Sacrifice, 32, 151 n. 40
of children, 151 n. 40, 152 n. 55
holidays, 102–103, 181 n. 81
Temple tasks, 70, 167 n. 4
Sadducees, resurrection and, 175
n. 49
Sages, wealth of, 114, 183 n. 3,
186 n. 36
Salvation, heathens and, 34, 149
n. 30
Sanhedrin, 30, 140 n. 48, 142 n.
59, 147–148 n. 16

excommunication and, 162 n.
119
Gamaliel II and, 1
meeting places of, 141–142 n.
56
powers of, ix–x
requirements for establishment
of, 28
Satan, 125–126, 191 n. 3
Scholars
fund-raising for, 50–51
poverty and, 137 n. 27, 140 n.
49
Sea bathing, 18, 142 n. 62
Seas. *See* Oceans
Seder, 15, 140–141 n. 51, 180 n. 71
Servants, 14–15, 139 n. 43, 139 n.
44, 139 n. 45, 139 n. 46, 140
n. 47, 140 n. 48
Seventy languages, 28, 146 n. 5
Sex differences, rationale for,
75–76, 171 n. 24
Sexuality and sexual intercourse.
See also Children; Marriage;
Women
adultery, 43–44
of animals, 93–96, 178 n. 68,
178–179 n. 69
childbearing and, 38, 97–98, 151
n. 47
marriage and, 31
temptation and, 59, 160 n. 112
Torah study and, 59, 160 n. 113
women and, 75
Shammai school, 71, 145 n. 1, 168
n. 9, 186 n. 31
marriage laws, 120, 188 n. 1
Shema, physical position for,
113–114, 186 n. 33
Shas (Six Orders), 29, 147 n. 10
Shavout, calendar and, 46, 154 n.
70
Sheaf ceremony, Passover and,
83, 174 n. 42
Shema, 2, 26, 132 n. 5, 146 n. 3
am ha-aretz and, 55, 158 n. 96
physical position for, 113–114,
186 n. 33

Sheol (hell). *See* Hell
Sickness. *See* Illness
Sign language, Christianity and, 88, 176 n. 59
Silence, importance of, 75, 170 n. 21
Sin, 36, 151 n. 44
  death of children, 38
  gambling and, 73–74, 169 n. 14
  illness and, 122, 190 n. 7
  love and, 34–35, 150 n. 32
  pain and, 64, 165 n. 124
  righteousness and, 101, 180 n. 77
Six Orders (*shas*), 29, 147 n. 10
Slander
  injunction against, 146 n. 6
  punishment for, 112, 185 n. 26
Slaves and slavery, 14–15, 139 n. 43, 139 n. 45, 139 n. 46, 140 n. 47, 140 n. 48
  death of, 35, 150 n. 34
  Egyptian bondage, 39–40, 152 n. 53
Sleep, 120, 189 n. 2
Snakes, 93–94, 178 n. 68
Snow, creation and, 57, 159 n. 103
Social structure
  priests and, 70, 167–168 n. 5
  wealth and, 168 n. 9
Soothsaying, 151 n. 40
Sorcery, 151 n. 40. *See* Magic
Soul, 33
  love of God and, 45
  nature of, 4
Sowing of seed, 46–47
Speech, importance of, 75, 170 n. 21
Spellcasting, 151 n. 40. *See also* Magic
Spies, 37, 151 n. 43
Strangers, dishonesty and, 71–72, 168–169 n. 11
Student. *See* Scholars
Suffering, value of, 65, 165 n. 125
Suicide, persecution and, 79–80, 173 n. 34

Sukkah, 14, 139 n. 46
  appropriate places for, 107, 183 n. 5
  rules of, 54, 157–158 n. 94, 158 n. 95
Sukkot, 8–9, 12, 136 n. 26, 138 n. 34
  activities and celebration of, 53–54, 82, 157 n. 92, 173–174 n. 41
  calendar and, 46, 154 n. 70
  sukkah covering and, 54, 157–158 n. 94
  Torah reading and, 181 n. 82
Summer solstice, 117–118, 188 n. 4
Sun
  creation and, 57, 159 n. 103
  movement of, 57, 159 n. 105
Survival. *See* Jewish survival

Tabernacle, 44
Tahnun, 162 n. 119
Talit, am ha-aretz and, 158 n. 96. *See also* Phylacteries
Taxation, Roman Empire and, ix, 133 n. 10
Teaching
  of Greek language, 76, 171–172 n. 25
  process of, 30–31
  teacher/student relationships, 28–29, 53–54, 103–104, 146–147 n. 10, 147 n. 11, 157 n. 92, 181 n. 82
Tefillin, 14–15, 29, 140 n. 47
  am ha-aretz and, 158 n. 96
  law of, 55–56, 158 n. 98, 159 n. 99, 159 n. 100
  Sabbath and, 65, 165 n. 126
Temple
  destruction of, 69, 70–71, 112, 129–130, 167 n. 1, 168 n. 6, 168 n. 8, 181 n. 81, 183 n. 2, 185 n. 28, 190 n. 8, 193 n. 3
  rebuilding of, Roman Empire and, 92, 177–178 n. 65

Watches of the night, allegory
and, 59, 160 n. 111
Water
creation and, 40, 152 n. 55
earth and, 57–58, 159 n. 106
Water ordeal
adultery, 43–44
punishment of, 160 n. 114
Wealth. *See also* Poverty
of Alexandria, 130, 193 n. 5
of Dosa ben Harkinas, 189 n. 2
of Eleazar ben Azariah, 107,
182 n. 1, 183 n. 3
evil eye and, 74–75, 170 n. 18
gluttony and, 48–49, 155–156 n.
80
law and, 97
love of God and, 45
righteousness and, 98–100, 180
n. 71
of sages, 114, 183 n. 3, 186 n.
36
social structure and, 168 n. 9
Torah study and, 184–185 n. 17
Weddings, 2
Wet nursing, 133 n. 12
Whores, 63–64
Wickedness, 30, 36, 37–38,
147–148 n. 16, 151 n. 42, 151
n. 44. *See also* Evil
foreskin and, 112, 185 n. 23
God and, 91–92
hell and, 74, 85, 169 n. 15,
175–176 n. 49
punishment for, 121, 190 n. 4
sin and, 101, 180 n. 77
survival and, 121–122
Winds, protection from, 74,
169–170 n. 17
Wine. *See also* Food(s); Libation
drunkenness and, 13
use of, 120, 189 n. 2
Wisdom, 28, 32
law and, 97
piety and, 110–111, 184–185 n.
17
as wealth, 114, 183 n. 3, 186 n.
36

Witnesses
calendar and, 19–20, 143 n. 66
Sabbath and, 18–19, 142–143 n.
65
testimony and, 14, 139 n. 44
Wives. *See also* Divorce; Marriage;
Women
co-wives and levirate marriage,
113, 186 n. 31
death of, remarriage and, 75,
170 n. 20
Women. *See also* Marriage; Sexuality and sexual intercourse;
Wives
conversion to Judaism by, 60,
161 n. 115
Greek language study and, 172
n. 25
ignorance of, presumed, 103,
181 n. 82
marriage and, 71, 168 n. 7
nature of, 47, 155 n. 73
promiscuity and, 100, 180 n. 73
sex differences and, 75–76, 171
n. 24
sexual satifaction and, 75
status of, 53, 59–60, 160–161 n.
114
Torah study and, 59, 160 n.
113
Woodcutting, 32, 148 n. 23
Work of the Chariot, 117, 187 n. 4
World to come, children of
wicked and, 74, 169 n. 16.
See also Afterlife; Hell
Wrath, 77, 172 n. 28
Written Law, 7. *See also* Law;
Oral Law

Yom Kippur, 19, 20
atonement and, 107, 108, 183 n.
6
calendar and, 46, 154 n. 70
celebration of, 191 n. 3
clothing and, 180 n. 71

Zion, creation and, 57, 159 n. 103

2 KINGS

2:12	166
4	179
4–5	174
8	174
18:19	156
21:1	65

ISAIAH

1:21	30
3:13	79
4:1	158
4:6	41
6:3	10
10:13	22
21:15	49
22:8	30
22:14	108
23:15	51
24:16	126
26:2	34
26:19	11, 175
28:9	83
28:19	50
30:15	73
30:18	38
34:4	33
36–37	156
37–38	169
40:27	77
42:24	84
45:7	7
49:7	73
51:14	112
51:15	112
51:21	112
52:3	73
52:7	72
54:2	114
54:17	88
57:16	74
59:2	36
63:4	51, 156
65:17	33
66:16	78

JEREMIAH

2:31	32
2:36	151
3:14	73
3:17	114
3:22	73, 108
4:1	73
9:25	112
11:15	72
17:6	110, 111
17:8	111
17:13	34
23:24	10
25:30	59
26:20–23	148
31:17	72
32:31	97
35:19	73
39:3	30
49:6	22
49:7	106
52:34	38

EZEKIEL

1:4ff.	187
1:28	4
4:13	92
16	150
16:2	35
16:49	111
18:32	96
25:14	48
37	138
37:12	101
38–39	160
40	131

HOSEA

4:6	38
5:16	8
6:6	69
14:2	34

RUTH

2:14	43
4:1	47

LAMENTATIONS

1:16	130
3:5	130
3:10	130
4:2	174
4:9	79

ECCLESIASTES

1:6	57
1:7	57, 60
2:4	108
3:16	30
3:20	56
4:2	77, 78
4:12	25
5:4	152
5:5	38, 170
7:1	119
7:15	121, 122
7:20	64
8:5	31, 38, 83
9:4	89
11:1	61
11:2	46, 109
11:6	46, 75
12:11	67, 82, 104

ESTHER

2:2	79

DANIEL

1	192
3:27	33
4:11	37
4:12	38
4:20	74

7:10	176
12:1–4	175
12:7	73

NEHEMIAH

8:10	49

1 CHRONICLES

12:33	44
17:21	181

2 CHRONICLES

12:13	65
12:24	116
24:20–21	148
33:10–11	65
33:11	169
33:13	74
36:10	29

APOCRYPHA AND PSEUDEPIGRAPHA

BEN SIRA

5:7	146
38:1	150

JUBILEES

2:18	158

NEW TESTAMENT

MATTHEW

5:17–18	132
6:12	192
14:15	192

BABYLONIAN TALMUD

BERAKHOT

Mishnah

1:1	132, 149
2:5	132
2:7	140
4:3	132
6:8	141

Gemara

3a	160
5a	172
6a	158
9a	184
13a	152
16b	150
17a	131
27b	144, 147, 182, 191
27b–28a	143, 168, 181
28a	132, 137, 182
28b	132, 164, 186, 189
34a	159
47b	158
48b	191
53a	139
61b	154

MAASER SHENI

Mishnah

1:5	161
5:9	161, 175

SHABBAT

Mishnah

5:4	183
16:8	137

Gemara

31a	146
32b	151
33a	190
54b	182
105b	146
115a	136
116a	133
116a–b	132
119a	176
144a	146
147a	142
151a	132
151b	131
152b	149, 181
153a	146

ERUVIN

Gemara

11b–12a	159
41a	168
43a	137
53b	181
54b	148
63a	147
64b	139
64b–65a	185

PESAHIM

Gemara

8b	191
25a	154
38b	149
49a	167
49b	158
50a	178
53b	147
68b	157
86b	167
117a	159
118a	185

YOMA

Mishnah

8:9	149, 183

Gemara

38b	149
53b	147
54b	159
86a	183

SUKKAH

Mishnah

2:3	158

Gemara

20b	139
27b	157
28a	158
41b	136
51a	167
51b	193
53a	167

BETZAH

Mishnah

2:7	183

Gemara

15b	155, 157
23a	182, 183

ROSH HASHANAH

Mishnah

1:5	143
1:6	140, 142
2:8–9	143

Gemara

10b	159
18a	132

TAANIT

Mishnah

2:10	157

Gemara

7a–b	176
9b	159
18b	178, 192
25a	191
25b	157, 190
31b	148

MEGILLAH

Mishnah

4:10	150

Gemara

9a	178
17b	132
21a	145

MO'ED KATAN

Gemara

27a	144
27b	144

HAGIGAH

Mishnah

2:1	187

Gemara

3a–b	181
3b	191
5b	176, 182
14b	187

YEVAMOT

Mishnah

12:1	136

Gemara

16a	188
25b	139
49a	142
62b	170
63b	185
63b–64a	152
86a–b	182
102b	136

KETUBBOT

Mishnah

13:1	174

Gemara

8b	144
26a	183

29a	142
49a	183
50a	134, 146
62b	183
112a	142

NEDARIM

Gemara

31b	185
32a	164
50b	176

SOTAH

Mishnah

3:4	160, 168, 170
5:2–4	191
5:5	191
9:12	168
9:15	148, 166, 175, 182, 186

Gemara

4a	153, 191
13b	154
17a	158
28a	138
48b	148, 190
49b	145, 166, 171, 186, 191

GITTIN

Gemara

48a	174
56b	131
57a	155
76a	167
88b	133

KIDDUSHIN

Mishnah

4:14	132

Gemara

29a–b	172
30a	172
31a	157
31a–b	157
32a	157
32b	141
49b	182
64a	142
68a	142
70a	149
81a–b	191

BAVA KAMMA

Mishnah

4:3	133

Gemara

83a	145, 191
84a	145
113a	134

BAVA METZIA

Mishnah

5:3	140

Gemara

49b	140
59a–b	161
59b	133, 142, 161

BAVA BATRA

Gemara

10b	187
25a–b	159
60b	168
74a	161
74b	161
81b	183
121b	148

SANHEDRIN

Mishnah

10:1	149, 175
10:2	169

Gemara

5a	131
11a	149, 190
17b	146
32b	131, 140, 146, 168
38b	164
39a	135
68a	163, 165
71a	157
90b	137, 175
90b–91a	138
90b–92b	175
92b	156
93b	156
94a	166, 191
97b–98a	169
99a	156, 166
99a–b	170
101a	164
101a–b	165
101b	169
103a	169
104b	138
107b	151
110b	151

MAKKOT

Mishnah

3:16	174

Gemara

11a	139
23a	185
24a	141

SHEVUOT

Mishnah

10:6	143

EDUYYOT

Mishnah

5:5	166
8:7	168, 173

AVODAH ZARAH

Mishnah

2:1	133
3:4	134
5:2	140

Gemara

16b–17a	162
17a	161
19a	185
23b–24a	157
44b	134
54b–55a	135
55a	140

AVOT

Mishnah

1:4	148
1:10	163
1:16	131, 188
2:3	163
2:5	146, 158, 168–169
2:10	167
2:10–11	145
2:11	167, 174
2:12	145
2:13	167
2:13–14	186
2:16	170
2:19	164, 187
3:7	135
3:14	189
3:21–22	184
4:12	188
4:15	186
4:19	189
4:22	175

HORAYOT

Gemara

10a–b	137

ZEVAHIM

Gemara

24a	151
116a–b	172

MENAHOT

Gemara

35b	158
99b	172
37a	191

GENESIS RABBAH
(*Continued*)

57:4	172
64:8	193
64:10	177
65:10	184
78:1	176
84:8	185
92:1	172
93:11	185

LAMENTATIONS RABBAH

Proem 27	154
Proem 33	148
1:1	178, 181, 182
1:2	138
1:16	193
2:4	143
3:10	193
3:15	193
3:23	176
4:2	174
4:19	193

LEVITICUS RABBAH

4:1	147
5:4	156
14:44	155
15:1	169
18:1	176
19:1	154
19:4	139
20:5	147
20:6	147
20:7	147
28:5	174
29:1	159
34:8	152
34:9	155
34:10	155
37:3	139

MISHNAT RABBI ELIEZER

p. 103	137

NUMBERS RABBAH

3:16	184
9:10	153
9:19	138
9:24	192
9:25	153
9:31	138
9:47	160
12:4	135
13:15–16	154
14:4	173, 181
18:21	132
19:7	148
20:18	153
23:2	152
61:3	154

MIDRASH HA-GADOL

p. 84	135

MIDRASH ON PROVERBS

Chap. 2	180
Chap. 5, beginning,	180
Chap. 5	186
Chap. 6	180
Chap. 9	141
Chap. 10	180
Chap. 11	180
Chap. 13	150
Chap. 17	181
Chap. 22	181
Chap. 23	181
Chap. 23, end	154
Chap. 31	187

MIDRASH ON PSALMS

1:17	159, 171
1:19	188
4:9	150
4:12	151
9:9	151

MEDIEVAL WRITINGS

About the Author

Dr. Judah Nadich served as rabbi of the Park Avenue Synagogue in New York City from 1957 to 1987. Since that time, he has been rabbi emeritus there. During World War II he served as senior army chaplain and was later appointed as the adviser on Jewish Affairs by General Eisenhower. He is the writer, editor, and translator of many books and articles, including *Eisenhower and the Jews*. Dr. Nadich was ordained by the Jewish Theological Seminary of America, which also awarded him a master's degree in Hebrew literature and doctoral degrees in divinity and Hebrew literature. He and his wife, Martha Hadassah (née Ribalow), reside in New York and have three daughters.